The 16mm Camera Book

Standard and Super

second edition

Douglas Underdahl

Acknowledgments

Thanks
Rosanne Limoncelli, Peter Gust, John Koshel, John Gurrin, Mike Casey, George Gal, Scott Bankert, Pat Kellogg, Paul Koestner, Nile Southern, T. Carl Schietinger, Bill Hale, Ian McCausland, Derek Whitehouse, Pete and Rich Abel, Gretchen Viehmann, Eric Schmitz. Special thanks to Gwen Montgomery.

DISCLAIMER:

Every effort has been made to assure that the information in this manual is correct, but the author and publisher assume no liability whatsoever in connection with any errors or omissions. It is strongly recommended that users conduct tests before making any assumptions about the workability of any devices, procedures, or processes described herein. The author and publisher would greatly appreciate any errors or omissions brought to their attention.

About the cover: What is it? Our apologies to Aaton and Arriflex for the computer composite of their two cameras. Guess which parts are which and recieve a warm, congratulatory handshake and a hearty hi ho from the author.

ISBN Number 1-57087-285-6

second printing 1996

To order additional copies contact

Long Valley Equipment (908) 876-1022

Preface

Sixteen millimeter is making a comeback. Long thought of as a medium for documentaries, college level film courses and TV newsgathering (before ENG) only, sixteen is now used for most music videos, many commercials and recently, TV series. Shows such as HOMICIDE, THE WONDER YEARS, MAJOR DAD, THE INDIANA JONES CHRONICLES, and IN THE HEAT OF THE NIGHT have switched to 16 and super 16mm and realized savings of as much as $50,000 per show. These shows saved more than just of film stock. Since a 16mm camera rig is smaller and lighter, in many cases a station wagon replaces a large camera truck, and the driver can be the assistant cameraperson rather than a separate operator. A number of features have been shot in 16mm and Super 16mm, and blown up to 35mm for theatrical release recently, with more than acceptable results.

At the same time that many producers are discovering that the 16mm format is more than adequate for their productions, others are betting that super 16, with its wider aspect ratio, will be the least expensive and fastest format with resolution good enough for HDTV.

How did sixteen get so good? Over the last ten or fifteen years, several manufacturers have introduced products that have enabled the 16mm format to take on higher quality: new, razor sharp lenses and equally new and improved color negative film stocks. At the same time, several camera makers have designed and marketed expensive, high quality 16mm cameras and camera systems that incorporate the kind of accessories - follow focuses, extension eyepieces, power zooms, etc. - that make high gloss productions possible.

But although these newer cameras and accessories are quite costly to rent (and nearly impossible to own), take heart; almost any older, less sophisticated 16mm camera has the capability to take advantage of the new optics and films stocks and produce high quality results.

Unfortunately, there are certain parts of the film budget that are next to impossible to sidestep. At the time of this writing, the cost of four hundred feet of sixteen millimeter color negative (about eleven minutes at 24 frames per second) with normal development, one light workprint, and the associated sound materials (1/4 inch tape and transfer to fullcoat and edge coding of the picture and sound) comes to well over two hundred dollars. Even on modest productions, this may be only a small part of the "in the can" cost, which includes such things as equipment and location rental, food, transportation, and donated human sweat. Add to this the unique performances of the talent that may be involved, and this short roll of film becomes, in many respects, irreplaceable.

Unlike video and audio tape, film cannot be played back immediately for examination. The lab and its costs are always involved between the times of filming and screening. A simple mistake such as an incorrect iris setting or shutter angle can result in disaster, one that cannot be corrected, ever. The same is true for problems caused by inattention to the gate of the camera such as emulsion scratches or hair exposures. An entire day's or even week's shoot may be dead. Perhaps even more frightening is the thought that an internally damaged camera may be used, and the otherwise competent operator proceeds to shoot unaware.

The purpose of this book is to:

a) minimize the possibilities of error, especially in regard to the use of a damaged camera system.

b) familiarize directors, producers, camera personnel, etc. with the capabilities and limitations of various equipment so that appropriate choices can be made to complete the job at hand.

What you'll find in THE 16MM CAMERA BOOK are chapters on camera functions, equipment testing, and technical discussions of the majority of all 16mm cameras and related equipment in wide use today. This book is not meant to take the place of those that tell you how to thread up a camera or change its speed (although much of this kind of information is included). Rather, you'll find something that isn't part of any other text in any detail: specific, to the point reviews about what each camera, lens and accessory *is good for*. Is one camera more dependable? One quieter? If one is noisy, how bad is it likely to be, and can it be silenced? Which lens/camera combinations can be used with which power zooms? The 16mm Camera Book answers these questions, and others, such as

How do I know that my camera will shoot in-focus?
Which part of my camera is scratching the film?
Am I getting a good deal from the rental house?
How much footage can I get from my batteries?

As with any technical text, there is always the risk that new equipment, techniques or even new systems may be introduced by manufacturers that render the work obsolete. Fortunately, 16mm is an age old format with not too many end users (compared, for example, to people using home video cameras). Because of this, the technology involved (although quite advanced in some cases) moves like a snail. Aside from the introduction of a new lens or filter, 16mm will likely change very little in the next few years, or even decade.

Unfortunately, this same small number of end users in 16mm also leads to problems. If you've already gotten your feet wet in the format, and are wondering why, for example, the cost of certain new 16mm cameras can equal that of a modest home, the reason is simple. Makers of state-of-the-art 16mm cameras often expect to sell only a handful, worldwide, each week. With these kinds of sales figures, the cost of each individual machine must be very great to offset the high costs of research and development, tooling and manufacturing (it should always be kept in mind, however, that this is the manufacturer's story).

Making a movie, even (or perhaps especially, depending on your viewpoint) in 16mm, is often frighteningly, jaw droppingly expensive. It is also one of the most difficult things a human being can undertake. I hope that The 16MM CAMERA BOOK makes things cheaper, and easier.

Table of Contents

The Camera

IMPORTANT NOTE TO ADVANCED READERS

If you thumb through this first chapter you may get the impression that the information is elementary. The text builds in complexity, however, until the end where an explanation of the most important camera test you can do is detailed. Skip the first part of this chapter at your own risk!

The goal of this chapter is to construct, part by part, function by function, a motion picture camera. This generic machine will serve to illustrate how and why cameras do what they do.

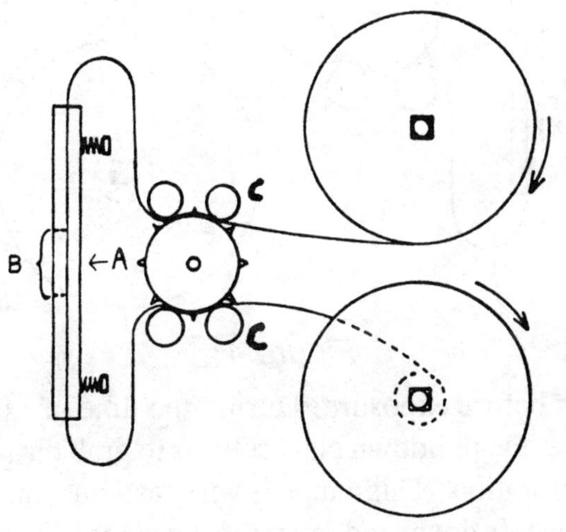

Figure 1

In the drawing above are two reels, and in this case they are called **daylight spools,** and they hold one hundred feet of sixteen millimeter film - so this is a sixteen millimeter camera. A daylight spool is simply a way of packaging film so that it can be loaded without the camera being in a darkroom or black fabric bag (called a **changing bag**) - that is, it can be loaded in what film manufacturers call **subdued light,** which seems to mean anything other than bright daylight. The sides of this spool are made of metal, and are opaque, so that the film that is beneath the outer four or five winds will not be exposed to light.

The upper reel is called the **feed**; it turns continuously clockwise when the camera is running. The lower is the **take-up,** it also turns clockwise and continuously. Some cameras have different paths and winds - this generic one has the ability to hold these daylight spools within the **body**, so it has what is called **internal load capability.**

The film runs over a sprocketed wheel at A, and the film itself has perforations that permit this. This is the only sprocketed wheel in this camera, and since the film runs to and from the **gate** (marked B) over and under this wheel, it is assured that the rates of feed and take-up will be identical. There are four **guide rollers**, C, that hold the film against the sprocketed wheel, and in most cameras there is some kind of release mechanism that moves these wheels away from the sprocketed wheel which allows you to thread the camera.

Before we go farther, the film itself should be discussed. Take a look at figure 2. It is easiest to think of film as composed of two layers, commonly called the base and the emulsion. The base is the clear plastic that gives the film it's shape, and strength. On one side of the base, a thin coating of light sensitive material is applied by the manufacturer, called the emulsion. It is this thin layer that is chemically altered by exposure to light - from the lens of the camera - then developed, becoming either a negative or positive image, depending on the film stock used and processing employed. (There are actually more layers of material on the film than just the base and emulsion, but for our purposes in this chapter, this will be enough.) It is always critical that this emulsion layer be facing the lens when the camera is loaded. The emulsion side can always be identified because it is dull; the base side is shiny.

For this film to be exposed correctly, a number of things must happen in the camera, at the gate:

The film must not be moving at the moment of exposure.

This seems strange. Film must move through the camera for action to be recorded. How can the film not be in motion during exposure?

Each frame of film, defined by the size of the **aperture** in the gate (marked B), must be held motionless at the precise moment of exposure, otherwise the image will streak across the film in the direction that the film was moving. (aperture is simply a nice way of saying hole). Imagine that you have put a dollar bill in a Xerox copier, and pressed the copy button, and instead of holding the bill still, you drag the dollar bill a few inches lengthwise. The copy will be a blur of the dollar bill. You may have seen film projected this way, but it was probably caused by misthreading of the projector. Everything looks blurry and streaky.

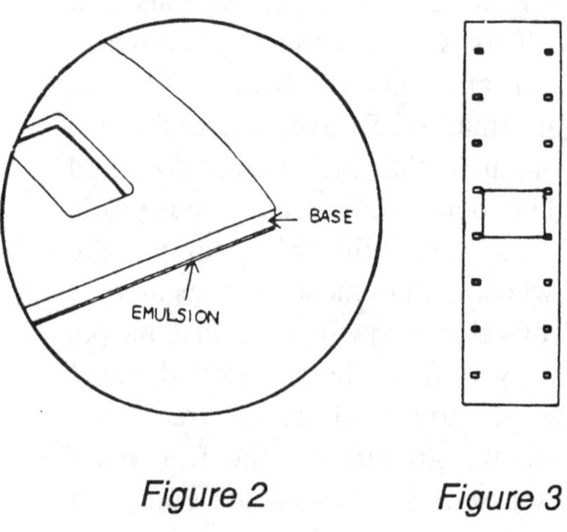

Figure 2

Figure 3

The "motion" in motion pictures results from the rapid projection of slightly different images. The individual images themselves are sharp. (Later, you'll find that for the motion to look smooth, a certain amount of blurring is actually necessary, a phenomena that stop-motion animators continuously struggle with. This blurring, however, is due to subject movement during exposure, not film movement.)

The system devised for stopping the film during exposure was invented by Thomas Edison. Small holes, called perforations, are placed at the side or sides of the film, and a certain number of perforations denote one frame. Usually, in 35mm, this is four perforations (although there are several other 35mm formats that use a different number of perfs per frame). In 16mm, there is one frame for every perforation. Take a look at figure 3.

A mechanical device called the claw (C in figure 4) engages a perforation, pulls the film down precisely one frame, then exits the film just before exposure. During the time of exposure, the pulldown claw returns to grab the next perforation. This happens very fast, but you can slow this down and examine the complete cycle by twisting the **inching knob**. This is a knob attached to the motor or drive system that lets you turn the camera by hand, advancing the film frame by frame.

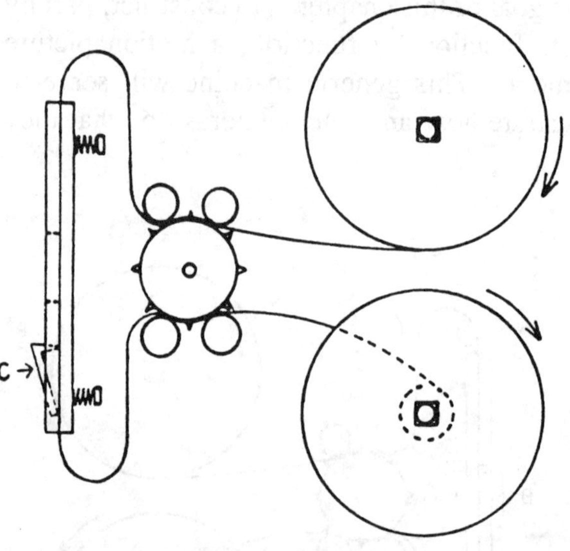

Figure 4

The standard camera speed - the rate at which both the camera and projector will run - is 24 frames per second (abbreviated in most technical texts as fps). This standard speed was finally locked in with the advent of synchronous sound (or so the popular theory goes), but for many years it may have been 16 or 18 or some other slower speed.

If you inch the camera manually, then run it at 24 fps, you'll note that the motion of the claw doesn't seem so gentle. In fact, the claw really has to slap the film through the camera to get it to stop and start twenty four times each second. The resulting racket produced is what accounts for most of a camera's noise. The design of the claw movement is paramount in producing a good, quiet camera.

This is the cycle: the claw engages the film, pulls it down, then exits during exposure. When the film is being exposed to light, the claw is returning to its original point to pull down the next frame, twenty four times each second.

The film must be held flat during the moment of exposure.

Film doesn't like to be flat. If you look at figure 5, or at a piece of film itself, you'll see that it wants to **curl** in the direction that it was

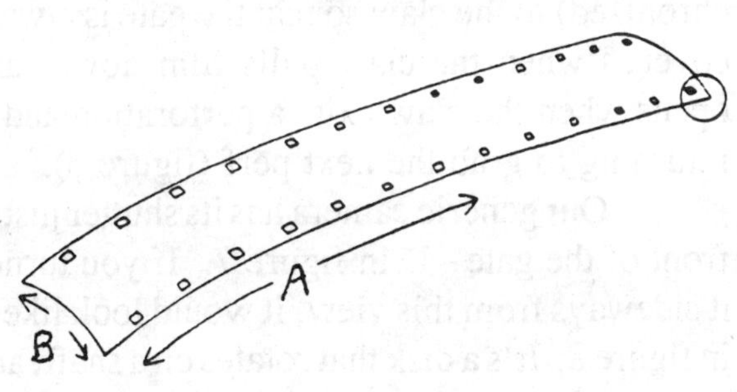

Figure 5

wound up on the reel, and it also wants to curl from side to side. The side to side curl usually results in the emulsion side being slightly convex.

Lenses for motion picture cameras are designed to give the sharpest image on a flat field, called the **focal plane**. If the film is not held precisely flat at the focal plane produced by the lens, it will have a poorly focused image when developed.

From a design standpoint, the film itself is a problem, because it naturally wants to curl. A sharp image projected on curled film results in an image that, when projected, is not all sharp. Perhaps the edges of the film are blurry, and the center is sharp, or vice versa. (You may have seen this in a movie theater, but chances are that it was caused by curved film in the gate of the projector, rather than the camera).

If you hold up a piece of undeveloped film, and look at your reflection in the dark surface of the base side, you'll see your image is distorted, like that in a fun house mirror. The distortion in this reflection is a direct result of the natural curl in the film. If you try to get rid of the curl, and make the image undistorted by flattening the edges of the film with your fingers - you'll find it quite impossible.

The only way to truly get the film to be flat enough to allow a sharp image to be recorded is to press the film between two pieces of flat, smooth steel. Nothing else - running the film through rollers, or holding the film only at the edges - will hold the film flat enough during exposure. These two flat pieces of steel are the **pressure** and **aperture plates,** and they are used in virtually all motion picture cameras. Camerapeople refer to them together as the **gate**.

The aperture plate is usually fixed motionless to the rest of the camera; the pressure plate presses the film against the aperture plate by a spring or springs, and either swings or slides back so that film can be loaded, or the gate area cleaned. The emulsion side of the film faces the aperture plate, so that this light sensitive layer is directly facing the lens itself.

This particular part of camera design should be a bit frightening to you. A ridiculously expensive, soft plastic strip of film is to be dragged between two pieces of steel (albeit highly polished). The steel is non-moving, and it contacts the film on both sides, all the way across, from perforation to perforation, not just at the sides. It is similar to audio tape being dragged across the playback and record heads in a tape deck.

Any dirt, or grit, or hair lodged in the gate can be disastrous. Even if dirt doesn't scratch or damage the film, or the gate itself, it may leave a permanent exposure on the film in the form of a shadow. If the pressure plate or aperture plate are somehow damaged, film running through them may be irreparably scratched.

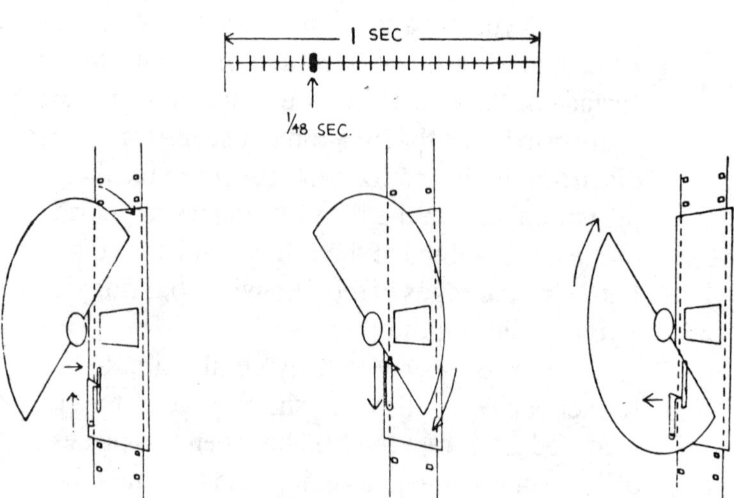

Figure 6

All this is leading us up to one thing: you must keep the interior of the camera spotless. Different camerapeople have their different favorite ways of cleaning cameras and lenses; mine are included in the chapter Testing and Cleaning.

A shutter must be synchronized with the pulldown claw.

What we have so far is a way to get the film to and from the gate (two daylight spools on spindles, a single sprocketed roller and two guide rollers), and a way to insure that the film is held flat (by the pressure and aperture plates) and motionless (by the action of the claw) during exposure. Its the "during exposure" part of our camera that we have to cover.

Remember that the claw is moving the film, one frame at a time, twenty-four times a second, past the aperture. A device called a **shutter** is needed so that when the claw moves each frame into position, the aperture is covered, and the film receives no exposure. If the film were to receive light from the lens when it was being advanced, it would be blurry and streaked, like the dollar bill copy in the earlier analogy.

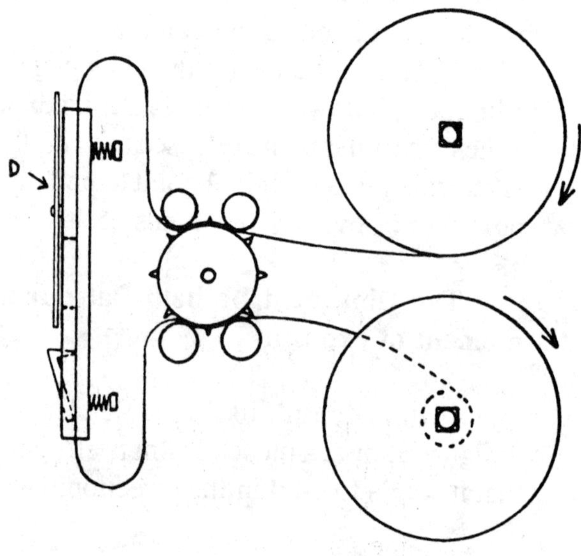

Figure 7

The shutter is linked mechanically (synchronized) to the claw so that the gate is always covered when the claw pulls film down, and opens when the claw exits a perforation and is returning to grab the next perf (figure 6).

Our generic camera has its shutter just in front of the gate - D in figure 7. If you turned it sideways from this view, it would look like A in figure 8. It's a disk that rotates on a shaft, and it revolves once for every frame of film exposed, and it rotates continuously (the film, which stops and starts and stops and starts 24 times a second, is said to be moving **intermittently**).

This disk has a certain amount cut out of it; in the case of A in figure 8, it's 180 degrees. When people describe a shutter, and they say it is 180 or 156 or whatever, they are referring to the amount of degrees out of a possible 360 that are *cut out* of the disk.

In the case of our generic camera, a 180 degree shutter rotating once for every frame of film, at twenty-four fps, will give us a length of exposure of 1/48th of a second. To visualize this, look at the scale in figure 6. The length of the scale represents one second, and it is divi-

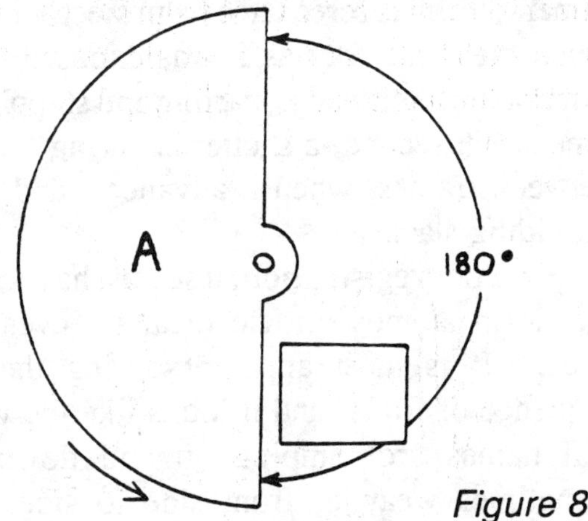

Figure 8

ded into twenty-four segments. Each segment represents one complete revolution of the shutter. The single dark segment represents the time that the shutter covers the gate, or exactly half of one complete segment: 1/48th of a second.

The mathematical formula for determining the length of exposure is:

$$\frac{\text{shutter angle}}{360} \times \frac{1}{\text{fps}} = \text{length of exposure}$$

To find out how this formula works for our shutter, divide 180 by 360, which is 1/2, then multiply this times 1/24 fps. The result is 1/2 x 1/24, or 1/48 of a second. Very simple math.

The length of exposure, expressed as a fraction of a second, is important because it will be one factor in determining the overall exposure of the film. (In the simplest of terms, this is the lightness or darkness of the resulting image when projected.)

Why 180 degrees? Why not a wider shutter angle that will allow us to film with less light? From a design standpoint, the length of time the shutter is closed (covering the gate) is important. Remember that each frame of film is advanced by the pulldown claw during this time. If the shutter angle is increased to say 240 degrees, only 120 degrees are used to cover the gate, and it is likely that this won't leave enough time for the film to be advanced in the gate. The claw will have to be made to move each frame in a much shorter period of time, and this might lead to other problems (ones that limit the fps range and make the camera noisy) as well.

What effect would a smaller shutter angle have? There are many reasons for choosing smaller shutter angles: 144 degrees reduces the effect of what some people call the roll bar when filming a video monitor. Narrower angles in general reduce the length of exposure so each frame of film is sharper when filming fast action, so camerapeople know to reduce camera angles when a "freeze frame" will be made from the shot in post-production. Expo-

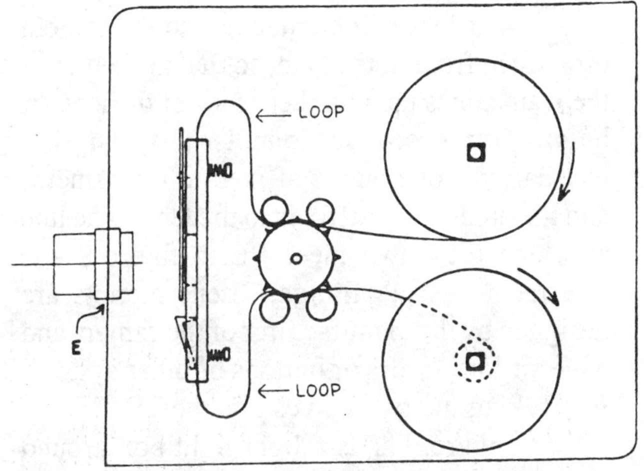

Figure 9

sure itself can be controlled by changing the shutter angle, but using the shutter in this way can have adverse effects on the moving image (to find out more about this, see Speeds and Angles).

A lens must throw a focused image on the film.

Lenses of motion picture cameras run the gamut from simple to extremely complex. Take a look at figure 9. The lens in our camera is simple: a barrel with two pieces of glass, called elements, inside it. If parallel light rays enter the lens, and are focused to a point, the distance from a place at the lens (called a nodal point) to the focus point is called the **focal length**. These parallel light rays are theoretically coming from an object at infinity. If this object were to move toward the lens, the apparent focal length would increase - the lens would have to be moved away from the camera to maintain this same focal point in space. This movement of the lens to maintain the same focal point is what you do when you focus a lens. Most of the time, a ring on the lens moves the elements in and out, and you can see this movement if you watch the glass inside the lens. This does not mean that the actual focal length of the lens varies with subject distance, because the term "focal length" applies to the situation when the object is at infinity only.

Our lens will be mounted to the camera directly in front of the gate, so that the center of the frame lines up with the center of the lens. A **lens mount** is used to accomplish this, and it has two halves - one that is affixed to the camera, and the other that is affixed to the lens. The line at which these two meet - E in figure 9 - is referred to as the **flange**. Lens mounts are designed by the manufacturer of the camera and have various levers or buttons or other systems for locking the two halves together.

Figure 9 adds a light tight box around the camera, one with a door that opens and closes to protect the film from outside exposure, and a motor to drive the sprocketed roller, the pulldown claw, and the shutter at a speed of 24 fps.

One thing should be mentioned - the **loops**. These are the segments of slack film between the gate and the sprocketed roller. They're necessary because while the film at the gate is running intermittently, stopping and starting twenty-four times a second, the sprocketed roller and the rest of the camera are running continuously. If the loops didn't contain this slack, the film would be ripped the first time the claw attempted to pull down a frame of film. Proper loop size varies from camera to camera, and is generally quite important. An over or under sized loop can cause the film to be torn, or scratched, or have poor registration when screened, a term used to describe the accurate positioning of each frame of film by the camera. Film is screened by a projector in very much the same way as it was exposed in the camera: intermittently, starting and stopping 24 times each second, a shutter covering the film between frames, when it advances, and loops providing slack.

Poor **registration**, it seems, has become the norm at most movie theaters, even new ones. It is most apparent during the title sequence of films, and it looks like the words and names are jumping up and down and sometimes weaving from side to side. This happens because either the camera (at the time of filming) or the projector (at the time of screening) was or is not pulling down each perforation to precisely the same location in the gate. The error is greatly magnified on screen, causing the image to be jumpy. It is almost certain that this sort of problem is caused by the projection system of the theatre, as only cameras and lab equipment of the highest precision are used in making multi-million dollar films.

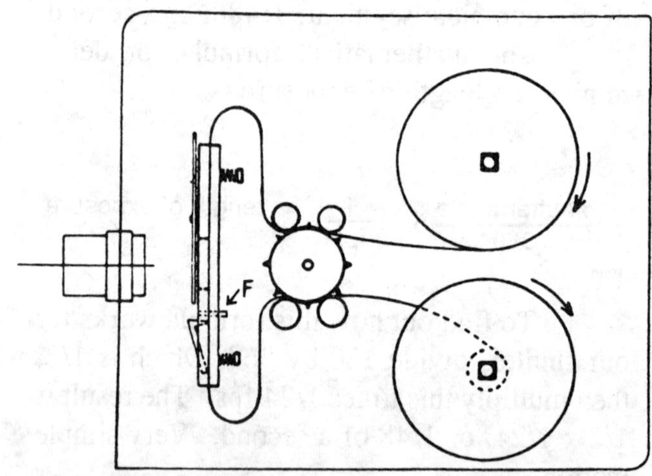

Figure 10

Although camera claws are usually designed so that they are coming to a nearly motionless part of their cycle (dwell) when they engage a perforation, they must make 24 cycles every second - such a speed that they are really slapping the film through the gate. Why is it that each perforation of the film will stop in the same precise place, every time? You might say that the action of the pressure plate keeps the film from moving after the claw has disengaged, and that is partially true. But the full answer involves another device, built into some movie cameras: a **registration pin.**

The registration pin (F in figure 10) is a device that is synchronized to the shutter and claw in this way: just before the shutter opens and the frame is being exposed, it inserts itself into a perforation and holds the film nearly motionless. Just after the gate is covered, the registration pin exits the perf, and allows the claw to pulldown the next frame.

Cameras with such pins are generally thought to deliver the best registration, and are favored for shooting critical material, such as titles or matte shots as well as standard footage. This is not to say that cameras without registration pins are apt to deliver poor footage. Some cameras have claws that are designed so that they act in both pulldown and registration functions. Others have fine registration in general, but are not quite precise enough for matte work, for example, which would be the ultimate test of registration in a working situation.

In the end it is important that you understand the function of the registration pin so that you can load and unload the camera. Often, cameras are built in such a way that you must inch the movement to a precise point in the film advance cycle to load it, otherwise the pin or the claw will not allow the film to enter the gate properly.

THE SOMEWHAT LESS SIMPLE CAMERA

is what we have now. Figure 10 shows all the bits and pieces - for the most part, all the bare necessities for making a sharp, steady image on our film.

What this camera now needs is a **viewing system:** something which we can look through in order to frame and focus the camera.

The best possible viewfinder would be one that would actually look through the lens that the camera is exposing film with. This is called **reflex viewing**, and you may be familiar with it from using a 35mm still camera. In the case of a reflex 35 still camera, a mirror is placed between the lens and the film so that an image entering the lens is bounced up, through a prism, and out an eyepiece. You look through this eyepiece and you see what the lens sees so you can compose your shot, and focus, and do other things like check depth of field - until you decide to make an exposure. When you press the button to take a picture, the mirror must jump up out of the way to allow light to go to the film. The viewfinder momentarily goes black, and you hear a loud "thunk" as the mirror plops down again.

Now we come to an interesting dilemma, one that hounded camera builders for many years: how can we possibly expose film and look through a lens at the same time?

Perhaps we could devise a shutter that would work like the one in our reflex 35mm still camera. It might work for a while, but at 24 fps such a shutter would bang itself off its hinges. It would also make a terrific amount of noise, and this is contrary to the goal of having a quiet camera for synchronous sound filming.

Initially, camera designers mounted a tube or box on the side of the camera, and carefully aimed it so that by looking through it you would have a good approximation of the actual frame being recorded. This **side finder** proved workable, especially when camera builders such as Mitchell made them with an elaborate system of cams that compensated for changing subject distance and lens focal length.

But there are specific benefits to actually looking through the lens used during filming. Framing and focusing can be viewed precisely, especially for telephoto shots, which prove tricky for a side finder to approximate. The actual look or feel that a given focal length lens gives a scene can be ascertained.

One answer was the **beam splitter** or **pellicle.** This is a thin piece of glass, partially silvered (mirrored) that is placed at an angle between the film plane and the lens - see figure 11. A percentage of the light entering the lens - say 85% - is passed by the beam splitter to the film, while the remaining 15% is sent to a small viewing screen. The operator watches the other

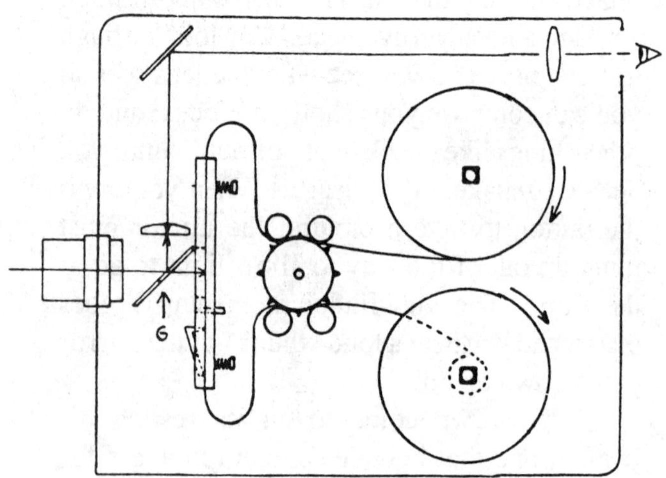

Figure 11

side of this screen and sees an image projected by the lens that duplicates that which will also appear on the film.

This works fine, and has a number of advantages. It is a true reflex system, and has all the advantages listed above. It is simple, has no moving parts to wear or make noise, and it can often be adapted to fit into existing cameras without too much modification. But it also has major drawbacks.

First, it robs some of the light, though very little, from the film. This is actually a small problem, but camerapeople always seem to be looking for faster lenses (ones that get more light to the film, and therefore require less lighting units on the set, for example). Secondly, the image in the viewfinder is not so bright. If only 15% of the possible light is being projected on the viewing screen, the resulting image can be very dark, especially when the operator is filming a scene that is itself dark. Thirdly, there is some degradation of the image, although slight. Anything placed between the film and the lens will soften the image somewhat, no matter how clear the material. Lastly, and most importantly, anything placed between the lens and film will optically change the distance by approximately *one third its thickness* (Richter Cine Corporation).

Recall how our lens focuses. As an object moves from infinity toward the camera, we have to increase the distance between the lens and the focal plane to maintain sharp focus, and this is done simply by the internal action of the lens when we focus.

There are markings on the lens in feet and inches (and often in meters as well) to tell us where to set our lens. Using a long tape measure to check subject distance and then setting the lens by its footage scale is the standard operating procedure for motion picture filming. This is called **tape focusing**. The

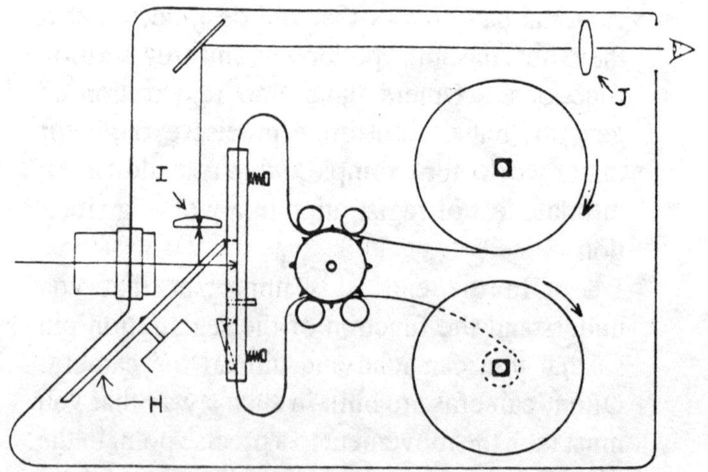

Figure 12

focus markings on the lens are based upon the distance the internal elements are from the film plane at any given footage mark, and if something is inserted that alters this distance, all the footage marks will be incorrect.

This is what happens when a beam splitter or pellicle is inserted, and it necessitates the use of special lenses whose footage scales have been altered to compensate.

For all these reasons, the beam splitter reflex system is thought to be less than the ideal.

Take a look at figure 12. Arnold and Richter took the shutter itself and set it at an angle to the film plane. The side of the shutter that faced the lens was mirrored, and bounced light up to a viewing screen, just like a beam splitter.

But unlike a beam splitter, the **rotating mirror shutter**, as it is called, took no light from the film, because when it rotated to expose a frame, there was nothing between the lens and film. 100% of the light was either sent to the viewfinder, or to the gate, depending on the position of the shutter.

Now, any lens can be used without footage scale modification, provided the rear element doesn't protrude so far into the camera that it hits the moving mirror shutter. There is no light loss.

But there are drawbacks. Since the shutter sends light alternately to the gate and viewing screen, the image seen when looking through the viewfinder flickers (the operator can stop the shutter in viewing position between shots, however). Perhaps the biggest drawback is that the mirror shutter itself requires high precision to manufacture and makes the camera costly.

But the advantages of the mirror shutter proved invaluable. Almost every modern professional movie camera uses it.

Take another look at figure 12. You can see the path of light as it either strikes the gate the or the **viewing screen**.

In most cameras, this is actually a piece of thin glass that has one side roughened, or ground, so that it is translucent and an image can be projected on it. This **ground glass**, as it's called, acts as a rear projection screen. You look through the viewfinder at the ground glass and see an image that is projected by the lens, bounced off the mirror shutter, onto the rear of the ground glass - a rear projected image. In most cameras the size of this image is slightly larger than one frame of film, and small black lines have been either printed or etched into the roughened side of the ground glass to outline the actual frame. Even in the case of 35mm movie cameras, the ground glass is quite small, so magnifying lenses located in the **eyepiece** enlarge the image for easier focusing and framing. With the addition of these lenses, our generic camera is almost complete.

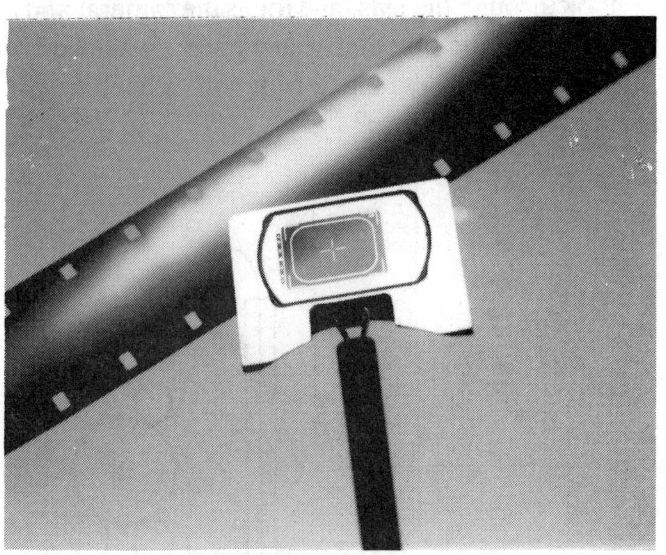

Arri 16SR Fiber View Screen

You may have noticed something about our reflex camera - the eyepiece is the back end of an open system. This means that a strong light could enter the eyepiece, light up the ground glass, and in turn light up the space in the camera that houses the mirror shutter and gate - and expose the film. To keep this from happening, cameras of this type need an eyecup to keep stray light from entering the eyepiece when the cameraperson is looking through the lens. As the operator, you must keep your eye pressed against this cup when filming, or risk fogging the film (exposing it to unfocused light).

If you wear eyeglasses, you must remove them, and adjust the eyepiece optics to compensate. In fact, every operator must do so. This is simply adjusting the magnifying lenses so that the lines or rough surface of the ground glass comes into sharp focus. If you have to shoot something and you can't have your eye at the finder, you have to find some way of keeping the eyepiece closed, and most cameras have either an external door or an internal dowser that accomplishes this.

A MORE COMPLEX CAMERA

is what we have now, in figure 12. It is a modern design, complete with mirror shutter. We can look through the lens, and focus the camera, and frame, and be sure that what we see is what we'll get when our developed film comes back from the lab. Or can we?

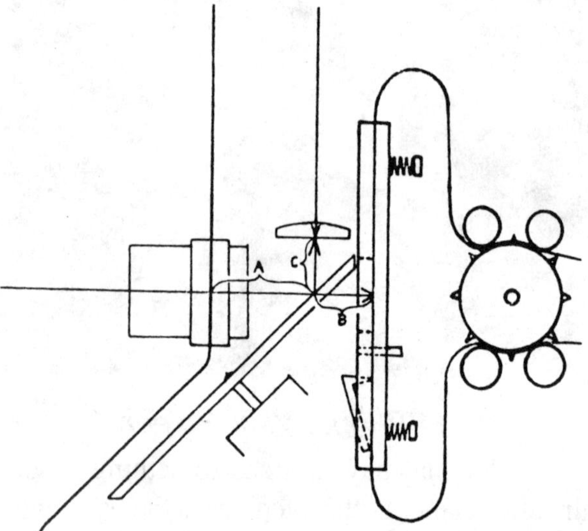

Figure 13

Think for a while about our ground glass. What we're asking of our reflex system is to project onto the ground glass an image that is the same as the one that will be projected onto the film. We're counting on this because we are looking at our ground glass to frame, and focus.

To see how this can go awry, take a look at the next diagram, figure 13. You'll see an important distance here - the **flange/focal distance**. Remember that we said that the flange is the place where the two halves of the lens mount meet. The focal plane is simply the place where the emulsion side of our film is, pressed against the aperture plate in the gate. The distance marked A - from the flange to the mirrored surface of the shutter, and B - the distance from the front surface of the shutter to the focal plane comprises the flange/focal distance. This is the distance over which you can think of the image being thrown before it comes to focus on the film. The distance from the mirrored surface to the ground (roughened) side of the ground glass - A plus C - is called the flange/ground glass distance.

When you **eye focus** a camera, you are relying on the fact that the camera is correctly adjusted, in this way:

$$A + B = A + C$$

Or, the flange/focal distance equals the flange/ground glass distance.

Take a look at figure 14. This is a bad, or incorrectly adjusted camera. The distance of C in this camera is too long. What happens when you eye focus this camera is this: you look through finder, see an image focussed on the ground glass, and adjust the lens so that the image is sharp. Then you hit the start switch on the motor of the camera, and film is exposed,

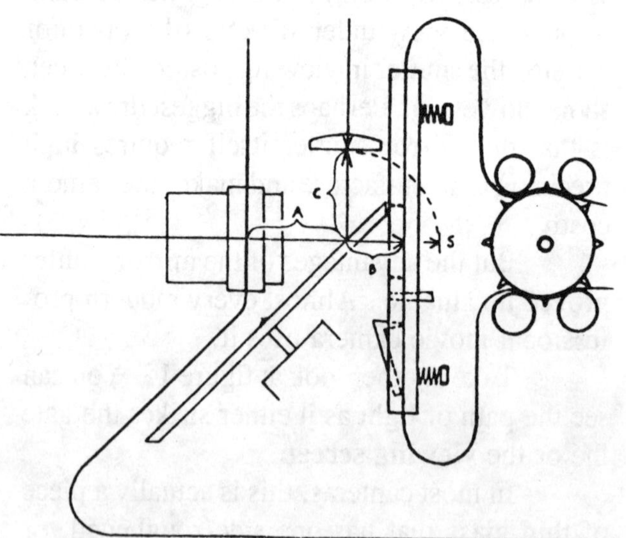

Figure 14

but not in focus. The place where the image is sharp in our camera is S - not at the film plane. In our bad camera, the formula is simply:

$$A + B \neq A + C$$

So, you get bad footage from this camera. Perhaps you should have tape focused it, and ignored the image being thrown on the ground glass. But how would you know to do this? And what could cause a camera to become bad - that is, incorrectly adjusted, so that the flange/focal distance does not equal the flange/ground glass distance?

Somebody dropped it. Or banged it. Or it received poor or no maintenance. Then they gave it to you.

This could happen at any time, or any place. A school, a friend, a small rental house or a huge rental establishment can all be sources of bad cameras, no matter how much money you've paid or what someone assures you.

It is up to you, or someone who is working with you (the Assistant Cameraperson) to do a specific test to make sure that this won't happen.

The test is called *comparing tape and eye focus*.

It is a test that compares the two different means of focusing the camera. If they agree, then you can be confident that you don't have a bad camera, that is, one where the ground glass is maladjusted, or the flange/focal distance is shortened, or anything else that might cause A+B not to equal A+C.

PERFORMING THE TEST TO COMPARE TAPE AND EYE FOCUS.

Make time and space to do this test. Even if you are loaned the camera for free, it's a poor bargain if it destroys your project. If you are at a rental house of any repute whatsoever, they'll have a special room or area where you can test the camera and lens before you leave.

Pull out your tripod, and check its functions: pan, tilt, spreader, leg extension - everything. Once you are satisfied, mount the camera.

Put something on the nearest wall to focus on: a dollar bill or a page of the script you particularly dislike will do nicely. The best thing to focus on is something called a Seimens star, and often rental houses will have charts that contain these already mounted on a wall for you to use. This done, get a light from your lighting package and aim it at your focusing dollar or page or whatever, and light it up. This will help you really see what's going on.

Select a lens and mount it, or if you are using only one zoom lens, mount that. Find a convenient mark on the footage scale of the focusing ring on the lens. This is usually the second closest footage mark on the scale (by closest I mean the nearest an object can be to the lens, and still be in focus). Don't choose the closest, as you'll need to twist the ring back and forth past whatever mark you've chosen to do this test, and usually lenses have a stop built into them near their closest mark. Don't pick a distance between the marks either, because it may be difficult to tell whether you are at 4' 8" if there is no mark for that distance.

Raise or lower the camera on the tripod so that the gate is level with the center of whatever you're focusing on.

Get out your tape measure. The best kind for this test, and for filmmaking in general, is a 50' fiberglass tape. The shorter metal carpenter's tapes are handy because they are easier to use by one person but their sharp edges can damage lenses and other equipment, and make actors and actresses understandably nervous on the set.

Using the tape, place the film plane in the camera precisely the same distance from the chart as the mark on the lens you've chosen indicates. How is this done? There is a symbol on the camera somewhere that tells you where the film plane is inside. It looks like this:

ϕ

Hold the tape up from the chart to this mark on the camera, and have someone drag the tripod back and forth until you get it right on. If no one is around to help, you have to use your foot to drag the camera back and forth (dangerous!), or set the tape down, then move the camera and check the distance over and over again.

Let's use an example: 5 feet. This was

the next closest mark on my lens (it focuses down to 4', then it stops), and now I've succeeded in getting my film plane exactly 5' from the chart on the wall.

Now I'll look through my viewfinder at the ground glass, and twist the focus ring back and forth until the image of the chart is sharp. There.

I look at the footage scale on the lens. Does it say 5'? If so, my tape and eye focus agree, and I can be confident that the camera/ lens system is correctly adjusted. Does it say 7'? If this is the case, I'll try again several times to make sure I've focused correctly. If I come up with 7' each time, or very close to it, something is wrong. There is no way for me to know where the problem is - it could be that one of the distances A, B, or C is incorrect, or the lens itself could be out of adjustment - or any combination of these factors could be the trouble. Without the use of special test equipment, I'm stuck.

I take the camera/lens off the tripod, and walk back to the person who gave it to me. I say "Tape and eye focus don't match. Tape is five feet, and eye is seven."

Unless the person I'm talking to is incompetent, s/he will take the camera/lens from me and ask me to wait while one of their technicians checks it out.

Why did I say what I said? You'll find that in rental establishments you are probably looked upon as just another know nothing filmmaker. So many camerapeople come into rental houses with inaccurate information (and a snobby artist attitude) that rental workers automatically react this way.

If you return with your questionable camera/lens to the rental person, you are just another problem - and actually, one of the worst kinds to such a business (worse would be if you went out and shot your film with a bad camera, then came back and blamed the rental house). What you are doing is calling into question the technical standards of the rental house as well as possibly creating a problem for the manager, who will have to find another camera or lens to give you if yours cannot be fixed (they may not have one!) Be polite, stand your ground. Once the technicians find the problem, you'll become different in the eyes of the rental person - someone who knows something! Be magnanimous, and let this person (and company) who almost ruined your shoot off the hook with a smile as they try to solve the problem. You are making friends, ones that could give you a better deal in the future, or help you out of a jam.

WHAT THE TECHNICIAN DOES

A) Collimate the lens

A **collimator** is a device that the technician uses to test the lens. It sends parallel (collimated) light through a beam splitter which

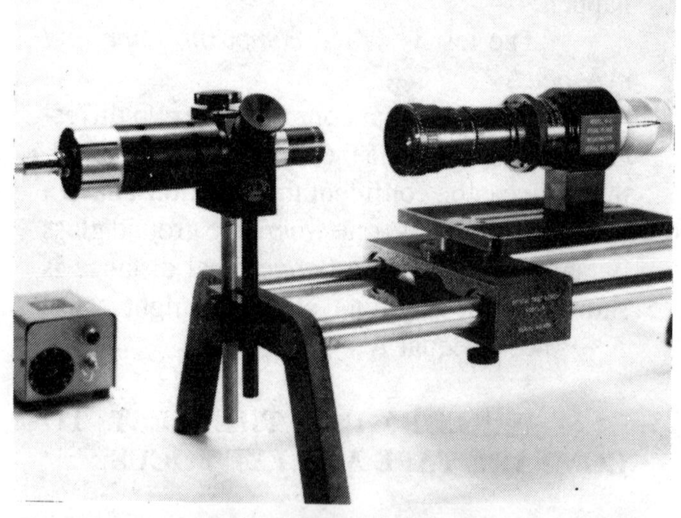

Richter Collimator

divides the light, sending half through the lens in question and the other half to a reticle. The light sent to the lens bounces off a mirror, then back to the same reticle. By setting the lens on infinity, then moving the mirror behind the lens with a special micrometer and looking at the reticle, the flange/focal distance for the lens can be measured by adjusting the micrometer until the image of the reticle is sharp. This distance should be the same as the factory standard flange/focal distance for the camera in question. If it is, then the problem lies somewhere in the camera. If it isn't, then the lens must be adjusted and re-collimated until it is focusing correctly. Then the camera should be tested for further problems.

B) Check the depth.

Depth is a term technicians use instead of flange/focal distance. Checking the depth involves the use of a gauge and gate plate. The gauge is inserted into the lens port of the camera. The flange part of the gauge rests against the flange part of the camera like a lens.

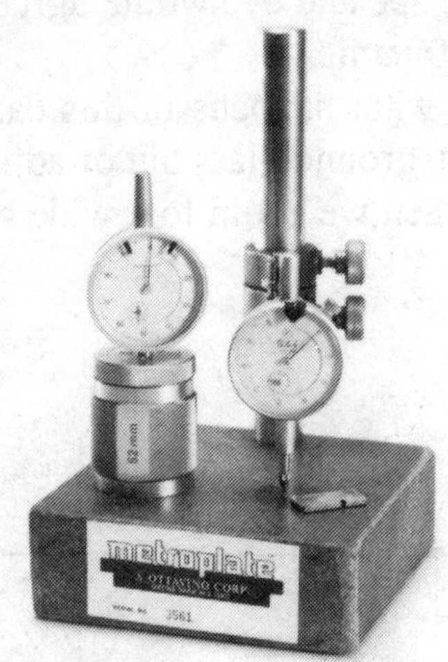

Arri depth gauge and granite standard

The pointed, spring loaded tip of the gauge rests against a steel gate plate which has been pressed against the aperture plate, inside the camera. The front surface of this plate rests in precisely the same place that the emulsion side of the film does when the camera is loaded. A dial on the gauge measures the actual flange/focal distance of the camera. Does it duplicate factory standards? If not, it must be adjusted so that it does.

C) Check the ground glass.

Once the depth of the camera is known to be correct, the technician must test the position of the ground glass. Unfortunately there is no gauge that can check the depth of the ground glass, because this depth is split into two parts by the mirror shutter. A shop standard lens - that is, one that is known to be correctly collimated and never leaves the shop - is mounted in the camera, and the technician proceeds to test the ground glass using the same test that brought the camera/lens into question in the first place: comparing tape and eye.

These three steps can be carried out in as little as ten minutes, so don't be afraid to ask for the technicians to do them, even if you're really rushed for time. Any significant discrepancy between tape and eye focus can indicate a problem and should be checked out.

But what is a significant discrepancy? At a distance of four or five feet, I would say three or four inches. If tape and eye are within two inches, fine. A half-foot difference is too much. Before you tell anyone that the camera/lens has a problem, make sure. Do the tape and eye test over and over until you are confident of your judgement.

THE ZOOM LENS

is a special case with regard to comparing tape and eye. To understand it better, we need to take some time and discuss lenses in general.

A **prime lens** is one that has two controls: focus and iris (the iris is the adjustable hole in the lens whose size is described in F stops). It has but one focal length. It could be a standard or wide-angle or telephoto prime lens, depending on this focal length. A **standard lens** is one that seems not to alter the image seen when you look through the viewfinder - that is, what you see when you are standing next to the camera and watching the scene and then what you see through the viewfinder look the same - no magnification or reduction. Each format - 16mm, 35mm, Vistavision, Imax, - will have a standard lens based roughly on the diagonal of the frame. For example, a 25mm lens is thought by many to be standard on 16mm cameras. A 25mm lens used on a 35mm camera is a wide angle lens for that format. Telephoto lenses are ones with larger focal lengths - 75,

150, 300 millimeters.

The **zoom lens** is one that has three controls: focus, iris, and focal length, or zoom. This added control lets the filmmaker select a particular focal length, or change the focal length during the shot. Zoom lenses are usually described by the range of focal lengths they offer: Angenieux 12-120mm, Zeiss 10-100mm.

To perform an accurate tape and eye test with a zoom lens, proceed exactly as you would with a prime: set up the camera, choose the next to the widest mark on the lens, set the film plane that distance from the lighted chart.

Twist the zoom control until the lens is at its most telephoto focal length. The lighted wall chart should appear greatly magnified, and this will make focusing easy. Compare the distance on the lens (eye focus) against the actual chart to film plane distance (tape focus). Do they agree? Unless the camera or lens is hugely out of adjustment, they always will.

Why is this? Before I can explain that, we have to talk about **depth of focus** and **depth of field**.

Many filmmakers understand what is meant by depth of field. It is the range of acceptable focus in front of the lens (in the scene to be filmed). A lens may be adjusted so that it has a depth of field that runs from 4' to 20', for example. This means that any object in the scene between these two distances will be in acceptable focus. Closing the iris of a lens down will increase the depth of field. In working situations, wide angle lenses have greater depth of field than telephoto lenses.

Depth of focus is the range of acceptable focus behind the lens, at the film plane inside the camera. If the emulsion side of the film should somehow move out of this range, it would be out of focus. Depth of focus is also increased by closing down the iris, but in regard to focal length, it is inversely related to depth of field.

A wide angle lens has great depth of field - some of them might render a sharp image from four feet to infinity at F 5.6, for example. But this same lens has a very tiny depth of focus. Consider the following chart based on lenses for 16mm cameras, focused at 6' and set at f2. The measurements given are the lengths of the fields of focus.

lens	depth of field	depth of focus
12mm	5'5"	.025mm
100mm	.5"	.20mm

The 12mm lens has a great depth of field and a tiny depth of focus. The 100mm has just the reverse: tiny depth of field and great depth of focus. So great a depth of focus, in fact, that even if the ground glass in the camera were .10mm out of adjustment, the image would still be sharp. Tape and eye would agree at a focal length of 100mm.

But what happens in this camera - the one with the ground glass out of adjustment by .10mm - when we zoom to a wide angle focal length?

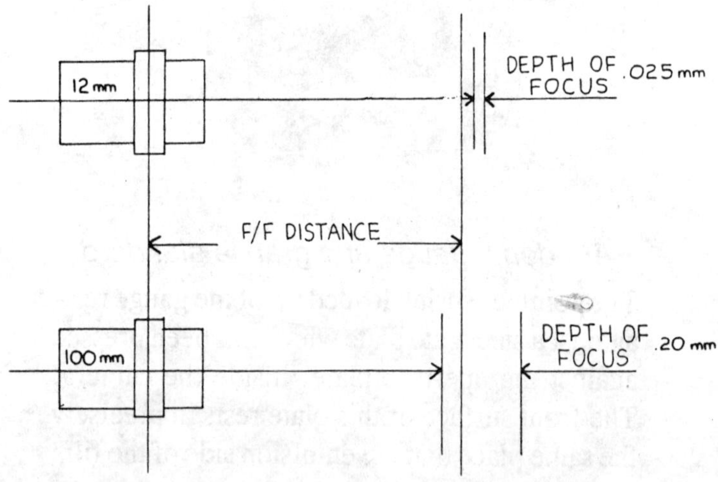

Figure 15

With a camera this badly adjusted, the image would probably start to go out of focus at 50mm, and look very fuzzy at 30mm because the depth of focus is not centered in relation to the flange/focal distance. As we zoom to a shorter focal length, the depth of focus shrinks and misses ground glass. Most camerapeople would now assume that something is wrong with the lens, since zooming to a wide focal length causes it to loose focus. But it is the position of the ground glass that is the real culprit. Figure 15 visualizes this.

To compare tape and eye focus with a zoom then, you must use the widest possible focal length, as this will give you the smallest depth of focus, and therefore assure the smallest testing tolerance.

The widest possible focal length for comparing tape and eye is almost never the shortest focal length of the zoom. In a 16mm camera set four or five feet from the wall, 25 or 30 millimeters is the widest setting that you can use and still see the chart well enough to focus. A wider setting does shrink the depth of focus further, but it also shrinks the wall chart in the viewfinder - and increases the depth of field. This combination makes for very difficult focusing.

So, testing a zoom lens takes a little more time.

Even if the concept of depth of focus is not clear to you, you'll be able to accurately evaluate a zoom lens if you understand how to do a simple tape and eye comparison using two focal lengths of the lens: the longest (most telephoto) setting and the widest (shortest) focal length that allows you to still see the chart well enough to focus. Both these focal lengths should indicate a focus the same as the tape focus.

A TESTED, COMPLEX CAMERA

is what we've ended up with in this chapter.

It is quite possible to build a camera that is not so complex.

Instead of a rotating mirror shutter, you could use a simple side finder; one that doesn't allow you to look through the lens. The lens might have three focus ranges - near, average, and far -instead of an accurate footage scale. It also might be permanently attached so that you needn't be bothered with focal length selection, or lens mounting. These kinds of simplifications make for an easier, simpler camera, but they also limit the flexibility of the camera, and consequently your creativity.

Another kind of camera could be built: one that has all of the good things in our generic camera, but also other complex things: for example, automatic exposure devices that interpret the lighting so that the nice silhouette you thought you were getting just turns out to be a dull, underexposed shot of your lead actress. Or they might have an automatic loading device that makes it very difficult to clean the gate, and jams occasionally.

Professional cameras have pretty much in them what I've described in this chapter, and no more. This is the way professionals like them to be - reliable, manually operated machines that are used by thinking, decision-making people.

Sync

Sync is short for **synchronization**, and it means recording sound during a take so that actors voices and other sounds can be heard when the film is viewed. How all this gets done is the subject for another very long book; even so, the process warrants discussion here because camerapeople must have an understanding of the requirements of post-production - otherwise, incorrect decisions may be made during the shoot that make the completion of the film very difficult, or even impossible.

To begin with, film is loaded in the camera. The film is exposed during the shooting session, and sent to the lab to be processed. A print is usually struck from the developed film (now called camera original) to be used for editing. This print can be edited and re-edited (spliced and re-spliced) until the final version is reached. This final edit, called "locked picture", will usually contain scratches, unintended splices (ones that were made for edits that were later undone) and other damage - but the camera original will not. The camera original, which has no damage, is **conformed** - or carefully cut together - to match the locked picture so that pristine, undamaged prints can be struck from it for final release.

The initial print which is struck for editing purposes (called a **workprint**) has a frame to frame relationship with the camera original. A machine called a **contact printer** assures this: the camera original and the unexposed stock which will become the workprint when developed are sandwiched together (hence the term contact) and exposure is made through the camera original to the film that, when developed, will become the print.

Sound is recorded during shooting on 1/4" audio tape. It is impossible to have a discussion of sync without mentioning a specific product: the **Nagra**. Walk onto a set anywhere in the world, and the camera could be an Arri, Aaton, Panaflex, Eclair, Moviecam, Cinema Products, etc., but the tape recorder will almost always be a Nagra. Other machines have been used - Tandburg, Uher, and Stellavox, for example - but Nagra has become almost unchallenged in recent years. Nagra builds its 1/4" tape machines to the highest standards, and specifically for the moving image industry. The only other recorder people occasionally use is a specially modified, crystal controlled Sony Professional Walkman (Sony, Stellavox, and Fostex DAT recorders are now being used more and more for film sound recording - see the DAT discussion in this chapter).

The Nagra runs audio tape at several different speeds, but the one used for filmmaking is 7 1/2 ips (inches per second). After the shoot, this tape is transferred to sprocketed, **magnetic film** - film the same size as the camera original (in this case, 16mm). This is a fairly simple procedure: the 1/4" is placed on a deck and played back while the magnetic film records it on another deck (called a dubber).

Now we have two records of the events of the shoot: a visual one on a film print (which matches the camera original frame for frame) and an audio one on magnetic sound film (which was dubbed from the original 1/4" audio tape). These pieces of material are then handed to either the editor or the assistant editor, who will attempt to align (sync) them, one to the other, so that they can be viewed in synchronization (by the way, film that has been synchronized with sound is synched, or perhaps synced, but definitely not sunk, just as pictures are hung but people are hanged).

But here is our problem: what if the speeds of the two initial recording machines - the camera and Nagra - vary? What if the camera is running a bit faster than 24 frames per second (the standard projection speed) and the Nagra at less than 7 1/2 ips? The workprint and magnetic film would not match. The person attempting to sync them up would find at a certain point in each take, sync would be lost - the words would begin to be heard sooner or later than the actors would be seen speaking

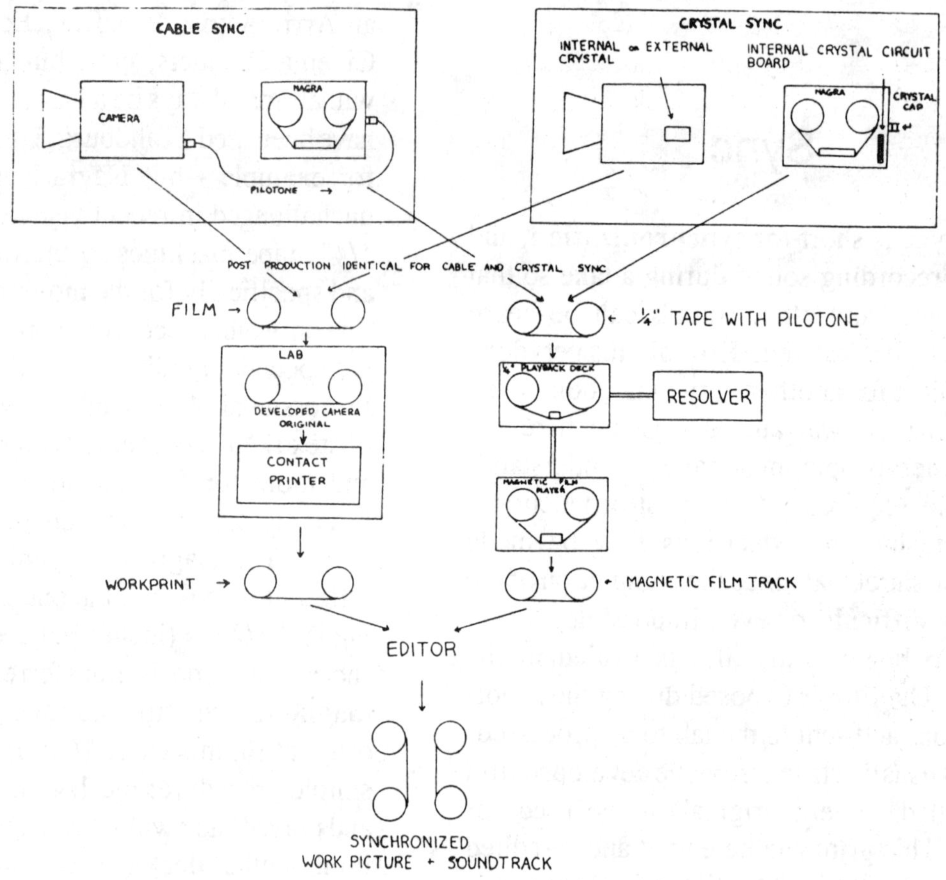

them, and this would get worse and worse as the take continued.

Why would this happen? Machines like cameras, phonograph turntables, tape decks and film projectors all have to run at a fairly precise speed. If a phonograph, for example, varies in speed too much, the listener perceives an annoying "wow", or variation in pitch. The phonograph must have a system which keeps its speed precise enough so that the listener is not disturbed. This is fairly easy to achieve, however, and turntables can actually run slower than 33 1/3 rpm, or faster, and even vary their speed considerably and the listening experience will be unhindered. But in motion picture making this kind of inaccuracy will make sync shooting impossible.

The standard 16mm camera load is four hundred feet, or about 11 minutes. Most viewers will perceive an error in lip sync (people talking) between the picture and sound of two frames. This, then, becomes the criterion: no more than one frame difference in four hundred feet (16,000 frames) between picture and sound.

Some means of assuring that the workprint and magnetic film have a frame-to-frame relationship must be employed. Over the years, there have been many different ways of doing this, but today, there are two: cable sync and crystal sync.

Cable sync works this way: a cable connects the camera and Nagra. The camera sends a tone - (60 Hz in the U.S., 50Hz in Europe), generally called **pilot signal** - via the cable to the Nagra, which records it on the 1/4" tape. As the camera and Nagra speeds vary in relation to each other, the pitch of the tone varies and becomes a record of both machine's rate of recording. When the 1/4" tape is transferred to magnetic film, a device called a **resolver** reads the pilot signal and adjusts the speed of the 1/4" playback deck so that the resulting magnetic film will be identical to the workprint, frame-for-frame.

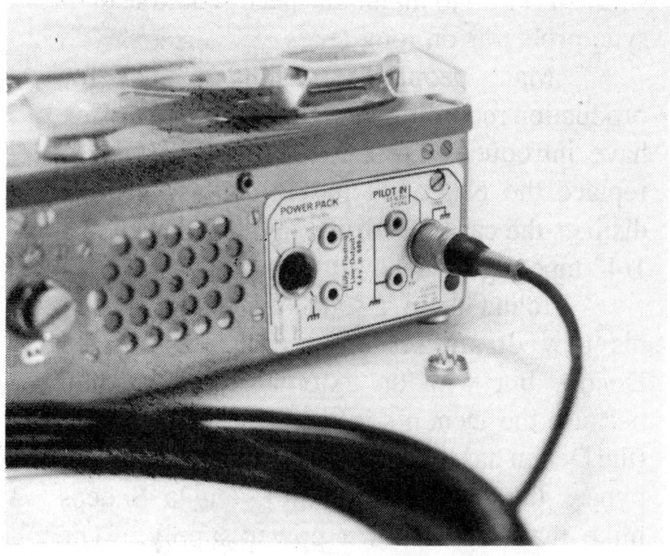

Nagra 4.2: Sync Cable and Crystal Cap

As a filmmaker you never actually hear this pilot signal. The head of the Nagra that records sound from each take is accompanied by a separate, dual gap neo-pilot head that records pilot signal. It is recorded as two signals which are out of phase with each other, so that only a resolver will be able to read it (this recording system is call **Neopilot** by Nagra). Playback on a standard, mono head tape deck will result in the two signals cancelling each other out, and the pilot signal will not be heard.

Using a cable between camera and tape recorder to carry the pilot signal works fine and was the standard means of shooting and recording sound until the middle to late Sixties. It has only one drawback: the cable itself. Connecting the sound and camera departments of the crew with a cable slows each down, and, for some takes (dolly and hand held shots) it can be a genuine roadblock. Multiple camera shoots (for rock concerts, events, etc.) become nightmares. Early on, several manufacturers came up with the idea of sending the pilot signal from camera to Nagra over a radio transmitter, but interference from CB radios and other sources made this approach less than ideal.

What if the camera doesn't vary in speed? What if a way could be found to control the speed of the camera so it didn't vary from the ideal of 24 fps over 16,000 frames? **Crystal sync** is that way, and here's how it works: a small quartz crystal - similar to the ones found in wristwatches - is installed in the camera. It generates a very precise frequency. The camera motor also generates a frequency signal which is then compared to that of the crystal. If there is any discrepancy, a special circuit alters the power to the motor (it is delivered in short pulses) until the motor generates a new frequency matching that of the crystal.

With crystal sync, the camera runs at 24 fps *very precisely* - so precise, in fact, that there isn't enough variation involved to necessitate a cable to the Nagra to record it - but pilot signal is *still* used. Another crystal, mounted on a special modular circuit board inside the Nagra, generates a pilot signal which is identical to any that would come from a crystal

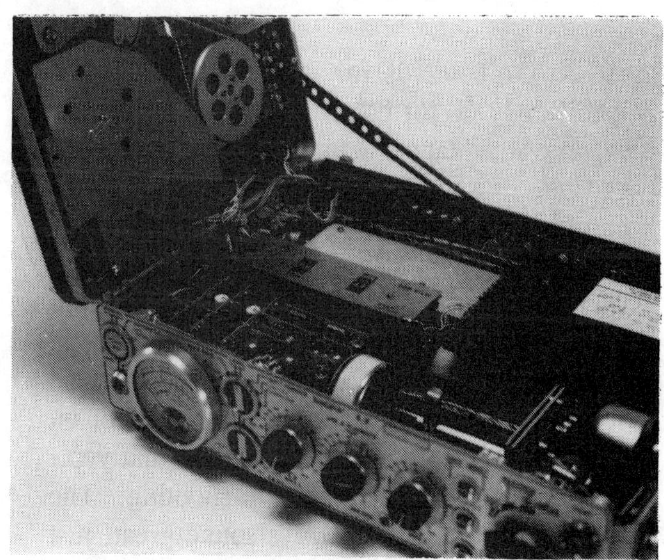

Nagra 4.2 Interior

controlled camera if it had a generator. The crystal board in the Nagra is activated by a small **crystal cap** that screws into the right side of the chassis in the same connector you use to plug in a sync cable. The pilot signal actually exits and then re-enters the Nagra through the crystal cap, and it is recorded and used to resolve the transfer. The process of resolving the 1/4" tape during transfer to magnetic film, then, is *identical* for either cable or crystal sync, since tapes made during either type of shooting have pilot signal.

The system of modular circuit boards inside the Nagra allows the user to custom design the machine to his or her specific needs. One of the most common of these option boards (aside from crystal) is an internal resolver. This allows the operator to use the deck as a resolver/ playback deck for transferring tapes to magnetic film as well as for playing back pre-recorded music (or effects) on the set during shooting.

The concepts of crystal sync, cable sync, and pilot signal are generally somewhat mysterious to the beginning filmmaker, since none are ever seen or heard, but there are indicators that will tell you that they are functioning, and there are *tests you can perform* to make sure that all is well - see the Testing and Cleaning chapter.

DAT

DAT stands for Digital Audio Tape - specifically a format that uses small audio cassette sized tapes (actually smaller) to record and play. Sound is digitized, or turned into numbers, and stored on the tape in the same way as a video tape recorder stores information - in frames. A DAT recorder is, then, just like a tiny VCR. Since DAT machines must drive the tape at a very precise speed to read each frame correctly (they read coded speed information on the tape itself to do so) you can see that yep - they can be used for sync film shooting! The advantages are many: DATs sound great, just like CDs, and they're small, light and, by Nagra standards, cheap. A near walkman sized Denon machine costs about $800. You can put up to two hours on a single tape compared to a standard Nagra's 15 minutes (a 5" reel at 7.5 ips) and a day's shoot can easily fit in your shirt pocket.

The disadvantages are that DAT machines are not as fall-down-the-stairs rugged as Nagras. Most are consumer grade machines that aren't built to stand up to hard use. They are also reportedly susceptible to moisture, so shooting in wet environments could be a problem. And something called error correction, or what DATs do to maintain speed, could lead to sync problems on long takes.

Many people are turning to DAT for production recording, and Stellavox and Fostex have introduced DAT models specifically to replace the Nagra on movie shoots. Nagra dislikes the cassette format and has designed a 1/4" tape digital deck all their own.

John Gurrin, a sound expert, tells me of his new dream set up: the walkman sized Denon, but with an external mixer/preamp because the Denon's internal pre-amp is poor (the Denon has line inputs, however, so you can bypass the internal pre-amp), and a Shoeps mike that has it's own power supply. The Shoeps is also tiny - like half a Tootsie Roll - and sits on the end of a carbon-fiber mic pole. The Denon, mixer and power for the Shoeps are attached to a small platform slung over one's neck, weighing no more than a few pounds, enabling the sound person to record and boom at the same time when necessary. A few extra batteries are stored in one pocket, a handful of DAT tapes in another (easily six or eight hours of recording time) and away you go.

SYNC WITH DAT

A DAT machine works as a recorder and resolver in one. Experts tell me that as long as the machine in question is in good repair and little error correction takes place, DAT machines will record and playback tapes with very little time change. One way people run into trouble, however, is when transferring to tape. Telecine machines like the Rank and Bosch actually run film at 23.976 fps. If you shoot at 24 fps, and transfer your film to video, the product will be very slightly off - actually .024 fps slower. The DAT tape, on the other hand, will not be slowed down by this amount because the playback machine isn't the Rank, or Bosch, but another DAT machine. If, on the other hand, you transfer from the DAT to magnetic film (either 16mm or 35mm) to be interlocked to the camera original at time of transfer, both sound and picture will be slowed down to 23.976 and therefore in sync. If you want to transfer from DAT directly to videotape, then synchronize, then edit, you should shoot at 23.976, or shoot at 24 and transfer your sound to mag film before transferring to videotape.

How to shoot at 23.976? Few cameras have this speed built in, but my guess is that many will have it someday. Right now, your best bet is to get a speed control such as the Media Logic 5 Digit Speed Control or the Cinematography Electronics Precision (see Speeds and Angles chapter). These let you change the speed of your camera in .001 fps increments, and every speed is crystal controlled. Unfortunately, many older sync cameras cannot be controlled by these units: the Arri 16BL (unless it has the Media Logic BL-Drive motor and Fischer interface), CP16R, and Eclair NPR and ACL. If you must use one of these cameras, you may be forced to shoot at 24fps and transfer to magnetic film before transferring to tape. Or, if you know that all your takes will be short, you can shoot at 24 with DAT for direct transfer and ignore the time difference.

Since the change is .024 frames per second, this means that every 41.67 seconds you'll be one frame out of sync. If you are shooting playback to a music video, where you'll be synchronizing to a pre-recorded track and more than likely cutting to a new shot every few seconds, this is not a problem. If you're doing long dialogue takes, however, you may want to find a way to get your camera to run 23.976 fps since an extra generation in the audio isn't a great idea, especially when it sounds as bad as 16mm mag does (in comparison with DAT) or costs as much as 35mm mag film.

Slating

Using either cable sync, crystal sync, or DAT, you can be sure the sound and picture films will be the same length for each take - but how do you know where each one begins?

Think about it: you have been given the task of "syncing up" the workprint and accompanying magnetic sound film. You thread up your editing machine (flatbed, upright or synchronizer-viewer-squawkbox) and try to match picture to sound. The first take contains some dialogue, and you can see and hear the person talking. The actor in question keeps turning his head, and another actor is also talking. You try to find a word that begins with a hard consonant and necessitates the use of the actors lips in a clear, visual way, like B or P, so you can figure out where to match the soundtrack with the picture. Finally, after twenty minutes of slipping the soundtrack back and forth, you get it - only to discover that you've synchronized the picture from take 1 to the sound from take 4.

The device that keeps this nightmare from happening is called the **slate**. Subject of countless comedy gags, it is invaluable because it tells the editor these things: where to sync the sound and picture, and what the scene/take/sound number is.

The part of the slate which has the writing on it is usually made of pressboard or plastic. A set of hinged clapsticks are affixed to the top and are striped with black and white paint so they can be seen against any background, dark or light. When these sticks are clapped together in a take, they tell the editor how to align (sync) the picture and sound tracks: the very first frame of noise from the clap on the sound track is locked to the very first frame of closed sticks.

Here's how the slate is used on the set:

The director will ask for quiet on the set, then inform the crew that he or she is about to call a take (as opposed to a rehearsal, which the cast and crew have supposedly been engaged in before).

DIRECTOR: Quiet everybody. This is a take. Is everybody ready? Camera?

The Camera Operator, or perhaps the Assistant Cameraperson will quickly, mentally check that the camera equipment is prepared to roll film. Many assistants use the acronym F.A.S.T. as a way of reminding them to check Focus, Aperture, Shutter angle, and Tachometer before the shot.

CAMERA OPERATOR: Ready.

DIRECTOR: Sound?

The sound person will do the same with the sound equipment.

SOUND PERSON: Ready.

DIRECTOR: Okay, roll sound.

The sound person will switch the Nagra to record, and when the machine has come up to speed, a small flag on the right front side of the Nagra will indicate so.

SOUND PERSON: Rolling.

DIRECTOR: Camera.

The Assistant Cameraperson - or sometimes the Camera Operator - starts the camera, and when it has come up to speed (on crystal cameras, this is indicated by the switching off of a small "out of sync" warning light), he or she will call out:

A.C.: Speed.

The person whose job it is to slate will call out the sound number, then clap the slate.

SLATE PERSON: Sound 32.

WAP! The slate is clapped. When the sound of the slate has died out in the room, and when the slate person has exited the frame and is not making any noise, the director cues the actors.

DIRECTOR: Action.

To be sure, there are many variations on this, but most crews follow this basic framework, and there are *important reasons* for doing things in the order mentioned.

The director has called for quiet, then let the cast and crew know that they are about to shoot an actual take. He or she might actually be misunderstood, because often the crew has rehearsed for a take along with the talent. Crew rehearsal is especially important for shots involving dollies and complicated subject movement requiring precision on the part of the camera and boom operators. It is a good idea to rehearse even for simple takes, because it lets everyone on the set know what is about to happen, and can turn up potential problems (a boom shadow, or a prop that will be an obstacle to the dolly, for example) before film is wasted during the actual take.

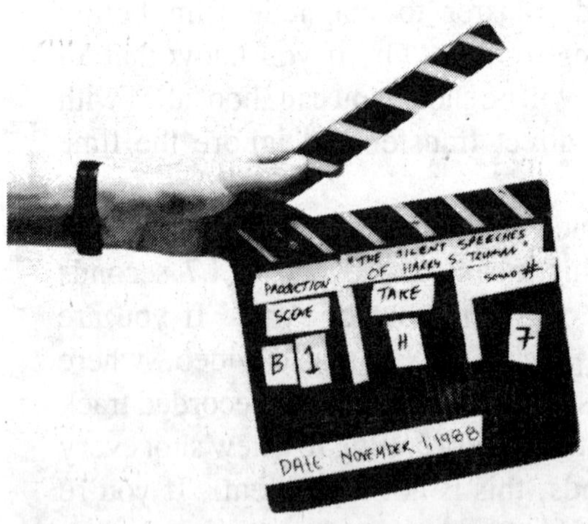

Slate

The director asks the sound and camera departments if they are ready - no sense in starting the shot if the focus marks haven't been finalized, or if proper recording levels haven't been found. Once both departments say they are ready, the director asks for sound to roll first. The reason for this is simple: 1/4" sound tape is far cheaper than 16mm film. Better to have audio tape rolling while the camera is coming up to speed than vice-versa.

The director calls for the camera to roll, and the A.C. (Assistant Cameraperson) will respond that the camera is at speed immediately upon switching it on. Cameras usually attain speed in under 2 seconds - often in as little as 1 second, so by the time the slate person calls the sound number and claps the slate, the camera will likely have been at speed for several seconds. If there is any problem with the camera after the A.C. has switched it on, he or she can yell "No sync!" at the start of the take, and the director can cut the shot. In this way valuable film and time is saved at the place where it is most crucial: at the head of each take. If you are shooting cable sync, you should be aware that there is no sync indicator on the camera. After both Nagra and camera are switched on, the *Nagra* will indicate that it is receiving good, usable pilot signal via the small, round flag on the front of the chassis. In this situation, the sound person calls speed for both sound *and* camera departments.

Once the A.C. has yelled "Speed!", the slate person knows it's time to mark the shot immediately. He or she will hold the slate in camera frame, call the sound number and clap the sticks of the slate together - then quietly and quickly, get out of the shot.

Sounds simple, doesn't it? Actually, the number of times and ways this is fouled up is surprising.

For example, the slate must be held motionless before and during the time the sticks are clapped. If it is moving during the clap, the single frame where the top stick of the slate has *just touched* the bottom - the frame where the editor will sync the first frame of the magnetic track has the sound of the slate -will be a blurry mess, and slow down the editor. If the slate is too small, angled incorrectly, or too dark in the frame, the information printed on it will be unusable. If the person slating is talking (calling the sound number) at the same time as slate is clapped, the editor will have a much harder time finding the very first frame of slate clap to sync to because the sound of the voice will be mixed in with the sound of the slate. Also, the top stick of the slate should be held open before it is clapped, then closed afterward - this way the editor can know instantly where he or she is when viewing the head of the take - before (slate is open) or after (slate is closed) the clap.

It is the job of the *person operating the camera* to make sure that the slate is recorded correctly - usably - in the frame. In the hurry of shooting this is often overlooked, but it actually takes very little extra time to make sure that the slates are framed and photographed correctly. The task of marking the slate itself is usually the job of the sound recordist. This person generally has less to do on the set than, say, the cameraperson or A.C., and because the soundperson will often be making careful notes to a log as the shooting commences, he or she should be put in charge of slate marking as well.

As to the *information* contained on the slate, and called by the person slating, it should be said that there are also many variations here. Ultimately, the person who will edit the film should control this, but here are a few guidelines:

Title, Producer, Director, Cameraperson - the broadest information on the slate: usually this information will not change during 16mm shoots.

Scene - if you have several scenes taking place on the same set, so that the editor might be confused as to which take belongs to which scene, record scene numbers on the slate - but if your scenes all look quite different (daytime at the beach, night inside a bar, etc.) the editor will know immediately by viewing any take what scene it is from, and recording the scene either in name or number will be unnecessary.

Shot - once again, the editor will usually be able to simply see, for example, that this shot is a close-up of the lead actor, that another is a wide master, etc. But also again, if there is likely to be confusion, record the shot on the slate.

Take - the second most specific information on the slate, it must be used in conjunction with the shot number, and sometimes the scene number (or name) to have any meaning. This is because you can have take number 4 in shot 7, scene 4, and take number 4 in shot 3, scene 5. Identical take numbers.

Sound number - the most important number on the slate, and the only one really necessary - *and* the only one that the slate person should call out. Sound numbers start at 1 (or 101, if you like) and ascend as each sound take is shot, hour after hour, day after day, never repeating, for the entire shoot. They are always different - no two takes will have the same sound number. The best way to slate, I believe, is to write nothing on the slate except the title of the production and the sound number, and write the latter so it is always visible - large, black on white, or white on black, whatever it takes so the editor can always see it on the editing machine screen. The slate person needs to do nothing more than wait until the camera department calls speed, then call the sound number *only* and clap the slate. If this is done consistently, the editor will have no trouble. On the set, it is the job of the sound operator (person working the Nagra) to keep track of the sound numbers and feed them to the slate person.

What about MOS (no sound) shots? When you decide not to record sound during a take, simply mark the slate MOS and hold it open and by the bottom stick (hand between the clap sticks) so that the editor knows there is no sound take associated with this picture. MOS takes have no sound number. For example, the order of shooting for a portion of the day might go like this: Sound 32, Sound 33, MOS, Sound 34, Sound 35. If you assigned sound number 34 to the MOS shot, the editor would probably spend a half hour searching for a nonexistent sound take. Whenever there is a sound number there is a sound take, and therefore both a picture and sound recording of it.

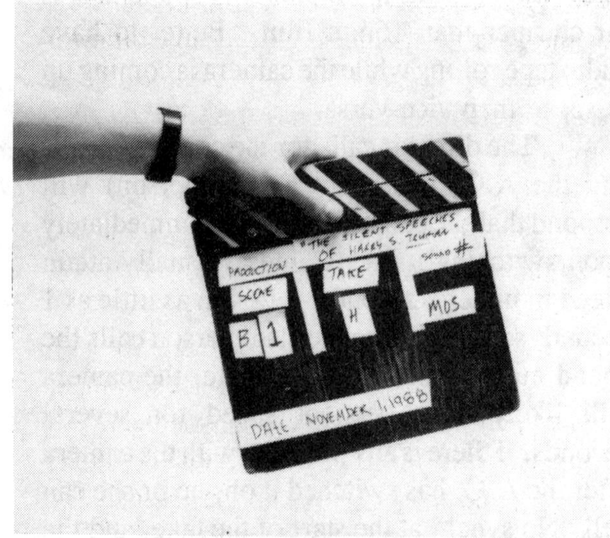

MOS Slate

Sound numbers can then be used as a reference for the entire post-production process: syncing, selecting takes for an assembly, etc. After syncing, they should be carefully logged along with camera original edge numbers *and* printed edge code numbers for each take before any assembling or editing is undertaken.

The reason for the logging process is sometimes difficult to understand at first, but it is simply this: say you've just edited a workprint for three months, and you've succeeded in getting the film through these stages: assembly (all the selected takes are put on one reel end to end), a rough-cut (all the slates are gone, and the material has something of a rhythm and is beginning to look like a movie), a fine-cut (the film is nearly done, very few changes will be made to the picture from now on), and finally, a locked-picture. This last stage means that no changes whatsoever will be made to the picture. At this time, you might turn the picture over to a sound editor, or edit the sound yourself, but in any case, the film and its accompanying sound track is going to be prepared for a mix: the dialogue will be separated to two or more tracks and others will be added for sound effects, voice-overs, room-tone, and music will be added. By this time, however, the dialogue tracks are mighty tired because they've been running back and forth, stopping and starting over the tape heads in the editing machine for three months. They sound worn and dead, just like any well used tape recording does. The solution is to *re-transfer* the dialogue from the original 1/4" tapes to fresh magnetic film. But how do you do this? The slates were cut off before the rough-cut! How do you tell which takes to re-transfer to mag, and how do you sync them to the locked picture? By using the **log**.

The log book contains two columns: sound number and printed code number. All that needs to be done to re-transfer and lay in the fresh dialogue tracks is to make a list of edge numbers for each take and correspond them, using the log, to sound numbers. This sound number list should be ordered from small to large, like this: 2, 5, 6, 12, 15, etc. When you play back the original 1/4" tapes for transfer, listen for the correct sound numbers and transfer the entire take for each. These can then be compared to each take of the worn sound track on a 6-plate flatbed editing machine, or even on a simple synchronizer with two magnetic sound heads and a squawk box, and laid in to form a

LOG:
" THE SILENT SPEECHES --- TRUMAN "

SOUND	CODE
101	AA0016 → 32
102	AA0032 → 156
103	AA0156 → 216
MOS	AA0216 → 374
104	AA0374 → 402
105	AA0402 → 431
MOS	AA0431 → 494
106	AA0494 → 552

Post-production Log

new, fresh dialogue track for use in the mix. It would be extremely difficult to re-transfer and replace the entire dialogue track without carefully recording and logging sound and edge code numbers, so when you plan on shooting 16mm you can save yourself a lot of time and aggravation by taking time to log these numbers. Many editors add a third column to their log - *camera original edge numbers* - so that they will always have a guide if they need to communicate with a negative cutter (for example, an important shot might be lost or chewed up in the editing equipment and need to be re-printed from the camera original rolls).

35mm shoots are a different story, because in 35mm it is possible to save time and money by asking the laboratory to print only selected takes from the camera original. Because of this, 35mm shoots need different, more complex slate marking procedures. In 16mm, all the camera rolls are printed head to foot, in which ever order the camera department numbered them. It makes the job of the editor much easier, then, to make sure the camera and sound rolls are numbered and then printed/transferred *in the same order,* so that Sound 50 follows Sound 49 in both the workprint and the transferred magnetic sound track.

Variations In Slating

Sometimes, it is better to slate at the end of the take, rather than the head. Slating can attract crowds on the street that can ruin a shot, or disturb an actor or actress attempting a difficult performance. To **tail slate**, simply prepare the slate beforehand with the sound number. The director has to remember to call "Tail slate!" before "Cut!", at which time the slate person will enter the shot, and clap the slate while holding it *upside down.* This lets the editor know that the take was slated at the end, rather than the beginning of the shot.

It's a good idea to have the A.C. (or the sound operator if you are using cable sync) yell "Mark it!" rather than "Speed!" because this tells the slate person exactly what to do, and lets everyone else know that the slate is about to clap, and that the action is about to be filmed.

Some filmmakers prefer to record information from the slate on the soundtrack *after* the

Nagra has been started, but *before* the camera is rolling. On cheap 1/4" tape they can call out scene, shot and take numbers, and then when the camera rolls, just the sound number and the

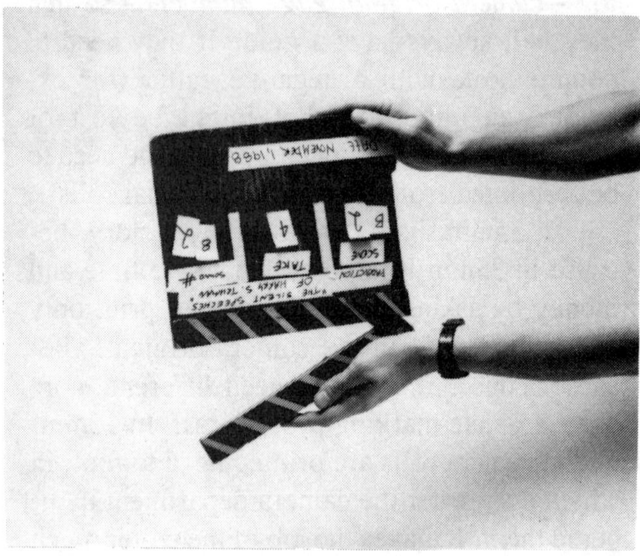

Tail Slate

slate clap. It is probably simpler and less time consuming to simply have someone record all this next to the sound number in a spiral bound notebook, then give it to the editor after the shoot.

Bloop slating - sometime after cable sync was devised, it became apparent that this same cable could be used to slate takes as well as be a means of keeping them in sync. Bloop sync works this way: when the camera is turned on (after the Nagra is running) the camera sends a short tone (a beep, or bloop) to the Nagra. At the same moment this tone is being recorded on the soundtrack a tiny light bulb near the gate inside the camera flashes on and off, fogging 4 to 6 frames of film. The editor merely finds the last frame of tone on the soundtrack and syncs this to the last fogged frame in the picture track.

This way of slating eliminates the need for the slate person, but it has serious drawbacks. There are no sound numbers associated with the sound or picture tracks (except when using a number bloop box, like the one above, which puts sound numbers on the picture only) so that unless the camera and sound rolls are printed/transferred in order, the editor may never be able to tell which beep goes with which flash. In addition, there always has to be that cumbersome cable between camera and Nagra.

Where this technique shines, however, is in situations where using a slate would be particularly annoying, or even destructive to the take - recording an interview with someone who is likely to freeze up in front of the camera. Using a slate would make this person feel even more under the scrutiny of the lens, and also that he or she has to talk *right now,* because the slate was just banged. By bloop slating, you could roll sound and talk conversationally with the person being interviewed until they said something that you wanted to shoot. The camera could then be started without breaking the moment with the noise of the slate.

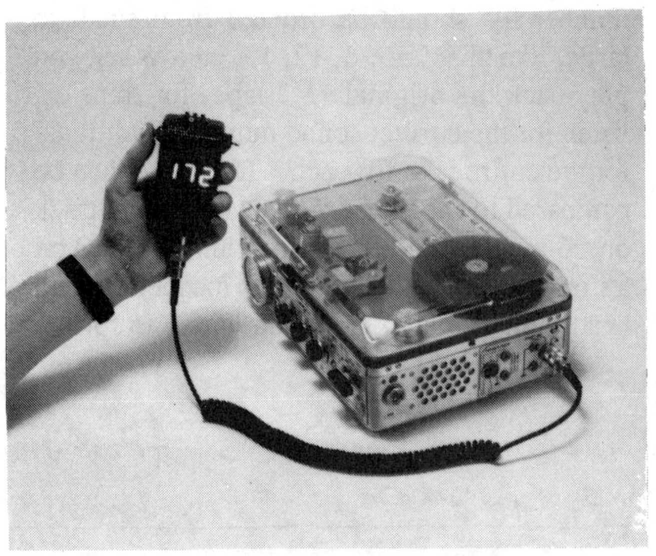

Audio Services Number Bloop Box

A variation of bloop slating can be done with crystal sync, and has many advantages. A small *handheld box* with a light affixed to it is plugged in to the Nagra (via a short cable) where the operator would otherwise plug in the cable for cable sync, or screw in the crystal cap. At the head or tail of a take, the sound recordist holds up the light box so that the camera operator sees it in the viewfinder. By pressing a button on the box, the sound operator triggers both the light and a beep tone generated in the Nagra (which is recorded on the 1/4" tape) at the same moment. The light on the workprint and the tone on the magnetic film sound track can then be synced together just the same as in cable sync bloop slating.

This device offers the unobtrusiveness of bloop slating but with the independent mobility of crystal sync, and is most often used to tail slate takes in documentaries. Once again, the sound and picture rolls must be printed/transferred in the same order for the editor to sync them efficiently.

TIME CODE

Just about the only sure thing about time code is that everybody thinks that everybody will use it someday. At this time, however, time code is not a single, simple, universal system in film production, but a number of *different* and somewhat costly systems. Eventually, there may be no confusion in any production person's mind when the term "time code" is used, but for now there is.

It is simply beyond the scope of this book to explain about binary coded decimals, user bits and flags, or drop verses non-drop frame. For this kind of detail, you should get your hands on Jim Tanenbaum's TIME CODE IN THE REEL WORLD II (see bibliography). This excellent book lays out all the different forms of code and operating instructions for almost all code capable cameras and recorders, and it is a genuine bear to deal with. As Tanenbaum himself states in his book, " . . . if you're not still a bit confused, you don't really understand time code."

The best way to introduce time is not to explain what time code is, but rather

What can you do with time code?

1) You can use time code to synchronize sound and picture during video transfer.

More filmmakers are using time code to sync up dailies while transferring to video than for any other purpose. This is because most film is shot to be transferred to video tape, then edited. Out of all the film exposed around the world, only a small amount is actually done with the goal of finishing with a projectable film print. Most people shoot film for TV series, commercials, movies of the week, music videos, and so on.

Recently, video editing systems have become **non-linear;** that is, you can edit on video as you would on film. For example, you can insert a three second shot into the middle of a ten minute segment without affecting the rest of the material. Older, linear systems forced editors to do such things as record all the shots that came after the three second insert, then replace them after the insert because there was no way to "pop in" three seconds of material on video tape without recording over something else. In film, splicing in three seconds automatically pushes all material that follows exactly three seconds. It is only recently that video editing systems that could accomplish this feat - non-linear - became widely used.

This being the case, many producers choose to edit on video for productions that will end up on video anyway. Why pay for the expense of a film picture print and film audio track, then edit on a slow, complicated editing table when you can transfer your negative and 1/4" audio tape direct to video? There are, of course, lots of reasons, not the least of which is that by cutting in film on an editing table you can create multiple sound tracks and do a "film style" mix, and that the rental of such and editing table might be as little as $500 per month, as opposed to about that same amount for only a few hours on a hot new non-linear video edit system. On the other hand, transferring direct to video saves a generation and therefore can deliver higher quality, and the digital audio capabilities of machines like the Avid have to be seen (and heard) to be believed.

The only fly in the ointment is sync. Before time code, transferring developed negative and 1/4" audio tape directly to video meant that synchronizing sound and picture had to be done in video, which is to say with video editing equipment. The picture would be on one video tape, and sound on another, and an editor would then combine the two after the film to tape transfer. But with time code, the process of synchronizing can be done during the film to tape transfer, saving time and possibly money.

SMPTE (*S*ociety of *M*otion *P*icture and *T*elevision *E*ngineers) time code has long been used as a reference in videotape, and it is now used in film. In videotape, SMPTE code is recorded on an audio track, and it is read by editing systems to find edit points (for sound and picture) and generate a numerical list of them - in short, to reference all post-production. It makes sense, then, for a film that will be finished on tape to have SMPTE code right from the start - during the shoot.

To accomplish this, a **time code slate** is used. It looks like a standard slate, except that it has large, bright L.E.D numerals near the clapsticks. At this point in time, the Denecke TS-1 slate seems to have captured most of the market. A cable connects it to the Nagra, which has a special SMPTE code circuit board inside. To shoot a take, the Nagra is rolled, and the circuit board in the Nagra generates SMPTE code. The board sends this to the slate, where it appears as numerals for the camera to shoot on film, and to the Nagra, where it is recorded on the audio tape. If the slate is clapped, the display will turn off. Often, a Nagra will be kept rolling (during a concert, for example) though, and the slate will not be clapped for a take, but rather simply shown to the camera with numbers ascending.

In post production, the camera original and audio 1/4" can be transferred directly to videotape, and the syncing can be done quickly using SMPTE code-reading systems.

When shooting dialogue, for example, the slate will display time code being recorded in the center of the 1/4" tape. When the slate is clapped, the slate will stop displaying code. In the transfer suite, the **colorist** (person who controls the transfer equipment and makes color corrections) will find the very last frame of code displayed, then enter the number into a control system which will then find the same number on the 1/4" tape. The playback deck with the 1/4" tape will then "chase" the film transfer machine, using the edit point the colorist entered, and the audio will lock to the film so that the video transfer will have both picture and sound in sync.

Transfer technicians talk about **pre-roll.** This is the amount of time that the 1/4" audio playback machine needs to back up, then run forward to lock to the Rank or Bosch (the film-to-tape machine) for transfer. Most technicians will tell you to turn the Nagra on for 5 seconds before clapping the slate to allow for pre-roll. In the early days of time code, the camera was pre-rolled also; this is now unnecessary.

2) You can use time code to eliminate the slate altogether.

What about the production that won't be finished on video tape? For standard post-production on *film*, SMPTE code offers little or nothing, because it isn't readable by people using a flatbed or upright film editing machine.

To remedy this problem, Aaton developed a different time code called CTR (*C*lear *T*ime *R*ecording).

CTR consists of three separate, addressable crystal clocks: one in the camera, one on the Nagra, and a calculator sized unit called Origin C. The latter is initialized with production number, date, hour, minute and second, then plugged into the camera, and then the Nagra where it feeds this time code information to their clocks. Now all three clocks are generating identical data. Tiny L.E.D.s in the gate of the camera expose this onto the film, and the Nagra's clock feeds this same data to the recording head when the Nagra rolls. For post-production, the code is read and then printed onto the 16mm fullcoat (magnetic film) by a third machine called the Adage. This code is simple, and man readable, and matches the code exposed on the workprint from the camera original. The sound and picture can then be synchronized just as one would match two already edge-coded work tracks.

CTR offers these advantages over standard slating and SMPTE slating: a) it eliminates the need for slating altogether, since the camera and Nagra clocks are independent and generate identical information - these clocks will run for up to 6 hours before they need to be re-addressed **(jammed)** by the Origin C unit; b) edge coding is eliminated since the Adage unit obviates it; c) syncing is much easier than with a standard clapstick - a flatbed or viewer is unnecessary because the information is printed right on the picture and sound tracks.

The advantages of CTR are quite obvious - no need to use a valuable production person to slate, no wasted footage - just call for camera and sound to roll, then call for action. Multi-camera shoots are much easier since all camera operators are freed from slating, and the editor's job is also easier - no poorly lit, badly focused or erroneously labelled slates to deal with. CTR can become the reference for logging for all post-production as well.

3) You can use time code to sync playback for music videos.

Playback is a term used to describe a situation when music or effects are played during shooting and talent dances, sings, or otherwise reacts in sync to it. Almost all music videos are done this way. This is usually accomplished by using a time code Nagra and a copy of the music on 1/4" tape with time code already recorded on the tape. A time code slate (once again, almost always a Denecke TS-1) displays the time code from the tape as it is played back. The camera is shown the slate, so that it photographs code, and the talent plays to the music on the 1/4" tape (often greatly amplified from the Nagra). The film and music can then be synchronized during the film to tape transfer, just as in example 1, or the editor can synchronize the music and picture later, which is generally pretty easy since most music videos are short, and the talent plays to the same section of music over and over again, take after take.

4) You can use time code to shoot on film, edit on video, then conform the original negative to the edited videotape.

Chances are pretty good that many people reading this chapter have experienced editing on videotape before or instead of editing on film, and therefore feel more comfortable editing with a few video decks and a monitor rather than a few trim bins and a flatbed. For these people, and for producers who need to have a conformed negative for transfer to not only NTSC but PAL or SECAM, or HDTV in the future, **matchback,** or conforming negative to video, is the way to go.

Time code's latest achievement is making matchback possible. SMPTE code can be exposed directly onto the film in the camera; at this time, AatonCode, which can be found on certain Aaton, Panavision, Moviecam and Arri cameras, and Arri's own SMPTE code, which can be used on Arri SR3 and 535 cameras, accomplishes this. Since the code is exposed onto the film and recorded on audio tape, it can be used for syncing during film to tape transfer and then burned in (a small window appears on screen with time code in it) on the video tape. After editing, the videotape can be viewed to generate a list of time code numbers at the head and tail of each shot. The negative cutter can then conform the negative because the numbers on the list are exposed onto the negative. Special time code readers are employed by the conformer to find the edit points.

Sometimes, a critical supervised re-transfer is called for. This refers to situation where a commercial, for example, has been shot on film, transferred to video, edited on tape, then re-transferred to video again to make critical color or brightness adjustments. This is done because once edited, the videotape can show shot to shot color mismatches that can only be corrected by re-transfer. In-camera time code which exposes code on the film itself enables the colorist to quickly find exact shots to be critically re-transferred because the negative can be scanned by a time code reader.

Keycode isn't time code. You can think of it as a sophisticated version of the edge code that film manufacturers expose into their stocks before you buy them. Keycode is Kodak's trade name for a barcode (like on food packages at supermarkets) that is exposed into all their film stock between sprocket holes. Keycode contains information on manufacturer, film type, edge numbers, feet, and frames. After development, Keycode can be read by machines made by Aaton and Cinema Products, and can be burned in to tape during the video transfer. Once the tape is edited, Keycode can be read back and used to cut the negative, or to find footage in the camera original for critical re-transfer.

A few notes:

- other manufacturers expose this same code into their stocks in accordance with SMPTE standards, but they don't call it Keycode, which is a Kodak trade name. The correct term is Edgeprint, but since Kodak was the first, most people use the term Keycode for all stocks.

- Keycode is machine-readable, but next to it are key numbers so negative cutters can work in the traditional manner.

- since the code is exposed into the stock and therefore not readable during the shoot, it can't be used for syncing up picture and sound during post production.

This last reason makes me believe that once (if?) all cameras expose their own time code, Keycode (Edgeprint) will be obsolete, because camera generated time code can be used for matchback *and* for syncing up during transfer (Keycode can't be used for syncing during transfer).

At this time, Aaton has developed a machine called the Linker2k that reads AatonCode and Keycode (without actually contacting the negative) and manages all the information in a database. Shortly, non-linear editing systems like the Avid, Editdroid, and E-Pix will be able to get this information from the Linker2k (via floppy disk) so that at any time during the editing process, any shot on in the non-linear editing machine can be found in the original negative quickly, and a cut list for conforming the negative will be compiled automatically.

Arri's Film Ident System seems to work the same way, reading and managing code in the telecine.

Right now, the Linker will automatically find audio time code to match camera time code during film to tape transfer, making syncing in the telecine suite as much as fifty percent faster. Arri's Film Ident System also outputs data to a slaveable audio playback deck and a time code generator/burn in device during transfer.

10 YEARS FROM NOW:

You shoot film, recording in-camera and in-DAT time code. The camera original is developed, then sent to the telecine for film to tape transfer. The camera original and DAT audio tapes are transferred to digital tape and automatically synchronized at the same time. The tapes are then sent to a non-linear edit system, which edits them digitally, and has enough information storage and handling capacity to be of broadcast quality (whatever that will be in the future). The non-linear edit system can handle at least one hundred digital audio tracks, so you can start and finish all your audio work, including a final mix, on this machine. Finally, the machine outputs a finished, broadcast quality tape, and a list on floppy disk that is fed to a brand new machine.

This machine reads the in-camera code contained on the camera original, scans the appropriate sections of film, then prints the information on one continuous piece of negative without ever having to cut the camera original. The final negative is developed, and even though it is a digitally sampled version of the camera original, the machine that scanned the negative has so much resolution and storage that the final prints, when struck from the negative, look identical to those contact printed from the piece of film that went through the camera on the shoot.

Audio from the version of your film that is on the video that came from the non-linear editing system is encoded onto the negative in Cinema Digital Sound, a new system being used today that records and plays back movie soundtracks digitally, on release prints.

Now, you have two copies of your finished film: one can be projected in theaters, the other shown on TV.

Sound great? I'm sure it will be. I think all this will happen in the next ten years; right now, there are machines that can scan in 35mm film, manipulate it, then print it back out on 35mm film. Many productions are using this technique for special effects, and sooner or later, someone will have the money to put an entire feature through one of these machines. Eventually, your camera original could be digitally recorded right from the start, so there would be no need to return to it after it is edited. The problem now seems to be that today's computers can't store and manipulate the huge amounts of data recorded on motion picture film. The info on one frame of 35mm film is enough to max out the entire hard drive of your personal computer.

So, that's my guess about the future. What about right now?

There's one big problem with time code (aside from the fact that it is new and complex and therefore scary). It costs a lot of money. What's that you say? It doesn't use up one more frame of film or one inch more of audio tape? Sure, that's true. You might as well record time code during your shoot because it doesn't use up any extra stock.

But the equipment, that's another story. If you want to use time code, you can't just borrow someone's dusty Arri 16BL and ancient Nagra to make your film. You have to go out and rent the hottest, most expensive Aaton XTR or Arri SR3, and get an expensive time code Nagra or time code DAT. Since this equipment is all new and sought after, you'll pay top dollar to rent it, and you'll have to spend a fair amount of time trying to figure out how to use the time code controls.

When you transfer, you can't just go to your friend Marvin, who has an old but trusty Rank telecine. You have to go to a film to tape house that has a Linker or Arri Film Ident System. These aren't cheap, so although you'll save time synchronizing during transfer, you'll have to pay more to use these facilities. It's just plain harder to "scrounge" up equipment and services if you want to use time code. This isn't to say that it can't be done, but the chances are slimmer.

Must you use time code? No. For example, you can sync film after your video transfer with a simple video editing set up. You can go back to the old fashioned slate and printed edge number set up, the system used for years, for synchronizing on film. You can do playback for music videos without time code; many people don't even use a Nagra - they do playback on a cassette boom box. I even know someone who is doing matchback from a VHS cassette without time code (he's cutting a film print to his finished VHS version on a flatbed), although I think he may be a bit crazy.

But there is one more important factor - time. Time code can really speed up the post production process, especially in-camera time code. So if time is important, time code could save money by speeding things up.

WORK BACKWARD!

The easiest way to learn about and benefit from time code is on a project by project basis, working backward. Go to the lab or editorial facility you intend to use to finish your project and talk to the technicians about what time code they use, and how they use it. You may find, for example, that it will save you quite a large sum of money because you want to cut your project on video, and time code will enable the dailies to be synced up during transfer. Or you may be shooting a low dollar project, finishing on film, and the extra expense of renting time code capable equipment negates any post production savings. Find out specific time code requirements and procedures by talking to technicians at the lab, film to tape transfer facility, and editing house. No two labs or post-production houses will be equipped exactly the same to handle time code.

Speeds and Angles

CHANGING THE CAMERA SPEED

People often use the term **speed** when they are referring to the frames per second - fps - of motion picture cameras. This can be somewhat confusing, because people also call lenses with very wide maximum apertures "superspeed" lenses, and the length of exposure that each frame of film receives is often referred to as "the shutter speed". More specific terms for the fps setting of a camera are *undercranking* (low fps) and *overcranking* (high fps). These terms come from the days when cameras were literally cranked by hand instead of wound up or plugged in and switched on.

Running the camera at low speed/low fps/undercranking produces a record of action that, when projected at normal speed, is speeded up. The opposite - high speed/high fps/ overcranking - results in a slow motion effect. It may be that audiences viewing Mack Sennet one-reelers were fooled by the cameraman's manipulations of the frame-per-second rate, but most film viewers today are quite hip to this phenomenon. At any rate, any change in the speed of the camera must be based on a understanding of the speed of the *projector:* just what is normal?

Before the advent of optical sound, projectionists would often vary the speed of the projector considerably if, for example, they thought the action of a film was too slow and boring. Many films were shot at 18 fps, or 16 fps, or perhaps even 20 or 22 fps. Today, however, 24 fps is the standard projector speed, and this generally is not varied. 16mm projectors made in the last 15 or 20 years do not have variable speed knobs at all; some may have two speed switches that allow the user to select between a "silent" speed of something like 16 or 18 fps, and a "sound" speed of 24 fps, but that's it. When you make a film to be shown in theaters on film projectors, you should therefore understand that the film will be shown at 24 fps.

With this in mind, here is a list of various camera speeds and the effects of them on the screened image when the projector runs at 24 fps (as it always will):

Single Frame - used by animators to photograph one image at a time; also by camerapeople who wish to show very slow change (example: flower blooming or building construction) speeded up on screen; An **intervalometer** is a device that controls the fps of a camera very precisely, at very slow speeds, from 2 or 3 frames per second all the way down to one frame every hour, or even day.

2-3 fps - results in wildly fast motion of everyday objects, such as cars, planes, etc., and people. Has exciting or comic (or both) effects.

4-7 fps - same as 2-3, but with less pronounced results.

8-16 fps - even less pronounced results; some action may be perceived by the audience as normal or not speeded up.

16-20 fps - often used to gain a slight amount of speed in cars, boats, planes, etc. Audiences are quite good at detecting this, though, so most filmmakers today use this speed range (and any slower ranges) for comic rather than dramatic results.

20-24 fps - audience will perceive very little speeding up; used in fight scenes and action sequences for short takes.

24 fps - speed at which the projector runs; all motion normal. Used for synchronous sound recording (lip sync).

24-30 fps - slows down action very little.

30-48 fps - film of extreme human action such as football, track, etc. will be perceived as slow and somewhat graceful; used by schools and businesses to analyze human action.

48-64 fps - human actions such as walking and talking are affected, appear somewhat slow; used in miniature sets to give a feeling of mass to buildings, water, etc.; also used to analyze action.

64-96 fps - extreme human and animal action becomes graceful, interesting.

96-150 fps - sporting events take on a graceful, dream-like motion; even non-extreme action - walking, gesturing - is very slow; most often used speed range in commercial filmmaking for beautiful slow motion effects.

150 fps and above - used to film explosions, stunts, fast objects like race cars and airplanes. Very high speeds used to film projectiles, shattering glass, humming bird wings, and so on.

The best way to choose a fps rate for purposes of changing motion is to simply shoot a test. It can be very difficult to estimate the results beforehand, because the actions of many objects are quite variable.

There are other reasons - aside from changing motion - that would lead you to change the fps rate of a camera. They are:

Change the Exposure. Say, for example, you need to photograph a man standing under a street lamp at night for a particular scene in a script. You take a light meter reading of the available light (most of it coming from the street lamp) and find that, for your particular film stock and length of exposure, you need to shoot at T 1.4. The lens you are using has a maximum aperture of T 2. Your options are 1) rent a superspeed lens (one that opens up to T 1.4 or wider), 2) change to a more sensitive film stock, 3) add light to the scene by setting up fixtures, 4) change the fps rate.

The first option, renting a superspeed lens, is undesirable for several reasons: first, it requires extra time (to pick up and return the lens) and money (to pay for the rental) and second, you may not like the shortened depth of field that results from shooting at T 1.4. The second option you deem out of the question; changing stock for one shot would more than likely be jarring to the viewer because of increased grain size (the light sensitive particles in the film emulsion). You could add more light to the scene - option 3 - but you would probably have trouble finding AC power for your fixtures on the street (rent a generator?) and you would also likely have to mount them quite high - 15 or 20 feet or more - to simulate natural street light. The last option may be the answer: slow down the camera. By changing the speed of the camera to 12 frames per second, you gain one F stop of light, because each frame of film spends *twice as long* in the gate as it did at 24 fps.

The problem with this last option is obvious: the man standing under the streetlight will look ridiculous if he moves: speeded up and/or comical. But if the script calls for no specific action, then this solution may be viable. If the actor is instructed to stand still, or move slowly, the shot can work, and the added time and expense of the other options may be avoided. For shots where there is no motion like landscapes, slowing down the camera can be a valuable tool for getting the correct exposure.

Increase/decrease depth of field. If you slow down the camera, increasing the length of exposure, you can then close down the iris of the lens on the camera to compensate and increase depth of field - again, in static or near static shots.

Shoot for video transfer. In this case, you've decided that you are going to transfer your camera original directly to video tape (at a post-production house that has film-to-tape facilities) for editing and for the final product. NTSC video - the standard in the United States, runs at 29.97 fps (30 nominal). You can shoot film at 24 fps and transfer to video, or you can make a somewhat higher quality, frame-to-frame transfer by shooting film at 30 fps. Those who choose the latter say that the image is sharper and clearer compared to the former; the drawbacks are increased film and development costs and limitation of post-production work and final product to video only. For productions whose final goal is video only, the technique of shooting at 30 fps can add a quality that some say is rivaled only by shooting 35mm.

A number of 16mm cameras have been modified to shoot 30 fps crystal sync. Aaton, GSMO, CP/R, NPR are the most common (ask the rental house or whomever you get the camera from if they have a camera that has been modified). The Arri 16SR has an 11 pin Fischer connector on the back of the camera that enables the user to plug in several speed control modules, some of which will run the camera at 30 fps. Later 16SR model II cameras have on-board switching between 24 and 30 fps (earlier cameras gave you a choice of 24 or 25 fps). Sometimes, certain cameras will be modified to run at 29.97 crystal instead of 30, more accurately matching the frame rate of all NTSC monitors. This enables the user to shoot the monitors themselves for inclusion in the final product without the "roll bar" that results from the difference between the NTSC scanning rate and most 16mm cameras, which run at 24 fps with a 180 degree shutter (see the next section for a more detailed explanation of this). Either 30 or 29.97 may be used when you intend to transfer the film to videotape.

If your film is MOS you can simply set your camera to 30 fps non-crystal if it has a variable speed control and transfer to and edit on videotape. It is only in the case where you will be recording synchronous sound during a take or playing back music that the actors will lip sync to (like on American Bandstand) that requires a camera to run at 24, 29.97 or 30 fps crystal for video transfer.

Remember, though: shooting 29.97 or 30 fps for video-only post-production and final product means just that: you'll only be able to show the work on video screens. People have tried to use an optical printer to turn 29.97/30 fps camera original to 24 fps without success (makes the movements of actors odd and jerky).

If you record sound on a DAT recorder, which will record and then playback at speed accurately enough that it is "self resolved", you may want to shoot at 23.976 for video transfer. This is because the Rank or Bosch scanner actually runs at this speed (see the DAT section in the Sync chapter).

SHOOTING A TV SCREEN

You've seen it in many films: the "roll bar" on TV screens. It isn't actually a roll bar at all (which is the black area that you see between frames when you monkey with the vertical hold on your TV) but an area of double exposure that occurs due to the difference in the exposure times of TVs or video monitors and movie cameras.

When you see this in films, what is it that you are supposed to believe? That the people who own the video screen in question (the characters in the film) aren't bothered by it? That it's supposed to represent bad reception? That in "movie reality", that's just the way TVs are? What it really means is that the people who made the film either a) didn't know how to get rid of the roll bar, b) didn't care that there *was* a roll bar, or c) didn't have the means to get *rid* of (or at least minimize) the roll bar. In truth, it is quite easy to shoot a TV screen on motion picture film and not have this annoying effect.

TV screens in the U.S. display information at 29.97 fps, but in lines: 525. In addition, each video frame is made up of two *fields* which supply half the total number of lines (either odd or even) for each frame: 262 1/2. The fps rate of each field, therefore, is twice that of the frame rate, or 59.94 per second. The resulting on screen time of each field is 1/59.94 of a second.

The sync speed of motion picture cameras is 24 frames per second - but the time of each frame is generally *half* this number per second because of the *shutter* in the camera which covers the gate between each frame. Shutters are generally rotating discs with a certain amount cut out of them (see chapter one); this amount is described in *degrees.* A camera with a 180 degree shutter, for example, running at 24 fps, results in an exposure time for each frame of 1/48th of a second because the gate is covered half the time (180 out of a possible 360 degrees) between each frame.

annoying roll bar in your footage (but perhaps you want the effect for some aesthetic reason, like whatever Soderberg was going for in *sex, lies, and videotape*).

180 degree shutter @ 29.97 fps crystal - Here you are simply matching the speed of the camera to that of the video screen, recording at a 1/59.94 exposure time, getting every *other* field of video (see the section in this chapter - *Shooting for video transfer* - to see how this is done). You can get results that are very close to this by shooting 180 degrees @ 30 fps crystal. The difference between 29.97 and 30 fps is slight, and the resulting roll bar may be negligible for most work. Keep in mind that if you

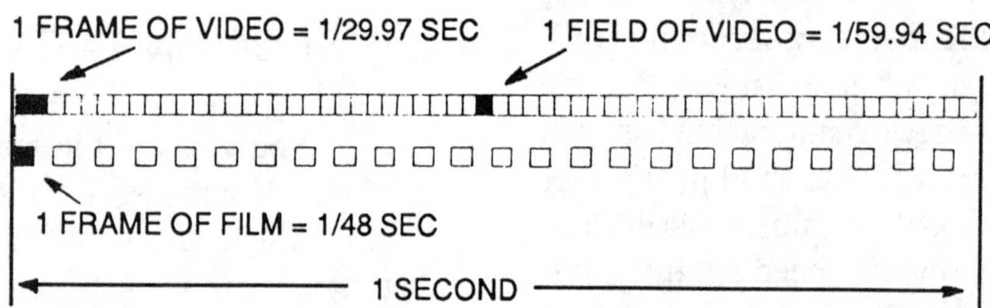

With the camera exposing frames every *other* 48th of a second and the video screen displaying fields (half frames) *every* 59.94 of a second, each frame of film records portions of *two* fields of video - but never *all* of two. Where the two fields overlap in the frame of film is where the roll bar will appear. By looking at the diagram, you'll see that no two frames of film record portions of two fields the same way, so that the roll bar, or area of double field exposure, changes from frame to frame, causing motion or roll.

Here are several different ways to deal with this mis-match between video and film exposure rates:

180 degree shutter @ 24 fps crystal - The first way is to ignore the problem altogether by shooting at these settings. You'll get the

plan to use this footage at the standard projection speed of 24 fps, all the action will be slowed down somewhat, and far from in sync - so for *film* post-production, this approach may be useful for MOS and/or short takes only.

144 degrees @ 24 fps crystal - By changing the shutter angle of your motion picture camera, you can minimize the roll bar and still shoot at 24 fps crystal for synchronous sound filming. A 144 degree shutter at 24 fps results in an exposure time of 1/60th of a second, or very nearly 1/59.94, the field time of video. You'll be exposing each frame of film almost the same amount of time as each field of video, and the resulting roll bar will be slight.

The CP 16/R and the Arri 16SR can be dismantled and fitted with 144 degree shutters for this kind of work - but these are expensive jobs. Often, rental houses will stock one of these two machines with a 144 degree shutter permanently installed for practical monitor shooting. Once altered, these cameras are still useful for standard filming; users simply open up their irises by about 1/3 of a stop, but many camera people feel that shooting with such cameras for standard scenes is undesirable because of the effects of strobing that results when narrow shutter angles are employed (see the following section on shutter angles).

Because of the small difference in the exposure times of each video field and each film frame (.04 frames per second), the faint roll bar *will* appear to move. The only way to stop it is to alter the speed of the camera to 23.976 frames per second (as discussed in *Filming Practical Monitors* - see bibliography). Media Logic and Cinematography Electronics make speed controls for the 16SR and Aaton that will accomplish this, and Media Logic can modify CP 16R cameras to accept their controls. Also, shooting this speed means a sync cable must send pilot signal to the Nagra or other recorder for sync shooting so that the sound can be resolved on transfer to 16mm mag stock.

145 degrees @ 24 fps crystal. Here the exposure time is 1/59.586 of a second - not as close to 1/59.94 as with a 144 degree shutter, but close enough so that the results are quite good. Mention is made of these settings because the Eclair NPR has an adjustable shutter which can be set to 145 degrees (sorry, no 144 as the shutter detentes are set for 5 to 180 degrees in 5 degree increments only) and many of these machines are still around and available to borrow or rent.

Most camerapeople set their exposures for practical monitor shooting by using a spot meter directly on the TV screen in question. They check a medium area of the brightness range and then adjust the set lights accordingly.

The best way to see the final results, both for exposure and roll bar effects, is to shoot a test, if time allows. You may find that, for example, a 145 degree shutter at 24 fps crystal is quite acceptable. Or you may want the complete elimination of the roll bar that only 29.97 fps can supply. If, however, you want to shoot at 24 *and* have no roll bar whatsoever, there is one last option: have your video converted to 24 fps. There are a few companies that specialize in this (call rental houses for leads), but this service can be quite expensive because of transfer and special equipment costs. Still, for films that have extensive and important practical monitor requirements, this may be the best way to go.

SPEED CONTROLS FOR CAMERAS

Early speed controls for film cameras usually consisted of a small box with a knob-operated potentiometer. The potentiometer could be twisted to send various frequencies to the camera in question, via a cable. This in turn changed the camera speed. These devices are still around, mostly for Arriflex cameras (the 16SR, 35BL, and 35III) and have the advantage of being inexpensive, and simple. They also allow the user to change the speed of the camera during a shot. But the speeds aren't crystal locked; they are only close approximations of the speeds they display on their dials.

Lately, a new kind of speed control has become available. This type has the ability to control cameras very accurately - in fact, any speed that you set will be crystal locked. Further, this control can be varied by .001 fps increments. This means that if you need to shoot at 29.970, or 23.976 or any other crystal speed within your cameras range, to you can.

People use this new type of control for

a) shooting under various speeds with HMI lighting, which requires all fps rates to be crystal locked to avoid flicker or pulsing problems;

b) shooting TV, video or computer monitors, which can have esoteric frame rates (like 30.024, or some such rate) without getting the so-called roll bar; and

c) shooting high speed or slow motion effects at

crystal locked rates.

A few years ago, the most common brand of this control was Cinematography Electronic's Precision Speed Control, and even today many people refer to any control of this type as a precision speed control. However, other manufacturers such as Cinetronics, Haflexx, and Media Logic have introduced their own units with other names.

The 5 Digit Speed Control III, made by Media Logic, has become popular with both camera owners and professional assistant camerapeople alike. It is the smallest control - not much larger than a pack of cigarettes - and most people simply put it on the sides of cameras with double sticky velcro. The 5 DSC, as it is abbreviated, has quick change cables that allow you to plug it into Arri, Aaton, Panavision, CP and Fries-conversion Mitchell cameras. It has two ranges: from 1.000 to 99.999 fps, and 10.00 to 999.99 fps (although no camera that it controls will run faster than 150 fps), and it has a **phase button** that allows you to shoot video screens and projections without seeing the roll bar.

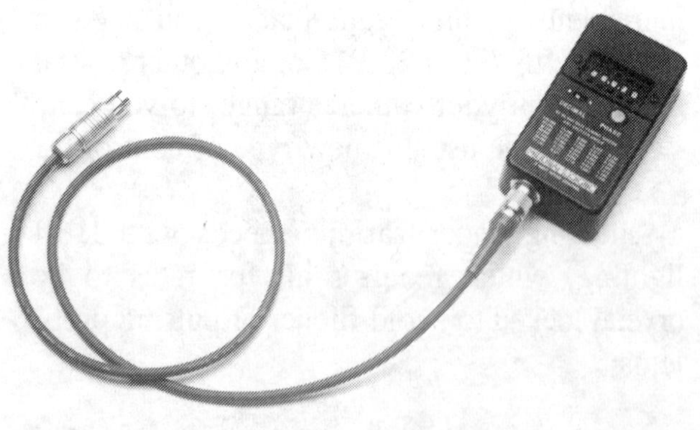

Media Logic 5 Digit Speed Control

The phase button shifts the speed of the unit by .2 fps. It is used this way: once you have started shooting a computer or video screen, you simply press the phase button until the small line (some call it roll bar) moves out of frame. Once out, release the button and the line will stay out for the remainder of the shot.

Before you start to shoot the video or computer screen, however, you must set your camera to run at the same rate as the screen. This is done by first making sure your camera is unloaded (no need to waste film while you adjust speed), then setting the 5 DSC to 30.000 fps as a jumping off point. Turn the camera on and point it at the monitor. You should see a faint, almost horizontal line moving up or down on the screen, over and over, through the viewfinder. Press the one's digit button on the 5DSC, changing the fps rate up and down, until the line moves at its slowest, then press the tenths digit, then hundredths, then finally the thousandths, slowing the line down more and more. When the line is stopped, your camera is running at the same frame rate as the video screen, and all that is left for you to do is move the line out of the shot with the phase button, as described above.

A few precautions when using this type of control, from any manufacturer. First, find out what your camera's maximum speed is by checking the chart below, or consulting the manufacturer. Some cameras such as those made by Aaton can be damaged by running faster than is recommended. Second, it is a bad idea to change the tens (not tenths) digit of the speed control while the camera is running, because by pressing this button, you can easily go from 0 to 9, which could make the camera jump from say 05.000 to 95.000 fps, causing damage.

Please note that this type of control is not good for smooth speed changes during a shot, because the frequency shifts are near instantaneous. Although this type of shift might produce interesting results, most users will want smooth changes in speed.

SOME MAXIMUM CAMERA SPEEDS

Please note that these are general speed

guidelines; to find out your camera's specific top speed, contact the manufacturer.

MAXIMUM SPEEDS

camera	fps
Aaton LTR 7	32
Aaton LTR 54	54
Aaton XTR, XTR+ and Xprod	60
Arri 16BLEQ	50
Arri 16BL+ Media Logic BL Drive	48
Arri 16SR I and II	75
Arri 16SR-HS	150
CP GSMO	64
CP16	36

MINIMUM SPEEDS

It has been my experience that with controls like the 5DSC, Aaton 16mm cameras will run as slow as 1 fps; Arri 16SR cameras can go as slow as 2 fps. The 16BL and CP cameras generally stop running smoothly around or below 4 fps.

INTERVALOMETERS

These devices run the camera really slow. You can see buildings erected in one minute, or watch clouds really race by, or flowers bloom. Many people have built their own devices for triggering single frame capable cameras (like Bolexes). The prime source for programmable, high quality intervalometers is Norris (see the resource list).

CHANGING THE SHUTTER ANGLE

Here are some reasons to change the shutter angle of your camera:

Shoot a TV screen - see the end of the section on changing camera speed for a discussion of this.

Change the exposure - If, for example, you change the shutter angle from 180 to 90 degrees, you have reduced the exposure by 1 stop (the new length of exposure at 24 fps is 1/96th of a second).

Fade or Dissolve - Some cameras, like the Bolex, have shutters that will close down completely. You can move the shutter control while filming (or have an assistant do it) and get a fade to black - reverse this for a fade in. You can also do a dissolve by combining a fade out and fade in, but you need to *backwind* the film in the camera, and keep a careful eye on the frame counter of the camera (once again, on Bolex cameras) to know where to start and stop. If your camera doesn't have a shutter that closes down completely, you can still do a fade or dissolve by closing down the iris; some lenses, including certain 25mm Schneider Arri Standard mount lenses, close down completely.

Reduce the shutter time to sharpen a planned freeze-frame - A frame of film that has been exposed at 1/48th or 1/50th of a second may have some blur due to subject movement. By decreasing the shutter angle, the length of exposure and resulting subject blur is reduced. A single frame from this camera original can then be "frozen" or held stationary and printed over and over again with the use of an optical printer, and the results will be less blurry than

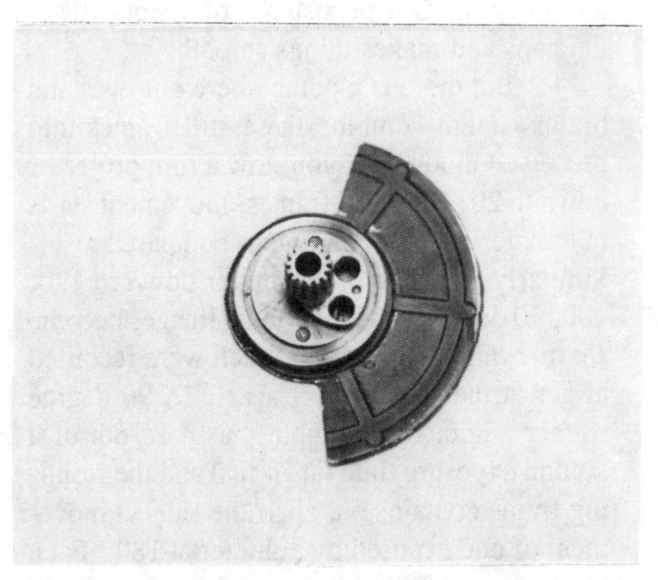

Bell and Howell Filmo Shutter

without a reduced shutter angle.

It would seem from the above that an adjustable shutter is a very useful thing to have on a movie camera - and it is, but only in one case: shooting a TV screen. For the others, there are either serious drawbacks or better/ easier ways to get the job done.

Changing the exposure by narrowing the shutter angle - to change the depth of field, or maintain the same T stop - is a bad idea because of what most camerapeople call the *strobing effect.* This is one of the most unusual effects in cinematography. There must be a certain amount of blur from subject movement in each frame *and* similarity between each frame for the movement to be perceived as smooth by the viewer on projection.

The whole of filmmaking depends on that tired phrase you've heard thrown around in film classes and in movie books called *persistence of vision.* Basically, it is the image that the brain and eye maintain of an object (or projection) after it is no longer in the field of view. Movies depend on this; there is no true motion in a film, only the rapid succession of projected *still* images. Our persistence of vision fills in the gaps and makes things smooth.

But there is a point where our eyes and brains cannot combine these still frames into perceived motion. If you slow a film projector down to 20, 19, or 18 frames, movement starts to look jerky or discontinuous compared to 24. Similarly, if you close a shutter down to 120, 100, 90 degrees, the individual images become sharper, and the times that each were recorded at get farther and farther apart. A 90 degree shutter angle, for example, has a 1/96th of a second exposure time (at 24 fps) and the resulting frame contains only half the subject movement of one exposed by a shutter at 180. Each 90 degree - 1/96th of a second exposure is 1/32nd of a second apart from the next in time. This means that if you photograph a person walking with a 90 degree shutter, 3/4ths of the action will not be photographed! The images wILL be relatively sharp and far apart in time, and when projected, the perceived motion would be jerky compared to that exposed with a 180 degree shutter.

This is why (among other things) King Kong looked like a puppet. He was not moving during exposure, and each frame of him was sharp. Model animators always come up against this problem, no matter how good they get (cel and drawn animators can add gap filling blur, but this is quite time consuming).

If you want to change exposure, then, it is probably better for your film to change the iris setting, or use Neutral Density filters. If, however, you think you want this jerky, "unreal" motion for a specific effect, by all means, experiment with narrow shutter angles.

Fading and dissolving can be done in-camera, as described above, and often, simple effects can be accomplished this way. But most professionals avoid this technique and fade or dissolve in post-production, either with a CRI or internegative, or when the film is answer printed. In-camera fades and dissolves are not easy to do; footage and frame counters can be hard to read and one slip can ruin both takes.

The last technique - reducing the shutter angle for a planned freeze-frame - can be effective, but the gain in reduced freeze-frame blur is traded for increased strobing in the portions of the shot leading up to and following the freeze. Also, most filmmakers decide on a freeze frame during editing, when they can stop the film in a flatbed or viewer, long after the decision to change the shutter angle can be made.

It should also be noted that **panning** a camera too fast will cause strobing even if the shutter angle is 180 degrees or greater. At a certain rate of camera movement, the image will begin to jump or skip across the screen because the successive frames will be too dissimilar. Camera operators follow the 7 second rule to avoid this: an object should take no less that 7 seconds to travel from one side of the screen to the other. This rule works no matter what focal length lens you might be using, because it concerns itself only with the recorded image. If you are *following* a moving object with a pan you can ignore the 7 second rule and pan as fast as you want, because the object itself becomes the focus of attention for the audience, and it will always be in the same place in the frame (more or less, depending on your camera operating skills).

HMI Flicker

HMI lights are a fairly recent development in motion picture technology. Compared to standard tungsten lighting, they are considerably more efficient (produce more light per watt), run cooler, and deliver a color temperature of about 5600 degrees Kelvin, which means they need no light robbing filtration to be used outdoors as fill or key. In comparison to carbon arcs, they are generally much smaller and lighter, need no constant monitoring of carbon, and won't fill a studio up with noxious fumes. They are also more costly to rent and maintain, and because they are A.C. arc discharge lighting, they can produce **flicker**, or non-constant exposure problems.

If you observe the light produced by an HMI, it seems constant, but it is actually pulsing. The number of pulses an HMI produces depends on the frequency of the A.C. line current that powers it; in the United States, this is always very precisely 60 Hz (60 cycles per second). Each cycle (one Hz) represents two surges of power delivered to the HMI, consequently there are 120 pulses of light emanating from an HMI that draws power from a 60 Hz source. If your motion picture camera speed isn't precise, and set at one of a certain number of very specific speeds, each frame of film many not be receiving the same number of pulses of light. The film will appear to flicker when projected.

This is the formula for determining **safe speeds** for any given line frequency:

$$\text{safe speed} = \frac{\text{line frequency x 2}}{\text{any whole number}}$$

For example: 60 Hz, times two is 120, divided by 8 yields 15 fps as a safe speed. Divide 120 by 7 and the result is 17.14285714, which can be rounded up to 17.143 fps. Another example: 50 Hz times two is 100, divided by 8 is 12.5 fps. One hundred divided by 9 is 11.11111111, which can be rounded down to 11.111 fps. The denominator, or number you use to divide double the line frequency, must be a whole number (no decimals) so that each frame of film receives the same number of pulses (or partial pulses) from the HMI, eliminating flicker.

Here is a chart derived from the above formula:

60 Hz line frequency, no flicker fps speeds any shutter angle

120.000	60.000	40.000	30.000
24.000	20.000	17.143	15.000
13.333	12.000	10.909	10.000
9.231	8.571	8.000	7.500
7.058	6.666	6.315	6.000
5.714	5.454	5.217	5.000
4.800	4.615	4.444	4.000
3.750	3.000	2.500	2.000
1.875	1.500	1.000	

By following the above and following tables, you can avoid flicker problems in your film. But keep these warnings in mind:

Each speed must be **crystal controlled!** The reason for each speed in the above table being carried to 3 decimal points is that even a slight variation in fps can result in flicker. A cable sync camera with a non-crystal governored motor will not do; neither will a crystal/variable speed camera set on a non-crystal controlled speed. There are several control units made by different manufacturers (Media Logic, Cinematography Electronics) that will crystal control the Arri and Aaton cameras to any of these 3 decimal place speeds; also, cameras such as the CP/R, GSMO and Aaton can be modified to run at different **crystal** speeds for HMI, video post-production (30 fps) and video monitor filming (29.97) speeds.

If the **A.C. frequency varies,** so will the pulsing of the HMI. How can this happen? Some less developed countries may have varying line frequencies. More likely is the situation where HMI's are fed from a generator that doesn't maintain a very precise 60 Hz. Even a slightly varying A.C. frequency can result in flicker.

50 Hz line frequency, no flicker fps speeds any shutter angle

100.000	50.000	33.333	25.000
20.000	16.667	14.286	12.500
11.111	10.000	9.091	8.333
7.692	7.143	6.667	6.250
5.882	5.556	5.263	5.000
4.762	4.545	4.348	4.167
4.000	3.704	3.448	3.333
3.125	3.030	2.778	2.500
2.000	1.250	1.000	

Many cinematographers like HMIs because of their power and efficiency, but there are also many who killed a shoot because they didn't take precautions against flicker. Be careful! If you have any doubts, shoot a test.

Below is a more complete formula (courtesy Media Logic). This version factors in shutter angle variations, giving extra safe speeds for peculiar angles such as 156, 172.8, etc.

$$fps = \frac{4LA}{360I}$$

where:

fps = frames per second
L = line frequency, e.g. 50 or 60
A = shutter angle in degrees
I = any integer >0, e.g. 1, 2, 3

For example, with a CP 16/R camera's 156 degree shutter, 4 times 60Hz times 156 degrees is 37,440, divided by 360 times 1 yields 104 fps as a safe speed for that shutter angle and line frequency. If you are shooting in Europe with a camera that has a 172.8 degree shutter, the formula might go like this: 4 times 50Hz times 172.8 is 34,560, divided by 360 times 1 is 96fps. Another speed would be generated by 34,560 divided by 360 x 4, which is 24 fps.

Recently, new HMI ballasts (the heavy boxes that HMIs are plugged into) have been developed that feed a square, rather than sine wave of current to the lights. This means that there is virtually no amount of time when the lights are not producing full output. Square wave HMIs then, are touted as flicker free for all shooting speeds and angles. One drawback, however, is that they can be noisier than the older sine wave HMI lights.

Super and Standard 16

The **aspect ratio,** that is, the ratio of the height of the frame to the width on television in the U.S. is 1 to 1.33. This was also the aspect ratio of film projected in theaters until sometime in the Fifties, when people began staying home, watching Milton Berle on tiny TV screens for free instead of paying money to go to the movies. The film industry panicked (as well they should) and attempted to make the movie theater experience bigger and better, hoping to combat the lure of the glowing tube.

forth for a number of years. Before I make my comments on super 16, let's take a look at what's really going on.

The super 16 format uses more negative and has a different aspect ratio than standard 16. By utilizing single perf film and extending the width of the frame .084", super 16 attains an aspect ratio of 1.66, rather than the standard 16mm 1.33. But the stock is no wider; it merely uses what might be considered waste - the second row of perforations in 16mm double perf stocks.

When standard 16 is blown up for 35mm theatrical release, it must be cropped severely to obtain a 1.85 ratio; the height of the frame must

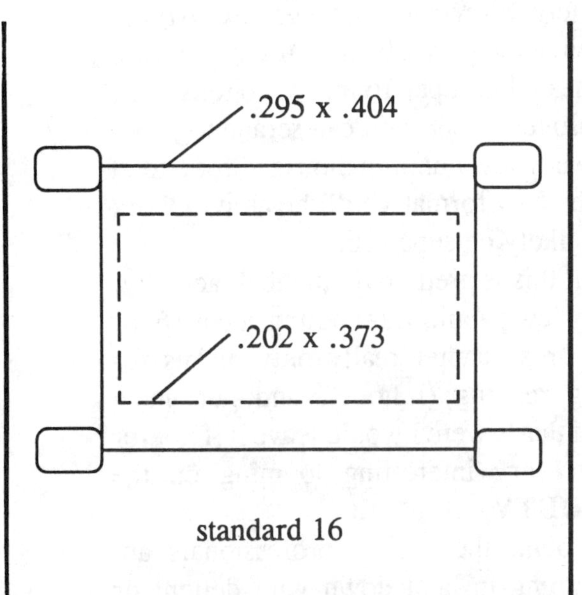

standard 16

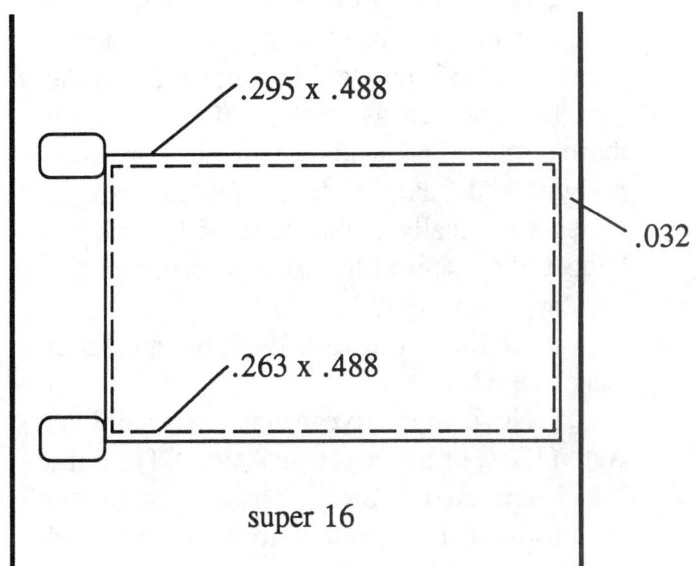

super 16

be reduced from .295" to .218". Super 16, on the other hand, needs to be cropped not at all for 1.66 release, and for 1.85 blow up, the height of the frame is reduced to only .263. Shooting super 16 for blow up to 35mm 1.85 rather than standard 16mm means you will use almost 50% more negative area.

Less grain, more sharpness, but still using the same 16mm film (as long as it is single perf) as usual? It all sounds great, but until recently, most people felt that super 16 was quite hard to justify. In fact, an article titled SHOOTING 16mm FOR BLOW UP in the 1980 edition of the American Cinematographer

New "formats", or ways of placing an image on 35mm film, were devised for projection in movie theaters. These formats widened the frame, and studios made up glitzy names like Cinerama, CinemaScope, and Vistavision to draw people back to theaters. These different formats have resulted in a number of different aspect ratios; today, the most popular are 1.66, used in Europe, 1.85, the most widely used format in the U.S., and 2.35, or "Scope".

Since 1970, when the format was invented, super 16 has been embraced by a number of filmmakers as a way to get to theatrical release with the least cost. The true value of the format has been debated back and

Manual stated that one should "Avoid the use of the Super-16mm format. The currently available 16mm negative materials . . . are characterized by such extremely fine grain, that the expanded Super-16mm format, with its endless list of complications and troubles is no longer considered justified."

The logic went this way: a) finding super 16 cameras was a pain, since for the most part they were specially modified standard 16 cameras that, once converted, couldn't be used to shoot standard 16, b) labs, edit tables, etc. were hard to find in this special format, adding to delays and extra cost, c) super 16 has absolutely no advantage over standard 16 for TV release, since cropping for video negates the widescreen format anyway, d) costs of the blow up to 35mm had to be figured in when comparing super 16 to 35mm, e) 35mm cameras like the Arri 35 BL became available, which were much more portable and hand holdable than previous designs, and finally f) film stock and camera rental are usually a tiny part of the overall budget of a feature film, so why scrimp on the very negative itself?

All this was true in 1980, but most of it has changed.

Now, super 16 cameras are usually the Aaton LTR, or better yet the Aaton XTR or the brand new Arri 16SR3. These cameras are switchable from standard to super 16, and although on Aaton LTR cameras the switch really requires a trip to a qualified technician, the Aaton XTR doesn't - it's user switchable. Arri claims its 16SR3 is too, and any of these cameras are far more mobile, less expensive, less costly and easier to hand hold than an Arri 35 BL 3 or 4, a Panavision Gold or Platinum, or the Moviecam Compact (although this last camera is really small and light). Labs such as DuArt films in New York advertise their expertise with 16 and super 16 blow ups regularly, citing hit films they have processed and printed. Edit tables such as those made by Steenbeck are available in super 16, and there are super 16 projection facilities available.

However, it is still true that for film to video, super 16 has no benefits, and that generally speaking, one must factor in the cost of the 35mm blow up and the fact that in 16mm, one cannot print selected takes as in 35mm. Also, it is still true that the cost of the film and camera rental is a very small part of the overall budget. Better to spend less on costumes, or extras, the argument goes, and get the quality of 35mm.

I hear the wheels turning in your head. You're thinking "In my micro-budget, independent first feature, the very biggest expense of production will absolutely be the camera rental, film and processing. If I can save thousands by shooting super 16 instead of 35mm, it could make the difference between making or not making the film". This reasoning is absolutely correct. Just because Arnold Schwarzenegger gets fifteen million per film doesn't mean that super 16 makes no sense. If, as an unproven talent, you can scrape together only a measly few hundred thousand for a total budget, the best format you'll be able to work with will likely be super 16.

All this is pretty hypothetical, actually. Since very few people are shooting super 16 for blow up, this chapter really only makes for interesting reading (I hope), and not much more, and that's were I would leave it if not for something very interesting looming on the horizon: **HDTV**

Around the world, professionals are either jumping up and down with delight or rolling their eyes in disgust at the thought of a sharper, widescreen television. At this point, High Definition Television that you can actually walk up to and touch is an analog system designed and broadcast in Japan and set up for special displays at trade shows elsewhere. Soon, however, the United States will set the standards for an all digital version that will also support the old NTSC sets everyone in this country already has, and when this goes down, some predict that High Def will charge onto the video scene as fast as Compact Discs did on the audio scene.

Personally, I think that there will likely be an interim format: widescreen NTSC. This format works just like our TVs - same channels using the same bandwidth, etc - except that the screen is wider. This system wouldn't be any sharper than today's TVs, but at eight feet I can't see the difference between a twenty inch standard TV and a comparably sized Hi Def TV. And the TVs themselves wouldn't be much more expensive than premium sets are now, unlike HDTV sets that will probably start at a minimum of five grand (or maybe much more). What I want is to be able to see movies - ones intended for theatrical release at a 1.85 aspect ratio - without the sides chopped off. Widescreen NTSC is good enough for me since I don't like to sit two feet from the screen and I don't want a huge projection TV in my basement, and it seems to me that, for the most part, these two situations are where I would really benefit from HDTV.

The aspect ratio of HDTV isn't set in stone, but everyone seems to pretty sorta kinda much agree that it will be 1.77, which is neither European theatrical 1.66 or U.S. theatrical 1.85 but in between the two, which makes nobody happy, but what the heck. One thing that is sure about HDTV is that there won't be a world standard anyway, because different factions (countries) have strong interests in protecting certain markets, and if a world standard exists, it will be more difficult for one group to dominate sales. Or some such nonsense. Piggy backed on the broadcast requirements of HDTV will be all the old standards, since governments will want to assure that consumers with old equipment won't be left out. All this will conspire to make widespread HDTV a mess when it does arrive.

Super 16, with its 1.66 aspect ratio, is an awful close match to 1.77 HDTV. Only a slight crop of the height of the frame is necessary. What this means is that the very minimum format for release on HDTV will be super, not standard 16. In fact, some TV series, realizing that future television syndication (where all the money is) may have to be of HDTV quality, have already made the jump to super 16. IN THE HEAT OF THE NIGHT, with Carrol O'Connor, is one.

Why not just shoot on Hi Def video for HDTV? For the same reason you wouldn't shoot Betacam for theatrical TV today. Video looks cheap. There, I said it. The film look is a prerequisite for productions that want to look high quality, and video - even Hi Def - doesn't make it. All you video people that have just thrown this book across the room and fished it out of the trash: go ahead, do it again, see if I care. While some people seem to think that Hi Def will mean the end to film, I say that the better the final display (in this case, an HDTV monitor), the better the initial acquisition must be, and that means film.

So, if you believe that HDTV is about to happen, or even if you think that it will happen but not in the next year or two, you might want to shoot that micro budget first feature in super 16 at least. Think about it: it could easily take you one or two years to edit, sound edit, mix, print and transfer your film, and by that time, HDTV could be here.

Nature filmmakers, the kind that turn in that incredible footage of cheetah kills or that icky bug mating stuff are understandably worried about HDTV. One of the main financial reasons to shoot nature is that it is timeless, like SNOW WHITE; a lion today is a lion twenty years from now, since they don't wear bell bottoms or plaid flannel shirts, and they don't say "groovy" or even "gnarly, man". If everything they are shooting now in standard 16 is substandard in ten years (or maybe even three?) they're in trouble.

Arri, having anticipated the super 16/HDTV connection, has made a 1.77 viewfinder fiber screen for the 16SR3, and Aaton, the first company to wave the starting flag on the whole affair has even come up with a new term: HD16. Pretty slick, eh?

Denz, a company in Germany that makes video taps and PL mount conversions, has introduced a standard 16/super 16 PL mount front for Arri SR one, two and highspeed cameras. Priced (at this time) at about $10,000, it offers excellent quality and upgradability at a good price. If you think that's pricey, consider that the body alone for a new 16SR3 is $46,000 (No mags, no lens). Bolex has introduced a super 16 camera, and can even modify some of their older units.

If you decide to shoot super 16, do yourself a huge favor: shoot a test. Most older Aaton cameras will not shoot super 16 without scratching the film. Kodak has introduced softer, more fragile emulsions, and Aaton had to make major magazine modifications to handle the change (see the Aaton section in the camera chapter). The Aaton XTR and Arri 16SR3 should have no problems, but I'd still want to shoot a test. Remember that the super 16 frame goes almost all the way to the edge of the film on the non-perf side; in fact, there is only about 30 thousands of an inch of room between the frame and the edge for film handling, both in the camera and at the lab. A shoot will tell you if your camera and the lab can really handle the format. Remember too that some lenses will cover the enlarged frame, and some won't, and while you should be able to see problems in the finder on the fiber screen, you might, in the heat of the moment, zoom to a focal length that vignettes; so again, a test is in order.

I clearly believe that super 16 will come on strong; it should be obvious by the title of this book. It seems to me that everyone is hungry for a change, for something new like cable TV or Compact Discs or personal computers. All these things burst onto the scene in the Eighties, and so far in the Nineties, nothing has happened that even comes close to these changes. So, I think it has to be HDTV, but it might be widescreen NTSC first. Either way, you'll want to shoot super 16 just in case.

Besides the super 16/HDTV connection, I like a widescreen aspect ratio anyway. Perhaps this is because I grew up seeing movies in the Sixties and Seventies, and I'm simply conditioned like Pavlov's dog. Or maybe it's because there is some genetic predisposition of humans to favor 1.85, film, cotton clothing, and real ice cream.

Testing and Cleaning

As stated in the preface, shooting film means you shoulder a certain risk that you don't when you shoot video or record audio tape. Film must be developed before it can be viewed; usually, it is developed and printed on another piece of film which is then developed and viewed. The film laboratory is where this all happens. The time and expense of laboratory processing that must take place before you, the filmmaker, can see the results is what comprises the risk inherent in shooting film.

The goal of this chapter is to help you test your equipment before and during the shoot so that you can make every effort to keep mistakes from happening.

Comparing Tape and Eye Focus

Equipment involved: the camera body, tripod and all lenses to be used.

When to do this test: upon receiving the camera and lenses; whenever damage to camera or lenses is suspected.

Test equipment needed: brightly lit focusing chart, tape measure.

This very important test is detailed near the end of the first chapter.

Scratch Test

Equipment involved: the camera body, all magazines to be used, battery.

When to do this test: upon receiving the camera equipment; at the head of every fresh roll of film for cameras with separate feed and take up compartments or after every other roll of film for cameras that do not; whenever camera or mags are exposed to dirty conditions.

Test equipment needed: unused film stock, small flashlight, magnifying glass or loupe.

Motion picture cameras can and often will put scratches on the film. The average viewing audience is quite accustomed to watching movie *prints* that are scratched, but not movie prints that are made from scratched *camera original.*

Scratches that take place in the camera, more often than not, cause the illusion of continuity to be destroyed.

For example: let's say you are shooting a scene involving two people having lunch at a posh restaurant. The two people are seated at a table, and the action in the scene revolves around a heated argument they are having. You spend most of the morning filming a wide master shot, one that covers all the action of the scene. The afternoon is spent on the first character's close up; the early evening on the second's. For each of these three segments, you used different camera loads, or rolls. The camera became dirty at the beginning of the third camera roll; subsequently almost all of the third character's close up has a large blue scratch down the middle.

In the editing room, when you try to put this scene together, each time you cut to the second character's close up, the large blue scratch pops up. Instead of a finished scene that gives the illusion that it was filmed all at once, the scratch jars the viewer, making him aware of the filming process.

When shooting color negative, a blue color indicates emulsion side scratches. A white color indicates base side scratches. Although base side scratches can sometimes be minimized when the A and B rolls are wet gate printed, emulsion side scratches are yours forever (there has yet to be concocted a liquid that will match the changing density of any given film emulsion). There are, however, digital video processes that can minimize scratches, but these are only useful for the video tape copies of your film, and are quite costly.

The testing procedure for finding scratch problems varies from camera to camera, but it is essentially this: look at a length of film that has been run through the camera and any associated magazine carefully with a light and magnifying glass to see if any scratches exist.

Any experiment that seeks to predict future problems must duplicate future conditions as closely as possible. This means that:

A) You *must* use film stock that has never run through a camera (or any other machine) before you use it for a scratch test. It could be an old short end that has been sitting in your friend's refrigerator for ages, or even one that has been exposed to light, but it cannot have been run through a camera before. If you use film that has gone through a camera previously, and you find scratches, it will be impossible to tell their origin.

On cameras that use mags with separate feed and take-up sides, you can use the first few feet of *every fresh roll of film*. Opening the take up side will not expose the fresh, expensive roll of film sitting on the feed side. Cameras with separate feed and take-up sides - Eclair NPR and ACL, Arri SR, Cinema Products CP16, and Aaton - are therefore better cameras in this respect. Cameras with single film compartments, either in the mags or in the body of the camera itself - Arri S and 16BL, Bolex, Scoopic - must be tested with a special roll of film that you use for scratch testing only, or with the first few feet of a daylight spool if that is the type of load you are using.

This may be hard for you to do - that is, track down some film that can be used for scratch testing purposes only (if your camera uses single compartment magazines). Sixteen millimeter raw stock is costly, and old, unused film that hasn't been run through a camera is hard to find. You may be forced to buy 100 feet of fresh film on a daylight spool and use this a few feet at a time. In any event, *don't use editing leader, print film, magnetic film* or anything else that isn't made to be camera original, because only camera original has the correct pitch (distance between perforations) and perforation size to run through motion picture cameras. Anything else will, at the very least, give you unreliable results for your scratch test, and at the very worse, damage the camera.

B) You must look at the film *after* it has entered the area of the mag or camera where it will be wound up on the take up spindle or core. Take a look at figure 1. The arrow marked A points to this area of film; B is incorrect. It is entirely possible that the camera will scratch the film after it has left the gate, but before it has entered the mag. If you get lazy, and decide to

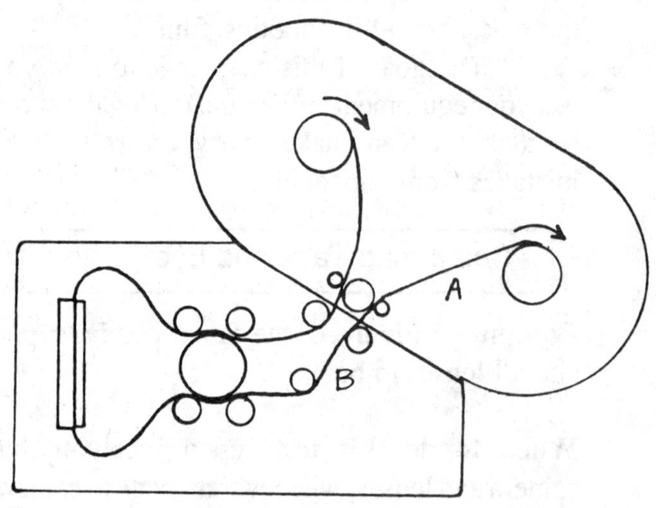

Figure 1

look only at the film at B (because you are using a single compartment mag and you don't want to have to go into the changing bag again) you are leaving it to fate that it will not be scratched when it enters the mag. Some cameras have simple felt rollers at this point; others have sprocketed rollers. Either type of mag is capable of scratching your film.

C) You must look carefully at the *surface of the film* - both emulsion and base sides - to see if the camera or mag is scratching. I've seen some people use a felt tipped marker to scratch test a camera. They scribble on the film, then run it through the camera. If the scribble is scratched, they reason, the camera is scratching. This is incorrect. Since the aperture and pressure plates are contacting the film all the way across both sides of the film, it is quite possible for the scribble to be rubbed off. The residue from the marker may also be burnished on the gate or pressure plate and cause problems. This is an invalid way to test, since in the future you will be running film - not *marked* film - through your camera.

Get a good flashlight and a loupe, or magnifying glass, and really examine the film. By angling the light off the surface of the film, you should be able to see even the smallest scratch.

D) You must look carefully at *several feet of film*. It sounds wasteful, but it is exactly the opposite. Some scratches are intermittent - they are, for example, two inches long, and they occur every one and a half feet. This kind of scratch could be the result of poor feed spindle tension, causing the feed roll to be repeatedly jerked instead of unwound smoothly, resulting in a little scratch every foot or so as the film jerks against a roller or pressure plate. If you looked only at six or eight inches of film, worrying about waste, you could be looking at a section of film between the scratches and miss them entirely.

If You Find a Scratch

If you are using a camera with more than one magazine, try the other mag. If the second mag is not scratching, the problem is likely in the first mag (although it may be the unique *combination* of mag and camera that causes the problem). If you find that the second mag is scratching also, unload everything and take a good look at the areas of the camera and mag that come in contact with the film. By now you should be nicely acquainted with the scratch or scratches. Are they on the base side only? In the sprocket area? Try to narrow down your inspection to scrutinize areas of the machine that touch this section of film only. If you find a bit of dirt - or even if you don't - clean the equipment in question, and re-test.

If you still have the same scratch or scratches, you can do one of two things: return the camera to whomever gave it to you and inform them of the problem and ask them to fix it, or locate the problem yourself and attempt to fix it. If you try to locate it yourself, and still have to ask the rental house or a technician to fix it, you'll at least be able to give a better description of the problem, and therefore be taken more seriously. Load the camera and mag with unused film and run off several feet. Stop the camera, and *very carefully*, with a pair of scissors, cut the film at the locations marked in figure 2. One by one, examine each section. You may find that the film is scratched between the take up spindle and the take-up side mag light trap, and the take-up side mag light trap and the gate, but not between the gate and the feed side light trap. You know, for example, that the scratch is on the base side, so the likely culprit is the pressure plate.

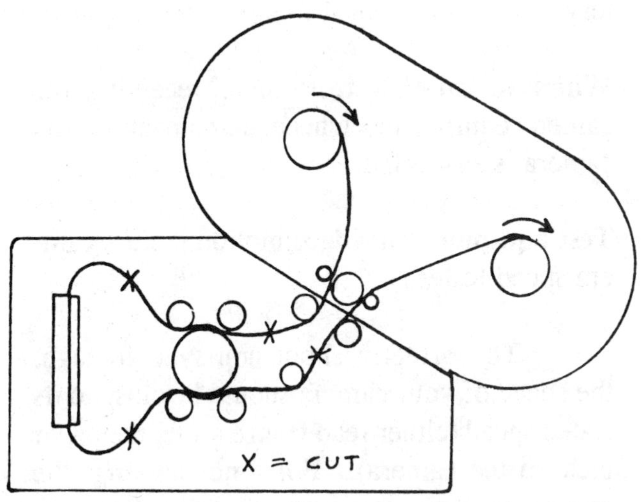

Figure 2

This is exactly the test a technician would do to find the problem. You can pinpoint a dirty pressure plate, or a non-moving guide roller yourself and fix it. Even if you can't repair the problem - and if it is much more than cleaning or perhaps tightening something, and you are not an experienced camera repair person, you probably shouldn't - you can be more informative when you ask the technician to. In the field, you may *have* to fix it, or the shoot will be dead.

Speed Test.

Equipment involved: Camera, magazine, battery.

When to do this test: upon receiving the camera equipment; whenever damage to the camera is suspected.

Test equipment needed: motion picture camera speed tester.

To correctly shoot non-sync footage, the speed of your camera should be close to its stated speed (either read from a scale, meter, or tach on the camera). For sync shooting, the camera must run at a precisely controlled constant speed. (see chapter 2, Sync). Testing the speed of your camera is the only way to be assured of this.

Many different devices have been made to check camera speed - strobes being the most common. Another device uses the sequential flashing of 6 L.E.D.s to test speed. Both these devices use the same principal: a pulsing light or lights of known rate are compared to an oscillating part of the camera that has a one to one relationship with each exposed frame. The strobe works this way: say you are going to test your camera at 24 fps. You select that speed on the strobe (older models may have this one speed only) and aim it at the camera claw when the camera is set to 24 fps. The light of the strobe is flashing 24 times a second, is crystal controlled, each flash having a very short duration - 1/3,000 of a second, or some such time. If the camera is running 24 fps also, the movement of the claw will appear to be frozen. If the pulldown claw appears to be moving (and it may "move" either forward or backward) your camera is not running at a precise enough speed for sync shooting. The strobe may also be used on the shutter, accessed from the lens port, or on a sprocketed wheel.

The L.E.D device is similar, but offers this advantage: the camera may be tested fully loaded (although rare, cameras may not be able to maintain an accurate speed when pulling film), and without pulling the lens . This device usually consists of a 6 unit L.E.D display. Each individual L.E.D is flashed in sequence 24 times per second. If you look through your rotating mirror shutter camera's finder at the display, and run it at 24 fps, you'll see that it appears "frozen". If there is any "movement" of the L.E.D.s - for example, one segment to the right begins to light while the one to the left fades - the camera is not running accurately enough for sync.

If you do this test long enough, you'll undoubtedly detect *some* inaccuracy. Over thirty or forty seconds, however, there should be no movement.

Media Logic sells two inexpensive crystal speed testers ($145) that test speeds of 24, 25 and 30 fps. One type is a six L.E.D display unit, and the other uses a single, ultra bright L.E.D as a strobe. Multiples of the base speeds - 48, 50, and 60 - can be checked by these units as well.

Battery Test

Equipment involved: all batteries to be used during shoot.

When to do this test: upon receiving the camera package; whenever the power of the batteries must be known.

Testing equipment needed: volt/ohm meter.

Nothing is more frightening on a shoot than the thought of being stuck without power for the camera. Those little black boxes - or that strange belt that looks like it belongs on a machine gunner - are the sole source of electrical power for most cameras. There are AC power adapters that enable cameras to run from household current, however, but these will slow down camera positioning on the set - and for exterior work, they're far more trouble than they're worth.

Motion picture cameras almost invariably run on 12 volts DC. The major exceptions are: Panavision (24 vdc); Cinema Products CP16 (20 vdc); the Arriflex 16S, 16SB and 16M (8.4 vdc); the Arri 16SR3 (24 vdc) and certain Arriflex 35mm cameras that need 20 - 30 volts to run at high speed.

Most batteries used to drive cameras are of the rechargeable, nickel-cadmium type. These are excellent because they can be recharged hundreds, or even a thousand times, and they *maintain their voltage* as they are used.

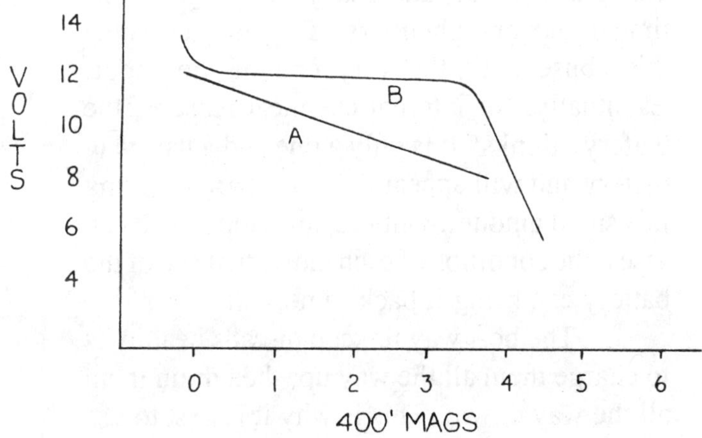

Battery Comparison

Unfortunately, the constant voltage output of these batteries is a source of consternation as well. Take a look at the diagram above. An ordinary carbon battery, marked A, will loose its voltage slowly, and quickly, compared to the ni-cad, marked B. Somewhere around ten or ten and a half volts, the camera we are using will not be able to maintain sync (run at precisely 24 fps) anymore. At this point, the battery is "dead". The carbon battery gives out after 2 mags (800' of film) or so, but the ni-cad drives 5 mags. Over those 5 mags, the ni-cad exhibits very little voltage drop. Since we use a volt/ohm meter (VOM) to test batteries, how can we tell how much charge a given battery might contain?

First, the VOM should be explained: this is a device that can be had at any electronics store for $15 (really good ones sell for much more, and have digital readouts, and do other things as well, but you don't really need this kind to just test batteries). It can test the amount of electrical resistance an object has (measured in ohms) as well as the electromotive force difference between two points in a circuit (measured in volts). Usually they have the ability to measure amperage, or electrical "volume" as well. For our purposes here, we need to see how much *voltage* a given battery has.

To do this, switch your VOM into the volts DC mode (as opposed to the volts AC mode, which you could use to test for power at a wall outlet). Although meters vary, this is usually done by rotating a knob on the front. There will be several ranges for measuring DC volts; choose the one for 0 - 50 volts. Connect the red lead coming from the VOM to the positive terminal of the battery in question; the black lead goes to the negative terminal. If you are uncertain about which terminal is which (positive or negative), simply connect the terminals at random: you'll have a 50-50 chance, and if you get it wrong you'll know because the needle on the meter will try to go backwards, off the scale.

What does the meter say? 13 volts? 9? 12.7? How do you interpret this reading?

Here is the problem - again refer to figure 3 . This ni-cad battery is very nearly twelve volts - *even when it is about to die*, at 4.5 mags. If you use your VOM to monitor the battery, it will always exhibit the same, or nearly the same voltage as it is used. If you get a battery from the rental house, and it reads 12.3 volts, how can you be sure it is fully charged, as the rental person says it is?

Firstly, when ni-cad batteries are fully charged, they indicate a slightly higher voltage - say 13.2 volts - for a 12 volt battery that normally indicates 12.3 when used. But this is not useful when you are on the set, wondering when the battery will die.

The only way to tell how many mags a battery will drive is to drain it completely, charge it all the way up, then use it on your camera, and see how long it lasts. Since you have to use it all the way up, you'll need two batteries - one on stand by.

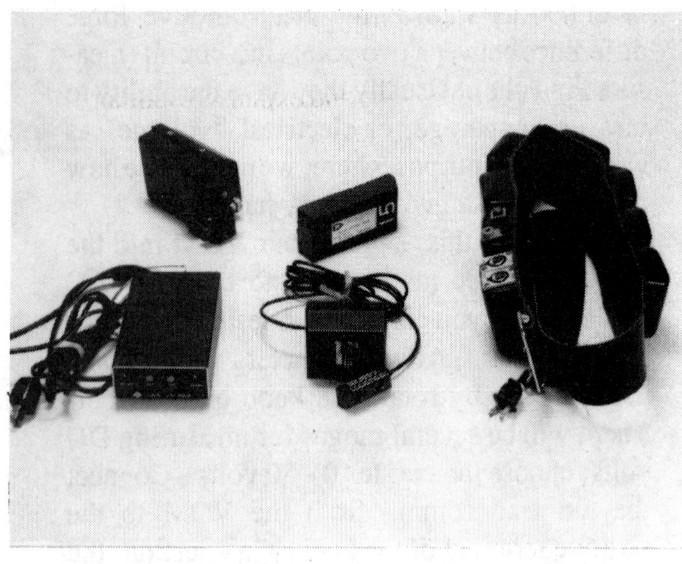

L to R: AVC Charger and On-Board for 16SR, CP Charger and On-Board, Cine 60 Belt

Here's how to do this: get two batteries and mark them #1 and #2, and charge them up if the rental house hasn't already done so. If a battery is completely dead, it will generally take 12 - 14 hours to recharge. (Some manufacturers have fast charge systems that consist of special batteries and charging units, and these might only take an hour to recharge.) Put battery #1 on the camera if it is an on-board, or connect it to the camera via a cable if it is a belt or block, and use it up during your shoot. You'll know when it is about to go dead because the camera will take much longer to get up to speed. This is usually best indicated by the **out-of-sync warning light** if your camera has one - it will light up when the camera is switched on, and take a long time to go out because the battery is almost dead and is having trouble getting the camera up to speed. When the out-of-sync light stays on an intolerably long time - say, three or four seconds, the battery is gone. How many mags did battery #1 drive? Four? Then this is how many you can expect it to drive in the future, under the same conditions.

Battery #2 may drive more, or less. Older batteries can be counted on for less mags, newer ones more. A battery that is misused - usually by repeated overcharging - will drive less.

Many batteries are pre-maturely aged by what many people do who use only one battery: **memorize** it. These people rent a single battery to save money, then charge it for three or four hours even if the rental worker said it was fully charged. Then they shoot a mag, or a mag and a half, and charge it up again, this time for six or eight hours. They may continue this abuse until the very end of the shoot. Eventually, for internal chemical reasons, the battery "thinks" it is only a one and a half mag battery and will appear to be dead after driving this small amount. Only repair people who can assess the condition of each individual cell of the battery can bring it back to normal.

The best way to keep ni-cads healthy is to charge them all the way up, then drain them all the way down. This is why it is best to use two batteries, one after the other, alternately charging and draining them, always having a back-up.

If you are planning to shoot in cold weather, you should expect far less from your batteries. Even if you wear your belt under your down coat, or stuff an on-board into your pocket and keep it warm, you'll probably drive half as many mags. This is because the camera itself is likely lubricated with oil and grease, and in cold weather these lubricants get more viscous, or sticky. It is harder for the motor to turn a camera when this happens.

Although a VOM cannot be your principle source of battery charge information - at least in regards to ni-cads - it can be used at the rental house, to see if the battery is really fully charged (remember, batteries put out a slightly higher voltage when fully charged) and it has many other uses as well: testing bulbs, cables, fuses, wall voltage, and fixing electrical devices in general if you are skilled in that area. No competent assistant cameraperson should be without one.

12V LITHIUM BATTERIES are available for use with 16mm cameras and will drive from 40 to 50 mags of film. They are not rechargeable. They have an extremely long (several years) shelf life. These are the lifesavers of camera batteries. Keep one in your kit for those times when all your ni-cads go dead or you can't recharge because you're in a location that has no A.C. current. You may have to run the camera several minutes without film to "activate" a lithium unit, expecially if you haven't used the battery for a while.

NEW CELLS - Buying a used camera? Does it come with batteries? Take some time to open up the batteries and check to see what kind of cells are installed. If you find a) consumer level nicads, like from Radio Shack, or b) a hodgepodge of mismatched cells, add the cost of recelling the battery (about $100-250) to the deal. Mismatched or consumer cells are an indication of poor repair. Consumer cells are seriously inferior to industrial, high amp-hour units, and anyone who replaces individual dead cells in a battery only is prolonging (and not for long) a dead battery. It's best to replace all cells in a ni-cad unit when the first dies (won't hold a charge) because new cells won't charge and discharge like old ones, or ones from other manufacturers. If a new cell charges faster than the others, it will be overcharged repeatedly while the others are undercharged, resulting in early failure. Replacing only the cells that won't charge with new ones begins an exasperating cell merry-go-round that can end up with far more expense and frustration, down the road, than simply replacing all the cells at the first sign of trouble (a dead cell).

BLOCK and BELT BATTERIES from manufacturers like Anton-Bauer, Frezzi Pag, Cine 60 and G+M are available for use with 16mm cameras. They won't mount on-board so you have to supply a standard 4 pin XLR cable. The main advantage of larger units such as these are increased running time, especially in cold weather.

CAR BATTERIES are almost always 12 volts and will work nicely for driving Aatons. But watch out! If you reverse polarity (cross your wires) you can do serious and expensive damage to the camera's circuits.

Many people keep track of the performance of individual ni-cads by giving them names. Battery #1, for example, is Susan, while #2 is Lou, and #3 is Margaret. It is much easier to remember that Lou is an invalid and will only run 3 mags fully charged than it is to remember that #2 is a bad battery. Other people stick with numbers, or use colors. Any one for tennis?

Video cameras are ni-cad addicts, so companies like Anton-Bauer and Frezzi have done considerable research in finding the best way to charge ni-cads for this large market. Anton-Bauer, for example, uses a temperature sensor next to each cell to detect the point at which any one begins to overheat, indicating overcharging. When this happens, the charger instantly converts from fast to slow charge, assuring quick charge times while protecting cells from overcharging. The Abel Cinetech ACT AX3 unit uses a microprocessor to sense a voltage change that occurs when any one cell is charged, switching from fast to slow charge. It has the ability to charge one 12 or 16 volt battery in only 20 minutes (rivalling the security of a lithium battery), or slow charge up to 3 batteries in 2 hours.

Recently, more and more film and video makers are turning to inexpensive, sealed **lead-acid batteries** to power their cameras. Available from several different manufacturers (Bescor is one), these units are generally designed for use with video cameras during long shoots where the camera's own on-board batteries just don't have enough power.

One Bescor model produces 6.5 Ah of power, which is like having one and one half standard 4 Ah Cine 60 type battery belts. At the time of this writing, this battery costs less than $50! If you want to use one with your camera, you'll probably have to modify it by soldering standard 4 pin XLR connectors on the charger and battery itself, or make an adapter cable, as the battery comes from the factory with feeble cigarette lighter style plugs.

Another advantage of this battery besides great low cost are that the battery is best used in exactly the opposite way that you would use nickel cadmium units. In other words, sealed lead-acid batteries will live longer if they are kept charged and not allowed to become completely discharged. Rather than use them all the way down, then charge them all the way up as you would with ni-cads, use them a little, then charge them a little. Or keep one fully charged as back up to your ni-cad on-board in case of emergency. If you discharge one completely every time you use it, you'll likely only get something like 150 cycles from it before it is dead, as opposed to 1500 cycles by only discharging it by one third.

Bescor batteries come in many sizes; the one described is a single 12V unit (no wiring from cell to cell as in ni-cads) and roughly the size of half a loaf of bread. Bescor has wrapped the battery in a nice zippered nylon case with a shoulder strap. You can find sealed lead-acid batteries for video use in most big volume consumer video outlets.

BATTERY WIRING FOR 16MM CAMERAS

Most cameras use a 4 pin XLR style plug. Long ago, these were all made by Canon, then by Switchcraft. The latest and bestest (and yet, least expensive!) are made by Neutrik. They'll all plug into each other, but parts among each will not interchange. If you are handy with a soldering iron and want to repair/adapt/make your own batteries or battery cables, here's the schematic, in all its simplicity:

PIN 1 = negative/ground/earth/minus/black

PIN 2 = not used

PIN 3 = not used

PIN 4 = positive/plus/red 12V

Hair Test

Equipment involved: the camera, lens and loaded mag.

When to do this test: immediately after the last take of every shot; when dirty conditions are suspected.

Test equipment needed: magnifying glass, flashlight.

Like scratches, hair or dirt in the gate caused by the projector is a familiar sight to audiences. Unless the buildup is very slight it will be incredibly annoying and destructive to the viewing experience. Now consider that this same problem can occur in your *camera gate.* Any dust, hair, or dirt in general can lodge itself in the gate (usually at the bottom) and block any underlying emulsion from exposure. A shadow of the debris is recorded, forever.

Problems of this sort are much more common in the projector than the camera because of poorly cleaned equipment, dirty or old prints, etc. But when they happen in the camera, they are far worse, for exactly the same reasons outlined in the section on scratch testing.

To keep dirt from lodging in the gate, you must keep anything that comes in contact with either the film, the film spools, cores, or the camera spotless.

The changing bag is usually the culprit. Unzip both compartments, turn it inside out and inspect it for damage. Shake it clean. If it is old and ratty - throw it away. Why risk it? There are good, anti-static ones to be had, as well as cheap fuzzy fabric bags that are destined to cause disaster. Buy/rent/borrow a good one, and once you've cleaned and inspected it, store in its own box or bag, all by itself, away from anything that might cause it to get dirty.

Fuzzy sweaters are out. So are dirty hands. When you use a changing bag, it's a good idea to roll up your sleeves and pull the bag up over your *bare arms* if you are wearing a shirt or jacket that you think is fuzzy. Remember also to pull the sleeves of the bag well up over your elbows. This accomplishes two things: it reduces the chance of light penetrating the elastic closure, and it gives you more working space inside the bag as there is less fabric bunched up around your hands.

The Hair Test itself is very simple: just after the camera has been threaded up, and at the end of the last take of every shot, pull the lens, clear the shutter, shine a small flashlight on the emulsion in the gate, and look for dirt. If you take your time and look closely, you'll be able to see even the tiniest debris without a magnifying glass. If you find nothing, you can tell the director that the take is good. If you find something, he or she might be mad at you for letting the camera get dirty, but not nearly as mad as they would be had you done or said nothing, and the problem turned up the next day when the dailies were screened, *after* the set has been struck, or the talent has returned home in London. Finding debris in the gate means the last take is questionable, and another take (or takes) is called for. Hair and dirt collecting in the gate is a fact of life - something to remind testy directors of when you insist on taking the time to do a good test.

Sometimes, you don't even have to pull the lens - this is nice to know because often there are matte boxes and follow focuses that have to be dismounted before you can remove the lens. Longer focal length lenses - 40 or 50mm and up - can be looked *through* to see the gate. It sometimes takes a little maneuvering with eye and flashlight, but longer lenses act as magnifying glasses and are actually helpful in letting you do a good Hair Test. Zoom lenses, because of their length and many elements, invariably have to be pulled, however.

Footage Counter Test

Equipment involved: the camera, all magazines.

When to do this test: upon receiving camera package.

Test equipment needed: short end footage, synchronizer.

Sometimes, footage counters on cameras and mags are inaccurate. Film stock is expensive (and so is time on the set taken to reload) so it's important to know just how much film remains in a given load.

To test footage counters on *cameras:* get a length of film - not used magnetic film or sound fill or leader, as these have a different pitch than film that is meant to be camera original and can damage the camera - and mark out twenty feet with a synchronizer (a device used in post-production to measure and align various tracks). First measure out five or six feet (for threading the camera) and make a mark on a frame with a Sharpie (indelible felt tipped pen). Roll off twenty feet, and make an end mark. Load this in your camera, roll until the first mark is in the gate. Reset the footage counter to zero, and roll until the end mark is in the gate. Check the counter - does it say 20'? If not, do the test again. You can multiply the error by either 5 or 20 to get the total error that will result in 100 and 400 foot loads respectively. Make a note of the error; write it on a piece of camera tape and stick it next to the footage counter. It might read like this: 100' on counter is 95'.

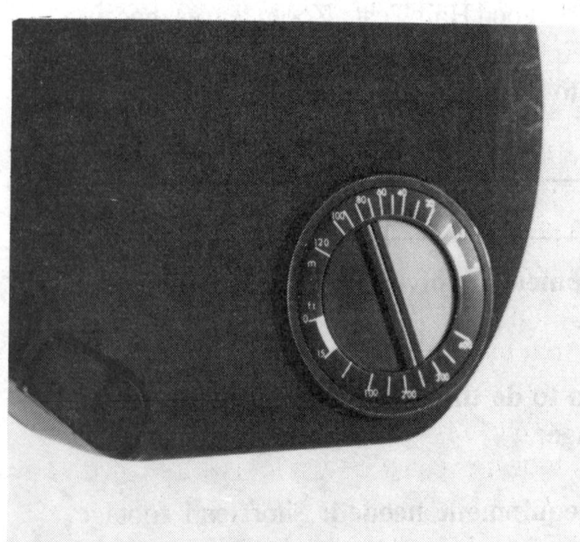

Aaton Footage Counter

You'll likely find little or no error with mechanical footage counters which are in the camera body itself. Subtractive counters in the magazine are another story. Subtractive means they tell you how much footage is left, rather than how much you've shot, and they invariably operate by means of a mechanical arm that swings a roller that rests on the film itself (in the sprocket hole area) on the take up side of the mag. These arms are often bent during loading, or else they slam down against an empty core when they are carelessly released (they're usually spring loaded and have a catch that gets them out of the way during loading) and this causes gears to slip, or parts to bend. Checking them is extraordinarily simple. Place an empty core on the take up side (or daylight spool if that is what you're using and the counter will operate with them) and lower the arm down until it touches it. If the counter says you've got 20' left, note this next to it with an indelible ink marker and camera tape (ex: 20' on counter is 0').

Registration Test

Equipment involved: the camera, lens and loaded mag.

When to do this test: when camera registration is in question.

Test equipment needed: chart, possibly a darkroom for rewinding film.

A registration test determines the steadiness with which the camera original will be recorded. Each perforation must be very precisely located (registered) at the moment of exposure by the pulldown claw and/or registration pin. If this does not occur, images will seem jumpy, or unsteady during projection.

Testing the registration of the camera is complicated somewhat by the fact that contact printers, optical printers, and projectors affect the perceived steadiness of the image as well. Other factors, such as variations in film stocks, tripod stiffness, and even the steadiness of the floor during the shooting (subway cars and walking people can vibrate the floor) can affect the validity of the registration test. To do a valid registration test of the camera, then, the variables introduced by these machines and conditions must be eliminated.

First, shoot the same camera original that you intend to use for your project. If you are purchasing a camera and are performing a general test for all stocks, then use color negative, because this is the stock that will probably be most used in the camera (unless you *know* that you will be shooting mostly reversal, for example, and you will be the primary user of the camera). A camera should, in theory, register reversal and negative, or color and black and white the same, but stocks do vary; pitch and thickness of the film may differ and affect registration.

Load the camera (or the camera and magazine) and place it on a sturdy, level tripod. It's a good idea to weight the tripod with sandbags to keep it steady and stiff during the test. Focus the lens on a well lighted chart. Don't use a standard focus chart (one with Seimens stars or resolution lines) for this test. Make up a special one. Get a piece of white cardboard that is large enough to fill the frame for the focal length and distance you've selected (25mm at 4 or 5 feet is fine) and draw an X across it, from corner to corner, with a black marker. Make sure the lines are dark and visible through the finder. Tape the chart securely to the wall, and note it's position with additional tape markers at the corners. Check the exposure with your meter, set the footage counters to 0'. Check the framing and focus through the finder, and lock the pan and tilt controls on the tripod. Make sure no one will be moving around the room (and possibly vibrate the floor), close the eyepiece door or dowser (you *shouldn't* be looking through the camera), and roll off at least 30' of film. It's also a good idea to start and stop the camera by plugging and unplugging the power cable from the battery belt. All these precautions are necessary to isolate the camera from any bumps or jostles that will appear as poor registration during screening.

The next step is to shoot the same section of film again - *double expose* it - but with the chart moved very slightly. What you'll see when you project the film are *two x's*, just slightly apart from each other: any movement of the x's in unison is a result of the *projector's* registration, while movement of the x's individually - one in relation to the other - is a result of the *camera's* registration.

At this point, the kind of camera you are using will determine how difficult it will be to complete this test. If the camera will run in reverse (like an Arri 16S or SB with a variable speed motor) or can be backwound with a crank (like most Bolex models) you will simply cap the lens, double check that the eyepiece dowser or door is closed, and backwind the film in the camera until the footage counter reads zero. Most 16mm sync cameras, however, will not reverse; in this situation, you may have to rewind the film in a darkroom that has film rewinds (hard to find) or in a changing bag manually (slow and tedious) to finish.

Once you've backwound the camera, move the chart. Just an inch will do. Don't pan or tilt the camera to reposition the X in the frame - once the camera has been moved, you've lost your reference as to where the original X was. The *tape marks* you stuck around the corners of the chart will tell you its original position, and tell you how to move it.

Run off the same 30 feet of film again, unload the camera and send it to the lab. Have the lab process and return the *camera original only.* Any print may have registration error added to it by a contact printer. Although this is unlikely, it is easily avoided by projecting the camera original, be it negative or reversal, and the additional expense of a print is eliminated.

When screening the test, try to concentrate on the two X's and their movement in relation to each other, rather than the overall steadiness of the frame, which admits error by the projector.

How important is this test? If you are laying out considerable money for a camera, or are embarking on a long and expensive film project, a registration test would be a good idea. But if this is not the case, you probably don't need to do this test. A film test for lighting will also be a somewhat valid registration test for the camera as well, and you should also know that registration problems are, in general, quite rare, and that camera registration has to be quite poor before it becomes bothersome.

There is one other, quicker way that some camerapeople use to test registration. A small, lighted pocket microscope is used to examine a perforation just before or just after the film has left the gate with the camera running. Any bobbing or weaving of the perf will be indicative of registration. It takes a trained eye, however, to translate this perforation movement, viewed through a microscope, to on screen registration, and some cameras like the NPR and SR won't permit this type of examination because the gate area can't be viewed with the magazine in place.

Pilot Signal Test

Equipment involved: The camera body, Nagra with tape, sync cable (if you are shooting cable sync), transfer equipment with resolver.

When to do this test: At the start of the production; when the recording of good pilot signal is uncertain.

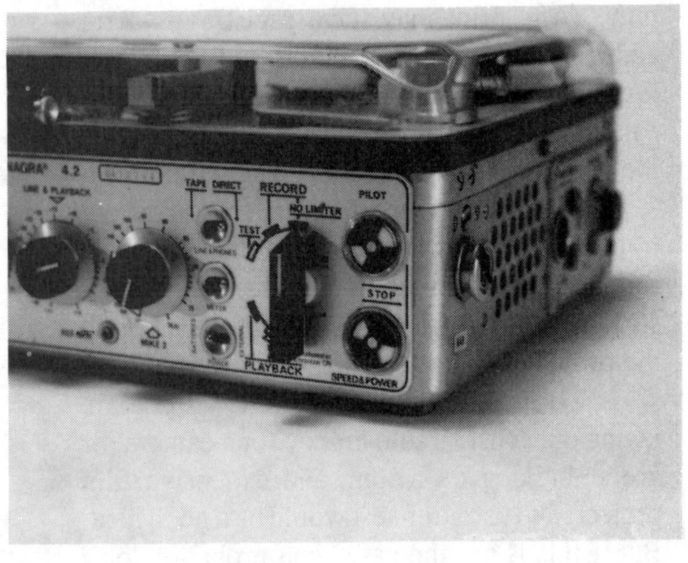

Nagra 4.2 Speed/Power and Pilot Indicators

Pilot signal is recorded on the Nagra, and it is vital whether you are shooting crystal *or* cable sync (see chapter II - Sync). To test pilot signal when shooting

Cable Sync - plug the camera end of the sync cable into the camera. This will almost always be a four or five pin Tuchel connector (sometimes male, sometimes female) which pushes in and then screws tight by turning an outer ring. The Nagra end of the cable will push/screw into the Nagra the same way. If there is a *crystal cap* on the Nagra, you'll have to remove it first. Tape it onto the carrying strap (or some other place) so you won't lose it. Turn the Nagra on. On the right front of the chassis are two round indicators called flags. When the Nagra comes up to speed, the lower flag will pop on. When the camera is then turned on and good, usable pilot signal is sent to the Nagra, the upper flag pops (turns white). If this doesn't happen, something is wrong either in the camera, the Nagra or the cable itself. If the top flag *does* pop on you can complete the test: wiggle the cable and the cable connectors at both the camera and Nagra and watch the pilot flag for any hesitation or movement. Often, the cable and connectors can be damaged internally, and work fine until the middle of an important dolly shot on the set. Get a spare cable and take it along.

Crystal Sync. In this situation, the pilot signal is sent from the crystal board inside the Nagra out through the crystal cap, then back inside the Nagra to be recorded on the tape for resolving in transferring the 16mm magnetic film. With the crystal cap in, simply turn the Nagra to Record. Both speed and pilot flags should pop on (older Nagra III recorders have a single pilot flag only). Test the camera by performing the speed test procedure in this chapter.

How do you know that Neopilot (what the pilot signal turns into once it is recorded on a Nagra) is really on your 1/4" tape? If the pilot flag pops on you can be fairly certain, but if you want to be absolutely sure, simply record a test, then play it back on transfer equipment that has a resolver. The resolver will have an indicator (sometimes a meter, sometimes an L.E.D. or light) which pops on when Neopilot is locked onto on the 1/4" tape. If you are going on a long shoot and are using an unfamiliar (hence questionable) Nagra, it's a good idea to test for Neopilot on the tape this way.

Framing Test

Equipment involved: the camera and lenses.

When to do this test: at the start of a shoot; any time the accuracy of framing is in question.

Test equipment needed: brightly lit wall, Scotch Tape (the Magic Transparent type), small mirror or prism.

Almost every cameraperson has, at one time or other, been the victim of a camera that didn't faithfully record the frame that appeared in the viewfinder. The dailies show the actors screen left, or to high in the frame - or worse, accompanied by light stands or floating microphones. At this point, the only remedies are expensive optical realignments (which generally degrade the image by adding another generation) or even more costly reshoots.

If time allows, you can shoot film to precisely test the framing accuracy of any camera. A well lighted wall can serve as the scene, with pieces of black camera tape placed to mark the four corners of the frame as seen through the viewfinder. The negative can be screened, saving the cost of printing, and any framing errors will be immediately apparent. Take care, however, that the framing of the projector in question is correct and isn't adding to or subtracting frame error (don't rely on editing machines such as flatbeds, uprights or viewers as these are often misaligned). If there is any doubt, inspect the negative *directly* by eye or through a magnifying glass.

If time does not allow - if the camera in question was only checked out from the rental house hours before the shoot, for example - there are other methods you can use to check the framing.

Cameras with rotating mirror shutter reflex viewing systems (CP/R, Frezzolini FR-16, Eclair NPR and ACL, Arri 16BL and 16SR, and Aaton) can be quickly sight-checked by pulling the lens, running the camera and comparing the views of the gate area and the markings on the ground glass/fiber optic screen. By positioning your eye along the lens axis - the center of the lens port - and looking directly at the gate, you'll see the lines of the ground glass superimposed over the gate when the mirror shutter passes. Any crookedness or misalignment will be apparent. Unfortunately, this method relies on the careful positioning of the eye, and even fairly practiced camerapeople may not be able to detect slight but unacceptable error (this may be because people tend to correct error by altering the position of our eye in relation to the lens axis). In any event, a much more critical test can be achieved by comparing the views *through* the viewfinder and *behind* the gate.

On cameras that have coaxial mags which detach at the line between pressure and aperture plates (Aaton, ACL, NPR and 16SR) this is a breeze. Set up your camera and any lens (a zoom is especially helpful here) on the tripod, and focus on a brightly lit wall. Remove the mag and place a piece of Scotch Magic Transparent tape over the gate, lightly so as not to leave any residue when removed. This tape is translucent rather than transparent, owing to its matte surface. It acts exactly like a ground glass! You can now look through the finder and pan your camera around to marks on the wall corresponding to, for example, the left edge of the frame, then lock the tripod and check for the same alignment on the tape in the gate (everything will be upside down and backward, though). This is, incidentally, essentially the method technicians use for testing and resetting cameras.

If your camera doesn't have mags that remove and leave easy access to the gate, you can still do this Scotch Tape Test, but you may have to use a small dental mirror or the like to see the tape in the gate. If you really want to be prepared, you can get a small right angle prism from suppliers like Edmund Scientific which will fit into the gate and give you a clear view. Cameras that have beam splitter viewing systems (reflex Bolexes, Canon Scoopics) and those with non-reflex viewers (older Bolexes and Filmos) can be tested this way also. Some of these cameras, though, have gate and pressure plate assemblies that make it extremely difficult to test framing in this way, and nothing short of a film test will be required.

Cleaning

Every cameraperson has his or her own methods of keeping equipment clean. What follows are mine.

First, get several 2" (or thereabouts) white **china bristle paintbrushes**. These can be had for less than a dollar at hardware stores. Use these to brush dust and hair from the insides of magazines and cameras, as well as cleaning anything that might be on the outside of lenses/mags/cameras/etc. The reason to get brushes with white bristles is simple: paintbrushes often shed individual bristles, and if they're white, you'll be more likely to see them against the black interior of mags and cameras before they do damage. You can use these brushes to clean everything except the mirror shutter and the lens elements.

Several good **camel hair brushes** can be purchased at any drugstore; they're designed to apply make-up, but they work nicely for removing dust from fragile surfaces: lenses, eyepieces and mirrors. This brings us to lens cleaning in general, and a bit of warning is in order here.

Most of the damage that happens to front and rear lens elements occurs when people clean them incorrectly. This is what often happens: the cameraperson sees some dirt, or dust, takes out a tissue and soaks it in lens fluid (or worse, drops the fluid directly on the lens) and begins wiping the lens. If any of the dust happens to be comprised of abrasive particles, these get wiped around and around until the lens coating becomes permanently scratched by them. The cameraperson then takes another tissue and wipes the lens clean and sees, to his or her horror, the several (or perhaps many) circular scratches in the lens coating. Replacement of these elements in some lenses can cost well over $1,000.

So that this won't happen to you, make sure you really need to clean the lens with a tissue and fluid in the first place. Blow the surface in question with a squeeze bulb (the biggest and best are sold for enemas at drugstores) then brush it with the camel's hair brush. If you still need to wipe the lens, pull a tissue from the pad and wad or roll it up, place a drop or two of lens cleaner on the tissue (not on the lens) and wipe the lens *gently,* and only *once.* Throw this tissue out, roll up another one, and finish the job. By first blowing, then brushing, and then wiping once lightly, you'll see to it that any abrasive dirt will be eliminated *before* you wipe the lens with any serious pressure.

The best lens cleaner I've found is made by Tiffen. It seems to clean best, and leaves the least amount of residue. Lens tissue is sold in packs and is fairly cheap. It's the only thing (besides a clean camel's hair brush) that should touch the front or rear elements of the lens. It's a good idea to store the tissue and brush in a separate plastic bag to keep them from being contaminated by dirt or finger grease during the shoot.

If you run about a thousand feet of film through your camera, you may find that the soft emulsion has literally burnished itself onto the pressure plate, and that this white deposit is so hard that the only way to get it off is to scrape it. The correct way to do this is to use a small piece of wood, like a **match stick** or **orangewood stick**, or a special plastic tool like the ones Arri supplies with their new cameras. Orangewood sticks are, like camel hair brushes, available in drugstores. They're intended to be used to push back fingernail cuticles. *Never* use anything made of metal as you will invariably damage the polished surfaces of the pressure plate.

Sand is the most destructive thing to which you can expose lenses, cameras and tripods, with the possible exception of complete immersion in salt water. This is because sand is so abrasive, and it is much harder than the metals used in cameras. If you must shoot in a sandy environment, shield equipment from blowing sand with umbrellas, foam core or B-board *and* wrap everything up with clear plastic. At the end of each day, carefully clean the equipment with brush and air, and inspect for any damage. Tripod legs can usually be sprayed off with water in the shower, then dried with a towel. Lastly, consider using less expensive equipment for shooting in sandy situations.

Salt water is death to almost all cameras and lenses. You can try to retrieve the piece and soak it in fresh water immediately, but this will probably have no benefit. Tripods, being less complex and often protected internally by a light coating of grease, can sometimes be saved. Since salt water instantly corrodes metal, the best thing to do is to remain calm, wave goodbye to the piece, then hold a brief but meaningful funeral.

THAT FUNNY CLUNK

D.P. PONYTAIL
Did you hear that? What was that funny clunk at the end of that take? It sounded like something fell off inside the camera. Turn the camera on and see if it's okay.

A.C. LEATHERJACKET
Seems to be okay. Let me check the speed. Nope, no problem.

D.P. PONYTAIL
Hmm.

A fatherly ANNOUNCER type steps between the A.C. and D.P., addresses the camera.

ANNOUNCER
What you have just witnessed is a possible tragedy in the making. Every so often, a small nut, screw, or other part will come disloged inside a camera, creating a one time noise. It will then likely fall to the bottom of the mechanism and not pose any problem until the camera is inverted or placed on its side. Sooner or later it will short out circuits or jam the mechanism, causing extensive damage. Don't let this happen to you. When you hear that first CLUNK, stop, and have the camera checked out by qualified service personnel.

D.P. PONYTAIL
Golly, he's right!

A.C. LEATHERJACKET
Gosh, we'll have it checked out pronto!

ANNOUNCER
You'll be glad you did.

Other supplies:

Alcohol - isopropyl - used for general cleaning. Don't use this on lenses or mirrors (use lens fluid only). Good for cleaning guide rollers, removing emulsion dust from the gate and wiping anodized surfaces.

Lighter fluid, a.k.a. Naptha - very good for removing sticky, gummy residue. The small Ronson-brand cans are sold everywhere and are very convenient.

Trichloroethylene - an excellent cleaner, often used in tape head and film cleaning products, it dissolves grease and removes it instantly. Bad news: implicated as a carcinogen (I avoid this cleaner almost entirely).

Lacquer thinner - removes grease, dirt, and gummy residue left over from adhesive labels and tape. Also removes paint, dissolves many plastics and fiberglass. The vapors are unhealthy to breath. Use only as a last resort, and test the area to be cleaned with a small amount on a cotton swab beforehand.

Lubricants - unless you own the camera or are going on an extended shoot, don't lubricate it. Chances are, the problem you are trying to solve (squeaks, noise) won't be corrected by oil or grease - you'll probably only make a mess as oil and grease have a tendency to travel, and fly off moving parts to places it doesn't belong (mirrors, lenses, etc). If you own the camera, follow the instructions given out by the manufacturers in regard to type of lubrication, schedule and lube points. The rental establishment/ owner can tell you how to lube the camera (if at all) during extended shooting periods.

Cotton swabs - watch out! These shed tiny particles of lint which can end up lodged in the gate. Some camerapeople advise against their use altogether, but they *can* be used to great advantage in certain situations - for example, cleaning one small spot on a lens, rather than wiping down the entire element. They'll also go into tight spaces where a lens tissue will not, and are indispensable for cleaning old dirty grease and gum (when soaked in lacquer thinner) from parts. You can wrap them in a lens tissue to contain the lint, but I find that by carefully looking at the area after cleaning, I can spot any lint residue left behind.

Chamois - a soft cloth that many camerapeople use to polish the gate and pressure plate after general cleaning. Also used as a wrap for rubber eyecups (it's more comfortable against the skin and breathes) and for polishing expensive automobiles (available at auto supply stores).

Canned air - Very convenient, yet expensive, and if the can is not held upright, a sticky residue squirts out. Sold in simple spray cans (like paint) with extender tubes (like you get with a can of WD-40) and as part of a "system" that requires the use of special cans and screw on valves (Dust-off, etc.) The former is preferable to the latter as problems can occur when screwing down the special valves, sometimes resulting in a slow leak - your can of air will be empty in a few hours. Bad news: some canned air depletes the Earth's protective ozone layer. Try to get ozone safe, non-CFC canned air. It is estimated that just one molecule of CFC can destroy as many as 100,000 ozone molecules as the heat of the sun cycles the CFC molecule over and over again.

Blower bulb - these come in several sizes, and with or without brushes attached.

Vacuum - use to clean cases, bags, etc. Much better than canned air because you *remove* dirt rather than just blow it around. Most vacuums exhaust fine dust and dirt back into the air, so be careful - use in a well ventilated area.

Tools

A few tool truths:

You can never have enough tools.

```
                DOUG
       Hi, my name is Doug.

A group of mostly men, sitting in
metal folding chairs, responds.

                GROUP
       Hi Doug.

                DOUG
       I'm a toolaholic. Look,
see, I just got this fantastic
cheese adjustment wrench set,
made in Germany, highest quality
chrome vanadium, and -

                GROUP
       Oooh, Aah, let me see, etc.
```

I love tools. A fine tool is more than a piece of

pretty sculpture, like jewelry or fine art. It represents the power human's have over their environment, and therefore the course of their lives. Anthropologists consider tools one of the most important artifacts of human existence. Besides, they look cool, resting in neat, shiny rows in your toolchest.

A bad tool is worse than no tool at all.

Even if a bad tool doesn't damage something (they often do, being made of soft metal that will strip screw or bolt heads, for example) they can break, causing possible injury to the user, or at the very least they use up more time than is necessary when repairing or building something. By throwing a bad tool away (so that you have no tool at all), you force yourself to buy a good tool, but if you keep the bad tool, you may end up using it, which is bad. So, a bad tool is worse than no tool at all.

The most expensive tool is the least expensive tool.

It's true that you don't need a backhoe to dig a flower bed (unless you have a really big flower bed). However, in most situations, the most expensive tool is, in the long run, the cheapest. A good, long lasting tool doesn't mess up your work and lasts longer (some for a lifetime). The only time I would go for a less expensive tool (but not a bad tool) is if I was storing it in a place that was a high theft or loss risk (like in the back of my truck).

With these tool truths in mind, here's a list of items you might want to have on a film shoot:

Swiss army knife - get Wenger or Victorinox, and go for one with a scissors, and tweezers, or you could get a

Leatherman, which is a beautifully made folding plier/multitool. But then again, why not have both? Remember the first tool truth! There are other versions of the Leatherman made by copycats, but I haven't tested any.

Hex wrenches - both metric and standard, from the very smallest you can find to about 3/8" and 9mm.

Jeweler's screwdrivers - jewelers actually don't use hardware store type jeweler's screwdrivers, but that's okay, because you don't really want a set of these really, really tiny slot type screwdrivers (or do you?). The quality of hardware store type jeweler's screwdrivers vary greatly; try to stick with Stanley or other brand name if you can.

Standard screwdrivers and wrenches - get them at Sears, but make sure they say Craftsman, not Sears, or you won't have a lifetime guarantee, which is the main reason to buy at Sears anyway. When you break a Craftstman tool, you just bring it in for an exchange, and while you're waiting in line, you might as well buy that power saw you've been wanting, and a box of garbage bags, and a jig saw blade, and here's one of them new . . .

Locking pliers - most famous are Vice-Grip brand, which is the original and highest quality, though copies can be just as good (or pretty bad). You should not be without at least one of these incredibly useful tools.

Soldering iron - the inexpensive Radio Shack type will do for occasional use; keep the tip clean when hot by rubbing it on a wet sponge or cloth. Also, use nothing but rosin-core solder on electronic repairs.

Flashlight - everyone seems to like the high quality Mini Mag brand AA units, but I think the cheaper pen-style are better because you can turn them on and off with one hand, rather than two hands or one and your mouth. A must for shining light off the film when checking for scratches.

Tape measure - a 50' tape for measuring

focus distance; get a fiberglass model. They are quieter and faster than steel and they don't have sharp edges. Also, a 16' x 3/4" wide Stanley Powerlock retractable is handy in funky focus situations (table top, etc.).

Volt-Ohm Meter - invaluable for testing cables, fuses, outlets, etc.

16mm Cameras

MOS or Sound?

MOS stands for either "mit out sprechen", "mit out sound" or anything else you may have heard about that means shooting film but *not* recording sound during a take. A MOS camera is, in the simplest sense, a camera that cannot be used for shooting synchronous sound because it makes too much noise.

This is not to say, however, that a given MOS camera is always an inferior or cheaper camera than a sound camera. MOS cameras should be thought of as special purpose machines. Often, they'll do things that sound cameras don't do, like run at high fps rates, or in reverse, or shoot single frames.

Engineering a camera to be quiet enough to shoot sound usually means that the claw and registration pin engage the film very gently, and in such a way that the camera has a very narrow fps range (say from 12 to 36) and cannot run in reverse. It may also mean that the camera is big and bulky compared to a comparable MOS camera because of sound deadening materials used in its construction.

MOS Cameras

Arriflex 16S and 16SB

reflex viewing
rotating mirror shutter - 180 degrees fixed
length of exposure: 1/48th sec. @ 24 fps
flange/focal distance: 51.975mm (52mm nominal)
fps range: 6 - 50, forward and reverse
accurate footage and frame counter
pin registration
power: 8.4 volts DC
lens mount: 3 port turret accepts Arri standard mounted lenses. 16SB model accepts 2 Arri standard and one Arri Bayonet mounted lens.
matte box: 2 stages, one rotatable, accepts 2" x 2" filters only
loading options: 100' internal daylight load or 400' with accessory magazine and torque motor.

The Arri 16St and 16St-B are the motion picture industry standard 16mm MOS cameras. The design has earned this distinction because of its ruggedness, high quality, compatibility and functional features.

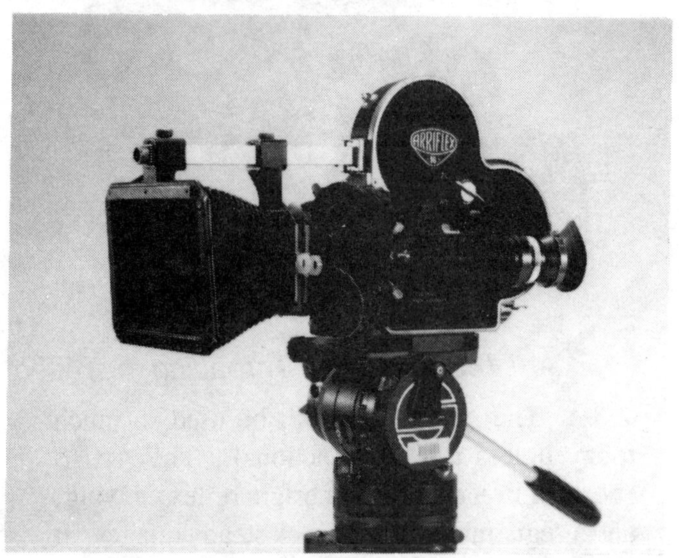

Arri 16S, Prime Lenses, 2x2 Matte Box

The Arri S, as its commonly called, is built like a tank. It would be hard to think of anything else that is so over built. The body and door are heavily cast in aluminum, rather than stamped, and all the moving parts are beautifully constructed. Repairing the Arri S is a breeze (compared to say, an Eclair NPR) because all the parts are identically machined from one to the next.

Even though the Arri S was designed over 30 years ago, it is still much in use today in 16mm work because of its compatibility with even the newest equipment. The 16SB has an Arri Bayonet lens mount on its turret, and this means the expensive, super sharp and fast new zoom lenses will fit on the camera. On commercial shoots, the camera package will often consist of an Arri SR or Aaton for sync shooting, and an Arri S for MOS, specialty or second unit shoots. All these cameras can work from the same lens package. Need to bolt a rig to the side of a motorcycle or a lightweight, handholdable machine for shooting a fight scene? The Arri S is the camera.

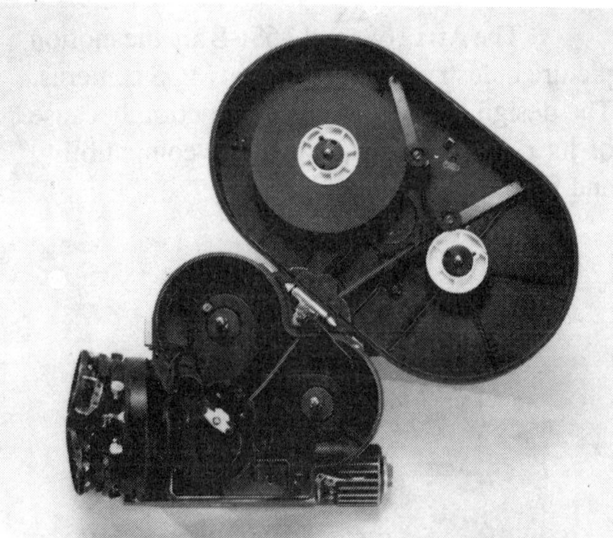

Arri 16S and 16SB Threading

The Arri S wouldn't be used so much today unless it were functional. The Arri S sports a mirror shutter for bright reflex viewing, and a registration pin for rock steady images. It will accept a 400' magazine and a variable speed motor. Without the magazine mounted, and with a prime lens, the camera is very compact; its built in hand grip makes it excellent to hand hold.

It is also very useful for shooting matte effects, and to a certain extent, titling. This is because the camera has an accurate footage *and* frame counter, and because the variable speed motor allows for running the camera in reverse to backwind the film for double exposures.

It has a few drawbacks: the fps range is only from about 6 to 50 frames. If the camera ran up to 80 or 90 fps it would be far more useful for shooting slow motion effects (a conversion done by the factory or an authorized technical facility involves the installation of a different tachometer and enables the camera to run up to 80 fps, but this is an expensive undertaking, and cameras which have already been converted are rare) . Secondly, it is very difficult to find a single frame animation motor for the camera.

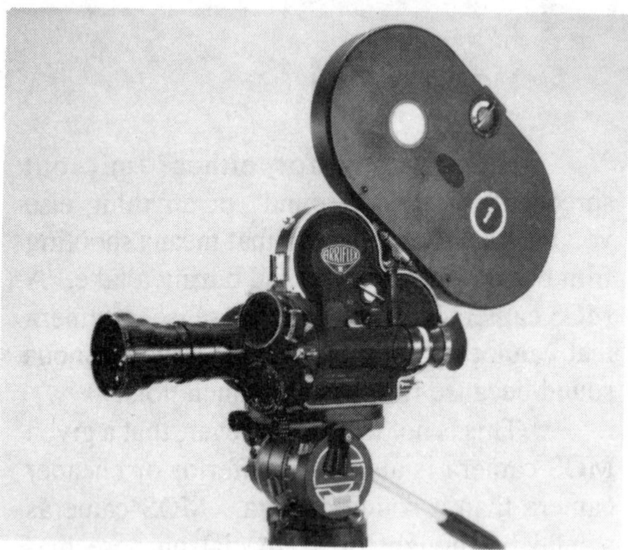

Arri 16SB, Angenieux 12-120, 400' Mag

Lastly, it is a very expensive machine as MOS cameras go. A good used camera with 3 prime lenses, matte box, battery belt and cable usually sells for about three thousand dollars. The 16SB usually goes for $500 to $1,000 more because its bayonet lens mount makes it able to accept all the newest, best lenses.

Arri 16M

reflex viewing

rotating mirror shutter - 180 degrees fixed

length of exposure: 1/48th sec. @ 24 fps

flange/focal distance: 51.975mm (52mm nominal)

fps range: 6 - 50, forward and reverse

accurate footage and frame counter

pin registration

power: 8.4 volts DC

lens mount: 3 port turret accepts Arri standard mounted lenses. 16M-B model accepts 2 Arri standard and one Arri Bayonet mounted lens.

matte box: 2 stages, one rotatable, ac-

cepts 2" x 2" filters only
<u>loading options</u>: 400', 200' and 1200' external magazines only

The 16M is an odd, rare bird. A cross between the Arri 16BL and the 16S, it's chief design difference from the 16S is that it will accept magazines which are very much like those on the 16BL - that is, ones which have the sprocketed rollers usually found inside the camera body built *into the mag itself.* This makes the mag more difficult to load, but you can change the mag on the camera faster because there is far less to thread up - only the gate. The main drawback to this is that the 16M sacrificed its internal load capability. You can't put a daylight spool in the camera body of a 16M. You have to load the camera mags. You can't easily hand hold a loaded 16M because the mags weigh so much.

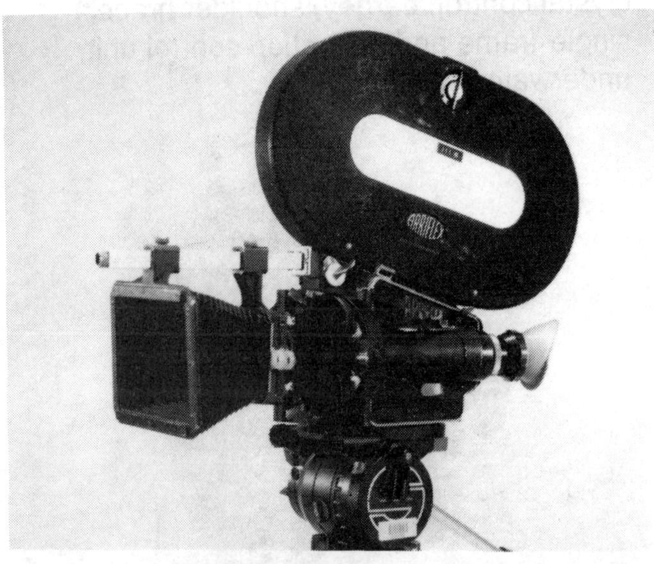

Arri 16M

Where this machine shines, however, is shooting on a tripod in situations where quick loading is a necessity, such as sporting events. A good amount of the footage shot at football, basketball and baseball events in the Sixties and early Seventies was shot on the 16M. A television broadcast of the 1988 Super Bowl revealed a glimpse of a 16M, held high overhead in one hand by the camera man, getting a shot of the winning coach as he left the field. The camera also has an excellent, hinged door (considerably nicer than the S door, which completely removes - where do you stow it during reloading?). If you come across a 16M and want to do some hand held work with it, don't despair: there are smaller, lighter 200' magazines which make the job quite easy.

Because the 16S has both internal and external load capabilities, it has won out over the 16M. Even longtime camera technicians have seen very few. Those that are around, however, are usually in excellent shape, as they've seen little use.

Beaulieu R16

<u>reflex viewing</u>
<u>Guillotine shutter</u> - 1/60th sec @ 24 fps
<u>electric drive, forward and reverse</u>
<u>flange/focal distance</u>: 17.5mm
<u>fps range</u>: 2 - 64.
<u>small/lightweight for hand holding</u>
<u>power</u>: 7.2 volts
<u>lens mount</u>: 3 port turret accepts C mount lenses
<u>matte box: none</u>
<u>loading options</u>: 100' internal daylight load; 200' external magazine

The Beaulieu R16 is an extremely lightweight camera that, due to it's pistol grip (with built in battery), is also very good to hand-hold. It's three port, C mount turret allows the user to interchange lenses, and since the viewing system is a mirror shutter type rather than pellicle or beam splitter, there are no worries about compensating for flange/focal distance (unlike with Bolex reflex cameras). It has a very wide fps range, from 2 to 64. It can run in reverse (but only with internal 100' loads) and this is especially useful because the camera has a both footage and frame counters. Many R16s were built to be used with a special Angenieux 12-120 zoom with provisions for attaching a power zoom and an auto iris. These electric devices are mounted in the "standby" C-mount ports when the zoom is screwed into the taking lens port. This system allowed the Beaulieu to be an excellent one-man machine capable of producing very smooth zooms. There is also a single frame control which allows for animation/special effect shooting.

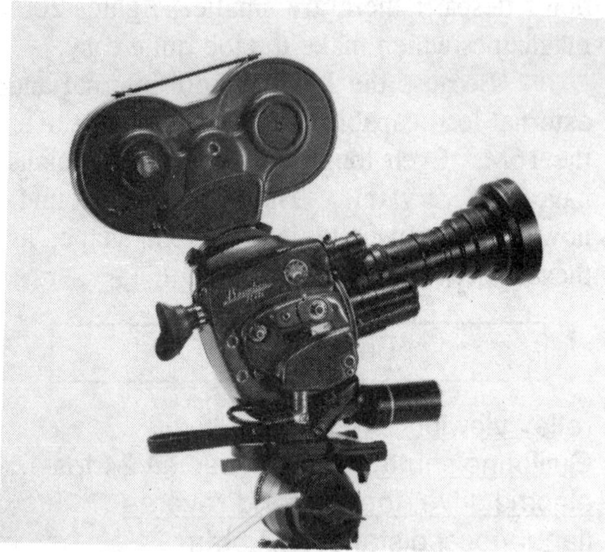

Beaulieu R16

On the downside, it should be noted that the camera is very lightly built, and needs to be carefully handled or problems will result. The C - mount turret is extremely susceptible to damage when long, heavy zoom lenses (like the Angenieux mentioned above) are mounted.

For years, Beaulieus were out of production - the company was out of the business of making 16mm cameras, and more importantly, spare parts. But recently, Beaulieu has come back, building an updated version of the R16 with nifty liquid crystal speed and footage readouts. This new machine is called the 2016, and it retails for close to $5,000. Owners of the older R16 now hope they will be able to find the parts and service they need.

Bolex Rex 4, Rex 5, EBM, SBM and EL

non-reflex viewing (earlier models)
prism beam splitter reflex (Rx models); light loss, 35%.
non-pin registration
rotating shutter - 133 degrees, variable (EBM and EL: 170 degrees)
Length of exposure: 1/80th sec @ 24 fps (EBM and EL: 1/67th)
spring drive: length of run 28 seconds at 24 fps; later EBM and EL have internal electric drive motors
fps: 12 - 64+ fps.
power: 12 volts for accessory motors and later cameras
lens mount: 3 port turret accepts C mount lenses; later models have single Bolex bayonet; adapter available for C - mount primes
flange/focal distance: C-mount 17.52mm; Bolex bayonet 26.46mm(optical 23.23)
matte box: holds gels only
loading options: 100' internal daylight load; 400' external magazine RX-5, SBM, EBM, EL.
Accessories: handgrips, electric motors, RX fader (springwound models only), crystal control, barney, shoulder brace, single frame and animation control unit, underwater housings.

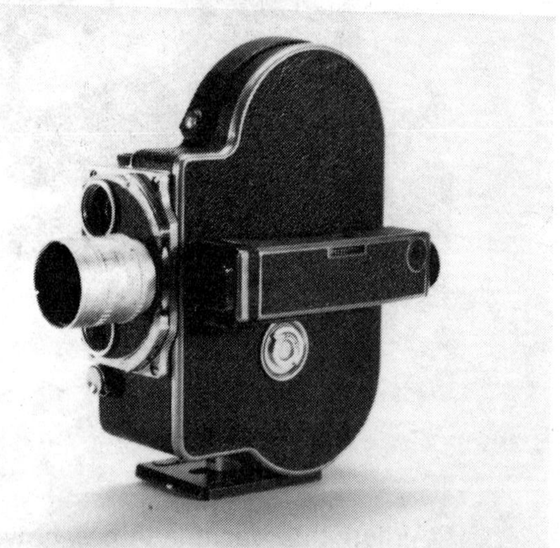

Bolex Non-Reflex

There are so many different Bolex models, with names like Rex 4, EBM, and SBM, made over so many years, that it is difficult to talk about them as a group. Fortunately, they are all based on essentially the same design (save the 16EL) and have many common features. The best way to talk about Bolexes is through time, following changes in design and accessories as the different camera(s) developed.

Long ago, Bolexes were non-reflex, spring wound, auto thread machines. Like other cameras of the day, they had small, three port, C-mount lens turrets, were compact and light, and were intended to be used by home enthusiasts. Despite this, these early machines contain a surprising number of sophisticated features. The Bolex company apparently thought that if the camera had accurate footage and frame counters, could be backwound, had a wide fps range, and could be run "single frame" (the film exposed one frame at a time), amateurs would grow into the machine instead of grow out of it. This strategy worked; Bolexes are probably the most popular 16mm cameras of all time.

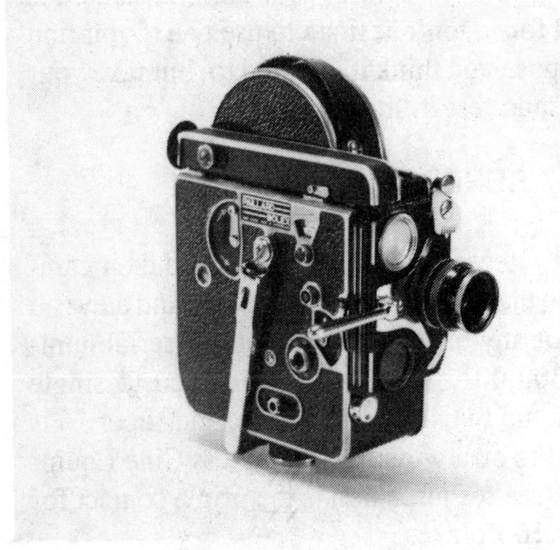

Bolex Reflex

The next stage in Bolex development seems to have been reflex viewing, and it was accomplished simply, with a beam splitting prism design. Cameras in this category have the letters RX in their description (RX-3, RX-4, etc.). The viewing system is so compact that it is actually difficult to tell reflex from non-reflex cameras at first glance (the front plate which holds the turret is thicker on reflex models). A small, battery driven electric motor was also introduced to eliminate the need for bothersome spring winding between shots, making longer takes and matte shots possible. Later motor models were introduced that put out a Pilotone signal that could be recorded on a Nagra for sync purposes.

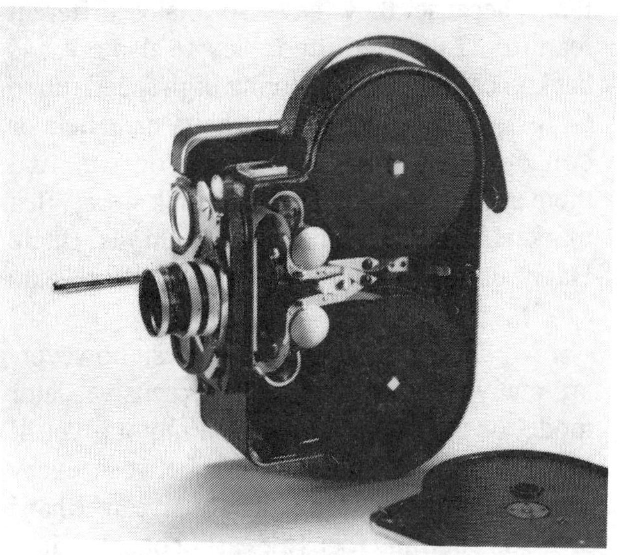

Bolex Threading

With the introduction of the RX-5, Bolex added a magazine port at the top of the camera and introduced a lightweight, 400' mag that had a small electric drive motor. The later H16 SBM added a well designed, strong bayonet lens mount that is nicely suited to supporting long, heavy zoom lenses. The H16EBM Electric incorporated a permanent internal electric motor (no bulky accessory motor hanging off the side) and a nifty handgrip/battery holder combination which made the camera much easier to hand hold and operate.

Finally, Bolex introduced the H16 EL, an extensively redesigned machine with a crystal controlled, internal motor and a built in light meter. With the H16 EL, Bolex tried to attract some of the sync shooting market share occupied by less expensive 16mm cameras: Frezzolini, Cinema Products.

What are Bolexes good for? Animators love them because they have single frame capability, and because many of them also have variable shutters that can be used for in-camera dissolves. They have behind the lens filter gels, great for long lenses and effects. They have auto thread systems that make it fast and easy to load 100' daylight spools in the body of the camera. You'll likely find one or more Bolexes at virtually every film school in the U.S.; they're reliable, and so much can be done with them because they have so many different features. Like the Filmo, they're also great as backup cameras, for shooting high speed (up to 64 fps), and for getting those hairy hand held or bolted-to-the-car-hood shots. You can find them everywhere: pawn shops, junk stores, flea markets, and your aunt's closet ("Oh yes, Uncle Harry used to be into that sort of thing years ago").

The drawbacks to Bolexes, however, are many. Unless you get an expensive, later model or use one of the add on motors, you'll have to wind the damn thing between every shot. Some models are reflex, but it can be hard to see through and focus the earlier ones because the magnification of the eyepiece is small. The beam splitter reflex system alters the optical flange/focal distance so that only special lenses marked "RX" may be used on these cameras if the focal length in question is less than 25mm. Shooting sync in exterior or noisy locations may work with the later machines or with the accessory, pilot signal producing motors, but if you are trying to make a narrative film with many quiet, interior scenes, forget it. None of these cameras is quiet enough; get a hold of a camera primarily designed for sync work. Lastly, Bolexes aren't as rugged as Filmos or Arri 16Ss; they need careful and consistently knowledgeable handling and care to live a long life.

If someone loans, rents, or offers to sell you one, take some time to go through the camera, just as you would any unfamiliar machine (see the Test chapter). You should try to find out just exactly which model it is. Almost all Bolexes have either reflex viewing systems or a critical focusing finder at the top of the camera. In the case of the latter, you must twist the turret so that lens you want to focus is in the uppermost position, view through the finder, and focus the lens, remembering (hopefully) to twist the turret back so that the lens you want is back in the middle or taking position before shooting. The only real problem with this set up is that many people mistake this focusing-only viewer for the reflex finder on later models; they're in the same exact place and look almost identical. Some cameras - the oldest - won't accept accessory electric motors. Is there an owner's manual with the camera? These can be invaluable when you are attempting to decipher the functions of all those little knobs and buttons on Bolexes.

In the end, the Bolex has a lot going for it; its low cost means it is within the grasp of many filmmakers - it's great to actually own a 16mm camera rather than have to pay a lot of money to rent an expensive, unfamiliar one. Most of the people who own one think it's great. They like the features, low cost and versatility of the machine, and since they are usually the sole users, they can see to it that the camera is cared for. Don't hesitate to use one if you find a purpose you think it is suited to, but take your time, and test it thoroughly.

SUPER 16 WITH BOLEX

Recently, Bolex has changed their cameras so that they can shoot super 16, and they can retrofit any bayonet models above serial number 300,001. Combining low cost, single frame, up to 64 fps, small size, and super 16 is bound to be a winner. Chambless Cine Equipment (see resource list) is the prime contact for super 16 Bolexes.

Filmo (Bell and Howell 70DR and 70HR)

non-reflex viewing
rotating shutter - 204 degrees fixed
length of exposure: 1/42.4 fps @ 24 fps
spring drive: length of run 36 sec.@ 24fps
flange/focal distance: 17.5mm
fps: 8, 12, 16, 24, 32, 48, 64.
small/lightweight for hand holding
power: 24 volts DC motor for 70HR only
lens mount: 3 port turret accepts C mount lenses

matte box: none
loading options: 100' internal daylight load; 400' external magazine, 70HR only.

These two cameras are both small, springwound, non-reflex, extremely robust machines; the 70HR differs from the 70DR in its ability to accept external 400' magazines and an electric motor. Other than this, both cameras are identical and can be referred to as one machine - the Filmo.

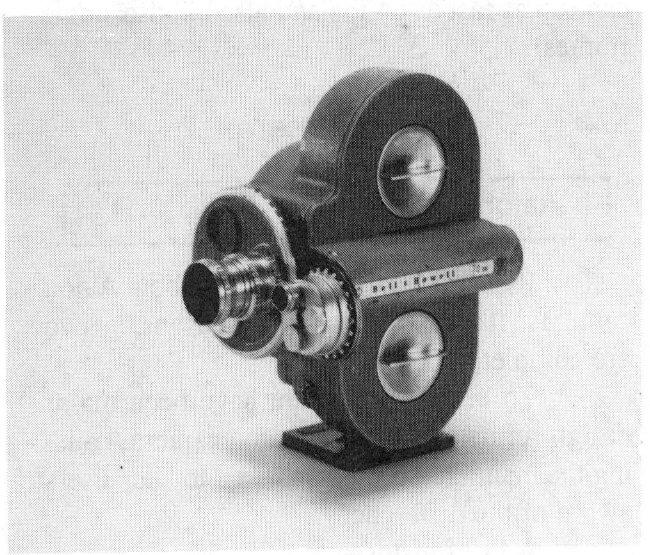

Bell and Howell 70DR

Filmos have 3 lens, C - mount turrets that interlock with a rotating, 3 mount viewfinder. When the lens mount turret is rotated, the viewfinder turret rotates as well, selecting a tiny objective that matches the focal length of the taking lens. At the rear of the finder is a cam operated adjustment for parallax correction. When wound with its external winding key or ratchet crank, the massive spring inside the camera will run 22 feet of film at 24 fps, or more than 36 seconds of film. You can back wind this camera for double exposures by using an external crank. Although you can't look through the taking lens *during a shot* (this is a non-reflex camera), you can twist the desired lens to a new position on the turret where a small critical focuser enables you to view through the lens (with magnification) and focus it. Filtering is accomplished by screwing small filters to the front of each lens, or by using the behind the lens gel filter holder (for lenses longer than 25mm).

When compared to modern, state of the art 16mm cameras, the Filmo is clumsy and unsophisticated. For most shooting situations, the spring drive quickly becomes a real pain: you have to make sure you've completely wound the spring to its maximum between shots, a tiresome affair that will also disturb any carefully aimed tripod setting (forget matte shots). The view through the side finder is small and you will always be wondering if you're getting on film what you're seeing through the tiny objectives. None of the accessories available for other cameras - matte boxes, follow focuses, rotatable or orientable finders - is available for this machine.

But Filmos shouldn't really be compared to modern cameras. Their charm lies in their simplicity and straightforwardness, and they prove themselves by being fine to handhold, nearly indestructible, and by not needing any batteries or power cables (no problems in cold weather). They can also cost very little to own; so many were manufactured that you might pick a good one up in a pawn shop or junk store for as little as $250 - maybe less. C - mount lenses are also plentiful, and you can find real bargains when outfitting your camera with a complement of them, although you may have trouble finding the accompanying viewfinder objectives. Many camerapeople own them as second or third cameras and use them where it would be too hazardous to operate their first cameras: on a boat, on a sandy, windy beach, strapped to a motorcycle, etc. They're great for shooting at 64 fps for slow motion effects. Although some cameras like the ACL and 16SR will shoot this fast, camerapeople are loathe to use them for this purpose because the speed accelerates camera wear and makes cameras noisy. You can use external magazines and an electric drive (if you can find them) on a 70HR, but these accessories actually defeat the goal of the design: supply the cameraman with a small, quick, reliable camera. Finally, this machine always works - it's great to have on a shoot as backup insurance if the main camera breaks down.

Canon Scoopic 16 and Scoopic 16M

prism-reflex viewing
shutter: 135 degrees fixed, model 16; 170 fixed 16M.
length of exposure, 24 fps: 1/100th sec. 16; 1/50 sec. 16M.
auto threading capability;
fps: 16,24,32 and 40 fps
small/lightweight for hand holding
power: 12 volts, small on-board batteries
non-interchangeable lens: model 16 supplied with Canon 13-76mm F 1.6 zoom; 16M with 12.5-75 F 1.8 macro
loading options: 100' internal daylight load; 16M also accepts 400' external Mitchell/CP magazine
built in exposure meter: parallax (non-TTL);

The Canon Scoopic is a 16mm camera with the heart and soul of a super 8. Once you use this machine, you'll see that this statement is actually a compliment. It self threads 100' daylight spools fast, hand holds beautifully, is very lightweight, and uses small on-board batteries that make it self contained (no bulky battery belts or bothersome cables) and quick to operate. The viewfinder is particularly bright (although the earlier model 16 has a confusing prism focusing screen) and the built in lightmeter, though not a through the lens type (TTL), is nevertheless very useful in simple shooting situations. Even though you can't change the zoom for another lens, the range of the zoom is very good, and it is quite sharp and contrasty. Although the overall construction is quite light, the machine has been designed to function so well that they actually are quite reliable. There's no need to force or wrestle with anything because the camera works simply and easily.

What this camera seems to have been designed for is the local TV news reporter on assignment who wants some footage of his/her story, but doesn't want to drag a film crew along (or doesn't have the money to do so). You won't find a frame counter, variable shutter or reverse switch on this machine; it's meant for fast and simple MOS newsgathering, and in this area, it excels. You can almost think of it as an updated version of the ancient Filmo; both were essentially designed for the same type of shooting. It's an excellent second camera to have on a production (especially the 16M model which can run as fast as 64 fps and also expose single frames).

Sync Cameras

Aaton 7, LTR, and LTR 54, XTR

It's hard to talk definitively about Aaton cameras. It seems that for many reasons, no two are completely alike.

To begin with, there have been major design refinements in the Aaton camera, causing the manufacturer to rename it to keep users aware of the differences.

A brief history:

Initially, the Aaton LTR 7 was manufactured. It ran film 24 and 25 fps crystal, and had several variable speeds ranging from 6 to 32.

Aaton began changing things almost immediately: they decided to make the doors on the magazines permanently attached by hinges rather than removable, and they made a lighter claw which enabled them to get the camera up to 54 fps. It was discovered that a particular gear that drives the mirror caused friction and heat buildup. This was remedied by installing a different set of gears that reversed the rotation of the mirror. This newer machine was dubbed the LTR 54.

Further claw designs were tried, and finally Aaton settled on a cast aluminum, steel tipped design. Concurrent with these changes were modifications which allowed the conversion of the camera from 16 to Super 16 to be carried out much faster by the technician (on later LTR 54s this can be done in as little as one half hour).

Finally, the latest design, called the XTR, has a mag drive system which uses a special magnet between camera and magazine - no metal to metal contact.

On top of these variables are individual options/functions which may or may not be installed in cameras: time code and 29.97 or 30 fps crystal locked speeds (there are probably quite a few more than this).

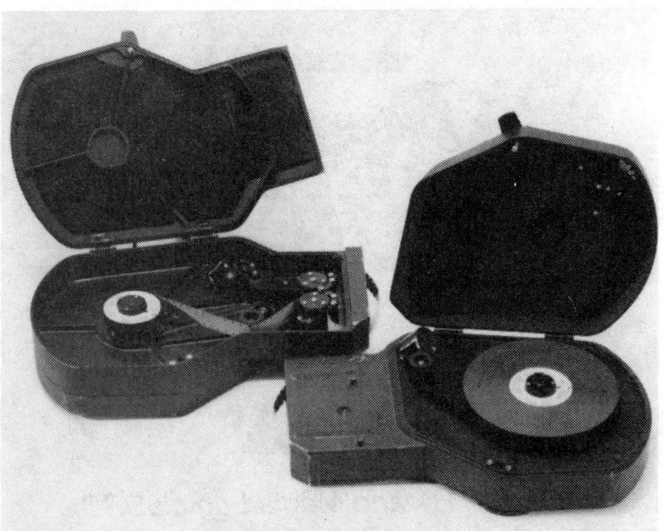

Aaton Threading

Somewhere in the middle of all this, Arriflex decided to sue Aaton for patent infringement over its orientable finder. Orientable finders - ones that keep the image upright when the eyepiece is rotated by the camera operator - have been in use for many years: Cinema Products and Angenieux have made them, as well as Arri and Aaton. But the Arri 16SR finder is unique: it can flip over to either side of the camera, making the camera a truly symmetrical machine. Very handy for shooting from the passenger side of English automobiles, and when there just isn't time or money to move a wall or other obstruction on the set (or if you just happen to favor your left eye.) Unique, that is, until Aaton incorporated it into the design of their 16mm cameras.

The results of the lawsuit in the United States eventually led to the dissolution of the factory authorized dealer for the region, Zellan Enterprises, and the discontinuation of the flip over finder on later models.

In the end, the innovation inherent in the Aaton story has been both a major selling point and a major setback. Whereas the Arri 16SR (the Aaton's only competition) has changed very little, the Aaton has undergone a constant change that has done two things: pleased owner/camerapeople, who want the latest, hottest machine for their money, and confused and confounded rental establishments who want simplicity and uniformity. What this means to

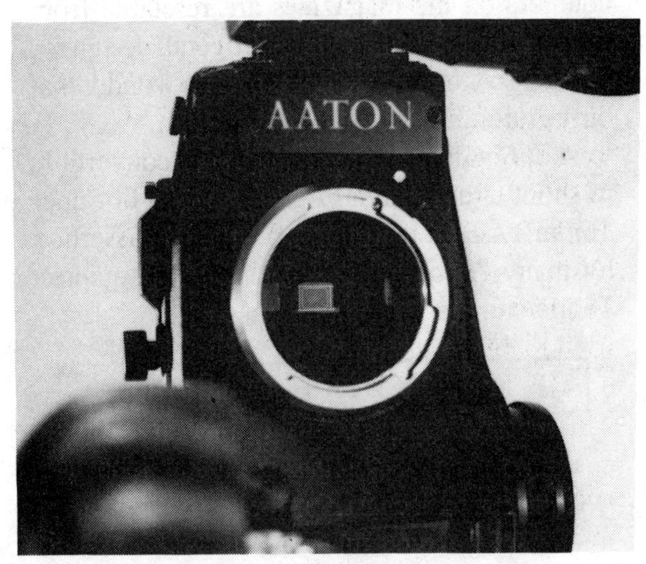

Aaton Lens Mount

you as the end user is that the Aaton you get (as either a rental, or a borrow, or perhaps a purchase, new or used) will probably be unique in many important ways. You must take time to find out just exactly which Aaton you are getting, and the best way to do this is to ask whomever is giving it to you. Which model is it? What speeds will it run? What is the shutter angle (could be a 172.8, 175 or a 180)? What are its power requirements? What kind of battery charger comes with it, and how is it used?

Overall, however, there are many things that can be said about all Aatons: they all have excellent ergonomics, which is to say that they're built to be used by people. They balance exquisitely on your shoulder, and like the Arri 16SR, Eclair NPR, and ACL, the mags are the quick change, coaxial type - but unlike those of these other cameras, the mags are considered by many to be the very easiest to load in the entire industry, 16 or 35mm. The viewfinder is extremely bright and sharp, and the video tap system has been designed-in rather than added-on, making mounting and dismounting quick and easy (and the tap itself amazingly compact). The flange/focal distance is very short, enabling the camera to accept many Nikon still lenses with the proper adapter (these are optically superb and very cheap!). The footage counters on the magazines are resetable from the outside of the mag, and the overall design for them is so simple and reliable it's a wonder that only Aaton has it.

Finally, the cameras are all convertible to shoot either standard gauge 16mm or Super 16mm. Added to the above list is the assertion by many Aaton users that this is the quietest 16mm camera ever.

AATON XTR+, and Xprod

The above cameras represent the latest evolution of the Aaton line.

The XTR+ can be configured with either Aaton, PL or Panavision mounts, though the Panavision is a proprietary unit only available through Panavision themselves. It also uses Aaton code. It has a CCD chip for video tap function that is is so small and light that it lives in the camera at all times. The camera also has a full 180 degree shutter.

Perhaps one of the nicest features of the XTR+ is the LCD data window mounted on the operator's side of the camera. It keeps track of footage in several mags (each is keyed with a magnet so the camera knows which one is being used), displays voltage, camera speed, and time code, and sets/displays ASA for the internal lightmeter,

The Xprod has an even more sophisticated LCD/control panel. It has all the functions of the display on the XTR+ but adds a built in crystal speed control that is changeable and accurate to .001 fps and will phase to monitors, projections, etc. (like the external Media Logic 5 Digit Speed Control or the Cinematography Electronics Precision Speed Control). The speed setting is changed by turning a jog wheel mounted on the camera, much like in video editing systems. The readout window can also be set to display either a subtractive or elapsed footage count.

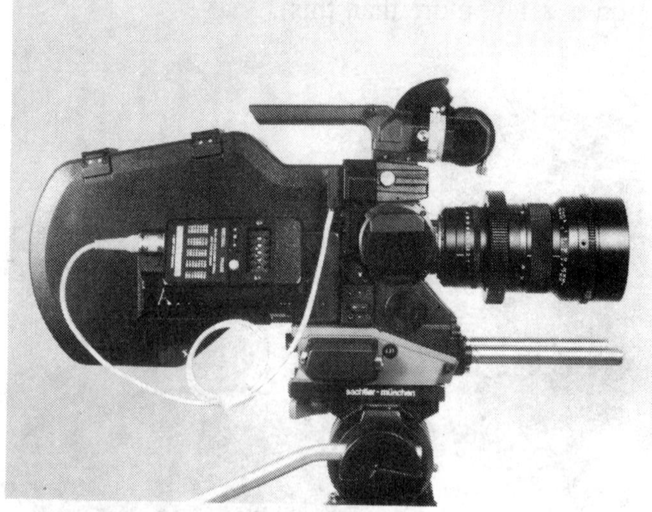

Aaton XTR+ and Media Logic 5DSC

The Xprod will also have (in September 1993) a three position mirror shutter in the future: 180, 172.8, and 144 degrees. The Aatonite-illuminated viewing system is new also; like Panaglow, it lights up the frame lines in the viewfinder so the operator can see them in low light situations.

Perhaps one of the best things about the latest Aatons are their ability to accept Nikon and Leica still lenses with special adapters. These lenses are excellent and inexpensive compared to prime lenses manufactured for movie cameras.

Aaton has also introduced lateral matte box rods. These are mounted on the side of the camera, rather than underneath it, so they don't dig into the operator's shoulder when s/he is hand holding.

Arriflex 16BL

reflex viewing
rotating mirror shutter - 180 degrees fixed
length of exposure: 1/48th sec. @ 24 fps.
flange/focal distance:51.975mm (52mm nominal)
fps range: 12 - 50, fwd and rev footage counters only - on magazine 0-500' subtractive, and on rear of camera, 0-9,999' additive
pin registration
power: 12 volts DC
lens mount: single Arri Bayonet mount, surrounded by special 16BL lens housing
blimp mount matte box: single stage, holds two standard filters or one Arri 16BL blimp glass, rotatable in 90 degree increments only; matte box is integral to special 16BL lens housing blimp; filter size for Angenieux 12-120, Zeiss 10-100 T3 and Schneider 10 -100 is 3"x3", Angenieux 9.5-95 requires 4"x4"
loading options: 400'and 200' external magazines only
accessories: crystal/variable speed units, offset finder, periscope finder, body braces, prime lens housings.

The Arriflex 16BL is, among other things, an incredible display of engineering tenacity.

When the Arriflex Corporation decided to create a quiet sync camera for 16mm use, it might have made the film movement inherently quiet. This was the path taken by other manufacturers of the same time period (late Fifties-early Sixties), most notably the French company Eclair, and the American company Bach Auricon. From a design standpoint, it makes sense. Building even a slightly noisy movement means that the overall design must include some sort of sound isolation material, and often this makes a camera bulky. But Arriflex used essentially the same movement it put into its 16S camera - one that sounds something like a Waring blender on low. To make the overall machine quiet, Arri suspended this movement on rubber isolators within an outer shell.

Unfortunately, any lens used with this camera must also be in direct contact with the noisy movement. It is critical to the proper functioning of the camera that this distance be held within very narrow tolerances. Isolating the lens from a noisy movement using rubber would be a disaster, as this flexible material could never be counted on to hold the lens at the correct flange focal distance. Since the lens must be in metallic contact with the movement - yep, you guessed it, the *lens makes noise,* and must be suspended by similar rubber isolators within its own shell.

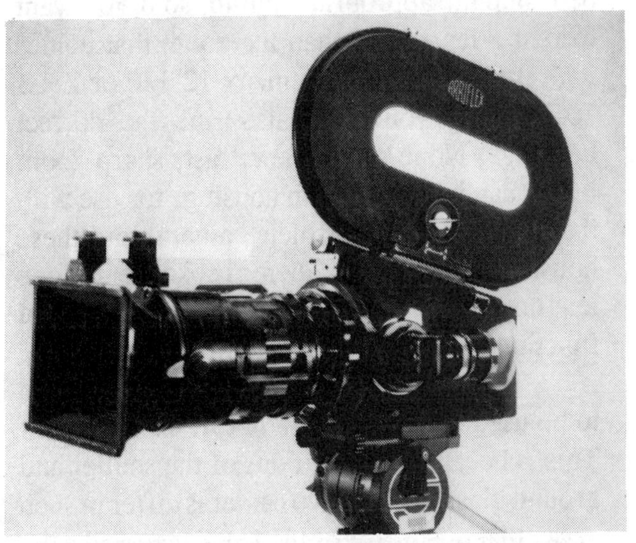

Arri 16BL

All of this makes for a very strange, and bulky camera. The lens is buried within a large blimp housing, and zoom, iris, and focus controls are large rings with winged activators attached. Although the data marks for these controls have been transferred to the outside of the housing, there are little glass windows built in case you don't trust them and you want to see the lens directly (they're always correct). The camera has one Arri Bayonet mount, but surrounding it is the large flange that engages the lens blimp housing. The matte box sits on the front of this housing and must contain a thick piece of optical sound glass to stop any noise produced by the lens from getting into the scene.

It is the kind of machine that seems preposterously unfunctional when you first handle it - but the more you shoot with it, the more you find that it *does* function. It is a tribute to the design and manufacturing abilities of Arri that they could actually make this camera work. Only a company with such high standards and abilities would even conceive of such a product, especially when the goal is to build a light-weight, hand-holdable camera for sync shooting. Many camera people consider it the best machine of its day.

More details: shooting interior sync with this machine means that any lens used must be inside the appropriate blimp, so if you want to rent a lens other than the zoom that comes with it (usually an Angenieux 12-120 or Zeiss 10-100 T3) you must also find the correct housing. None of the new, fast, sharp zoom lenses can be rented with housings for use with the 16BL; it is an obsolete camera, and these housings do not exist. There are excellent prime lens housings, however, and most primes fit and function well within them - but they are scarce.

Some wide angle prime lenses designed to be used on the 16S will not fit on the 16BL. This is because the positions of the shutter and ground glass in these two cameras differ in such a way that the mirror of the 16BL may strike the rear element of some wide angle (25mm and shorter) primes while easily clearing that in the 16S. To find out if a particular prime will work, do this: inch the 16BL so that the shutter is covering the gate (move it into viewing position). Adjust the focus ring on the lens so that it is on infinity - this way the rear element will protrude its farthest into the camera. **Very carefully**, and **slowly**, slide the prime in question into the mount. If you are holding the lens release down fully (a small rectangular button near the viewfinder) and the lens will not completely seat, you know that this is the wrong prime for the 16BL and it can't be used.

The magazines are of the single compartment type, and are difficult to load because they contain sprocketed drive wheels. Once the mags are loaded, however, the camera can be threaded quickly because there are no sprockets or rollers inside the camera body itself. Only the gate needs to be threaded. The correct loop for the 16BL is set when loading the magazines - 40 or 41 frames. These are the kind of magazines that require a good deal of loading practice time in the changing bag before the actual shoot.

There are three different motors available; two run 24 fps forward only (unless controlled by an external unit) and one runs 24 fps forward and reverse. Sync shooting is accomplished two ways: with one end of a **sync cable** attached to the Tuchel connector at the rear of the camera and the other to the tape recorder used, or with an **external crystal/variable unit** which feeds power to the camera from the battery belt.

The 16BL seems to be a very un-hand-holdable camera when first encountered, but with the addition of a few accessories, it isn't so bad. These are 1) a body brace, which places the weight of the camera on your shoulder and stomach, and 2) an offset finder, which is an optical elbow of sorts that moves the position of the eyepiece nearer to the front of the camera. This means that the camera will sit farther back on your shoulder when you hand-hold it, and you can use your hands to stabilize the shot rather than heft the camera. Still, if you have to shoot hand held all day long and for several days, you'd be better off using something else - an NPR, or maybe a CP (better yet - an Aaton or a 16SR if you can afford it).

As of the previous publication of this book, 1989, the following was true:

There are three different crystal/variable control units made for the 16BL: Cinema Products, Jensen and Audio Engineering. Like any other accessory for this camera, these after-market devices are no longer manufactured. Arri, it seems, never made one for the camera themselves, and when I commissioned someone to build an updated unit, I found out why. Apparently none of the motors was made to really function well - that is, run reliably - when

controlled by a crystal unit. They simply were not designed for it. Any of the units mentioned above works, and each does essentially the same thing: make the camera run 24 (or 25) fps crystal as well as variable, from about 12 to 50 fps, but every so often, for reasons no one can fully explain, the camera will race past 50 fps when turned on. This situation may last a few minutes, or an hour, or perhaps never return to normal and require a trip to the technician. Once on the repair bench, the problem usually vanishes, and the technician cannot make it occur again. He or she is forced into writing the most feared words in the camera owner's vocabulary:
no problem found.

This means that there is a problem, but since it cannot be found, it cannot be repaired.

All three units do this, so be prepared - carry a sync cable. Test it before you get onto the set. It is a good idea to have a second sync cable because they are fragile.

Now, however, there have been several developments in the 16BL crystal situation. Three separate manufacturers, recognizing the value of the camera (especially when compared to the escalating costs of new Arri or Aaton cameras in the last few years) have come up with new gadgets for controlling the 16BL:

1) Roessel CPT, in Queens, NY, has designed an elegant crystal for the 16BL that replaces the rear electronic panel. You, the user, simply remove four screws at the rear of the camera, pull out the Arri control panel (the old electronics assembly that includes a Tuchel plug for attaching a sync cable to a Nagra, a running light, a "bloop" sync light, and a remote on-off plug) and replace it with the Roessel control. The camera is then plugged into the control via an external 9 pin Amphenol connector (same as on standard 16BL power cables) and a much more rugged 4 pin XLR (a.k.a. Canon) style power cable can be used - a cable which also happens to be the standard for all 12 volt 16 and 35mm cameras. The Roessel Control has built in crystal speeds of 24, 25 and 30 fps, as well as variable speeds for 5 to 50, and a digital readout of speed.

2) Tobin Cinema Systems, of Seattle, WA, has introduced their TCS TXM-9, a crystal for the 16BL that replaces the rear electronic panel on the camera just like the Roessel crystal (Alan Gordon Enterprises also sells this unit). It has no digital readout of speed, but offers these crystal speeds: 23.976, 24, 25, 29.97, and 30 fps. It has a variable speed range of 18 to 50, and - like the Roessel - allows the use of the better, standard 4 pin XLR type cable. In the near future, they plan on offering the TXM-9F which has a Fischer connector installed so that users can plug in an external control, and the TXM-9/25 which will have the same speeds as the original TXM-9, but will work with the European 25:50 gear set.

3) Media Logic, of Manhattan, NY, offers their BL-Drive Motor, a crystal controlled unit that replaces the old standard Arriflex motor entirely. It offers built in crystal speeds of 24, 25 and 30 fps, and with the addition of Media Logic's 11 pin Fischer interface, allows the use of any Arriflex compatible speed control. The cost of the motor is $1250 and the Fischer interface $150.

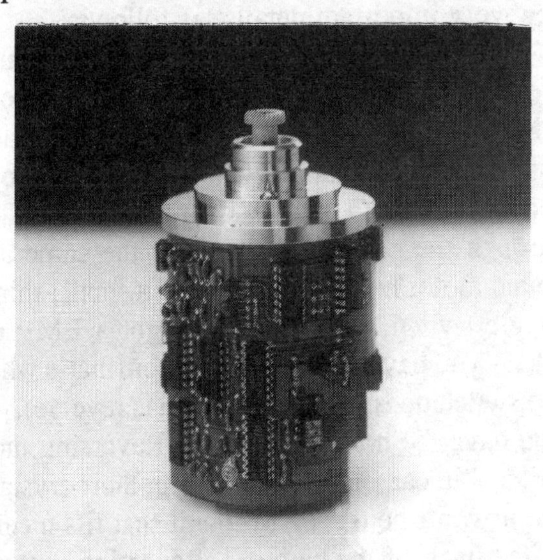

Media Logic BL-Drive Motor

So, which to buy? Well, as Co-owner of Media Logic, I have my prejudices, but here's what I think.

The Tobin Cinema TXM-9, if it performs well (no reason to think it won't) is a better bet than the Roessel, because it has more useful crystal speeds and costs, at the time of this writing, $895. The Roessel does have a digital readout, but it doesn't really tell you anything the analog tachometer that's built into every 16BL does already, since it only reads out to two digits (no tenths, hundredths, or thousandths of a frame) and it doesn't have speeds like 23.976 (useful for shooting with DAT tape recorders which aren't resolved during transfer like 1/4" with NeoPilot transferred to magnetic film, since telecine machines run at 23.976) or 29.970, which is useful for filming NTSC monitors without getting the roll bar, or for direct film to tape transfer (the Tobin unit has these speeds). The Roessel costs about $1400 - certainly no bargain. So of the three, it looks like the best would be the Tobin, except for a few very important details, as follows:

a) You must use both the Tobin and Roessel controls with Arri Universal motors EMP or BLE. These motors are the only ones that can be controlled with a crystal without modification and can be identified by looking through the clear plastic cap on the camera's round motor housing. If you see a small, shiny toggle switch, you've haven't got a EMP or BLE - you have a Reversing motor (that's what the switch does, runs the camera is reverse). If you have the non-Universal or Reversing motor, Tobin can modify it to accept their crystal, but it won't be the TXM-9 unit that fits nicely in the back of the camera. Reversing motors have to be used with their older TXM-7 unit that is a big box screwed to the motor housing. The TXM-7 unit costs $875 with only one crystal speed (of your choice); one extra crystal speed is another $50 and variable or non-crystal speed capability from 5 - 50 fps is yet another $50, and the camera and motor must be sent to Tobin for modification.

b) The Tobin TXM-9 must be used with cameras that have a gearset that runs the camera at 24 fps and the motor at 3000 rpm. You can see what gearset your camera has by opening the loading door and looking at the back of the cavity. You'll see two gears under a clear window. One gear is large and made of steel; the other is smaller and made of white nylon, and is mounted on the motor. The larger gear will be engraved with one of the following: 24 - 50, 24 - 60, 25 - 60, or 25 - 50. The first number is fps; the second is pilot signal Hertz. The Tobin TXM-9 needs the 24 - 50 gearset, which is the most common. Shortly, Tobin says they will have model TXM-92/25 which will use the European gear set. Your gearset may have the second number ground away.

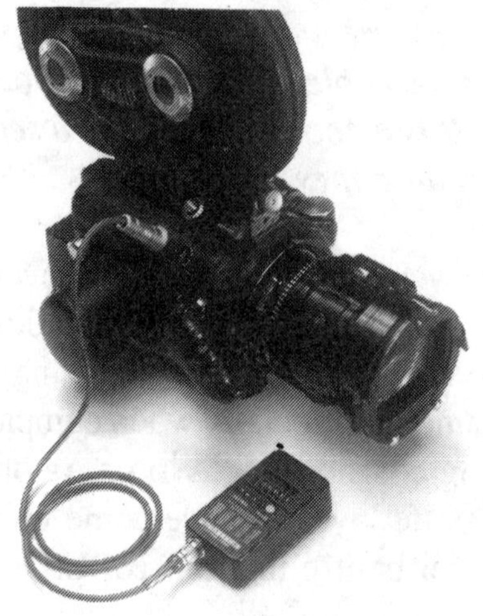

Arri 16BL with Media Logic Fischer Interface

This was likely done to alleviate the fears of camerapeople who thought that the camera would output 50 Hz pilot signal with this gearset; actually, this setup can put out 50 or 60 Hz. The only way to be sure of the signal is to test it, which you certainly won't want to do since pilot signal from the camera is obsolete anyway. If your Hz number on the large gear is ground away, simply count the teeth; 50Hz has 50 teeth, 60Hz has 60.

c) You can't plug in an external control unit to either the Tobin TXM-9 or the Roessel; you will, Tobin says, be able to plug in any Arri type control into their soon to be release TXM-9F.

So, if you have a EMP or BLE motor and don't care about an external control, you probably want the Tobin TXM-9. If you want external control capability, or if you don't have an EMP or BLE motor, get the Media Logic. If you have a non-reversing motor and want external control capability at the lowest price, you might go for the Tobin TXM-9F when it comes out, but you'll only save about $300 over the Media Logic BL-Drive, and you'll still be using your old motor (which is probably at least twenty-five years old).

Why would you want external control capability? Say you want to shoot at 15 fps crystal, then transfer to video in sync, so that each frame is transferred twice, giving you an unusual visual effect. Or perhaps you have to film a computer screen for a software company. In this situation, the video monitor won't run at the NTSC speed of 29.970. A Tobin or Roessel unit won't run at 30.125, or 28.990 (except, once again, the promised Tobin TXM-9F when plugged into an external control), or some other esoteric computer speed, so you'll have to rent an Aaton or Arri 16SR that does accept an external control. The Media Logic 5 Digit Speed Control and the Cinematography Electronics Precision 1 and 2 controls all offer the ability to change speeds by .001 fps, and each speed is crystal locked. What's more, these controls allow you to *phase*, or very slightly change the speed of the camera until it is locked to the monitor, frame for frame.

The Media Logic motor, with the Fischer interface, will also allow you to automatically lock the camera to any video signal with the Cinematography Electronics Synchronizing Control.

In addition, the Media Logic BL-Drive incorporates a modern, efficient motor that requires less power and makes less noise than any of the original Arri motors. This means a quieter camera and less battery changes on the set.

If you have the EMP or BLE motor in your 16BL, you might find that the Tobin TXM-9 is all you want. But if you have a reversing motor, my advice is to go for the Media Logic. The Tobin TXM-7 is just too limited and bulky, and just as expensive as the TXM-9. If you want your camera to have state-of-the-art speed ability, you want the Media Logic. The extra capabilities may mean the difference between getting the job and having to rent a 16SR.

Arriflex 16SR I and II

reflex viewing
rotating mirror shutter - 180 degrees fixed; 144 available
length of exposure: 1/48th sec. @ 24 fps (180 shutter) 1/60th sec. @ 24 fps (144 shutter)
frame counter: none
flange/focal distance: 51.990mm (52 nominal)
footage counters: on rear of mag, 400'-0 subtractive; on left side of mag, 0-400' additive
fps range: 6-75 with accessory speed control forward only
pin registration
power: 12 volts DC
lens mount: single Arri Bayonet mount
matte box: Arri: two stage, 3x3 or 3x4 filters; Chrosziel: same as Arri but is not compatible with 9-50 Cooke Varo-Kinetal
loading options: 400' external quick change co-axial magazines only
accessories: extension finder, various speed controls, follow focus, power zoom motors, sliding base plate, various matte boxes, video tap.

Before anything specific is said about the SR, one book must be mentioned: John Fauer's 16SR BOOK. If you plan on using this camera this text is a must. Well written, full of excellent drawings, it is a complete guide to the entire system, and it also includes practices prudent to camerapeople using *any* 16mm camera, not just the SR.

That said, the 16SR is the premier 16mm sync film production camera in the world today. It is also the standard 16mm *rental* camera everywhere. It has earned these distinctions because it is one of the two most versatile, flexible, rugged and advanced 16mm cameras made today (the other is the Aaton).

It hand holds like a dream because of the placement of the viewfinder in relation to the balance of the camera. This finder is also the most advanced of any camera - 16 or 35. You can swing it up, or down, or away from the camera by 20 degrees, and the image stays upright - an **orientable** finder. But it will also **flip over** to the right side of the camera and

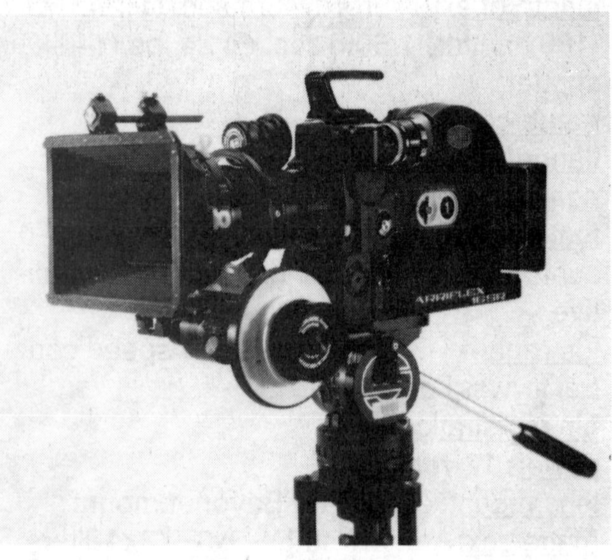

Arri 16SR I

operate there just like it does on the left, making this the only truly symmetrical professional movie camera - great if you happen to favor your left eye, or if you want to place the left side of the camera near some sort of unmovable obstruction. This camera has compact, *coaxial mags* that hold four hundred feet of film and can be changed in less than five seconds.

It is also the heart of a very well thought out *camera system:* matte boxes, follow-focuses, video taps, zoom motors, extension finders, speed controls - every conceivable accessory that the working cameraperson needs can be attached to the camera quickly, and easily (with the possible exception of the video tap which is somewhat tedious to install).

The 16SR has undergone very few changes since its introduction. The most important is the introduction of a version II machine, which is said to be quieter than the version I, making this later design more sought after and more expensive. This change, however, has had very little impact on compatibility. Virtually al the accessories that work with the very first camera made will work with the last one off the line.

The camera's major drawback, however, is its cost. In 1989, when I finished the first edition of this book, a standard camera package that included the camera body, two mags, two on-board batteries and chargers, and a Zeiss or Cooke zoom cost something like $35,000. One day's rental for the camera body, one mag and an on-board plus charger - no lens, no tripod - is $175.00. And most rental houses complained that Arri has raised their prices so much that amount was actually too low. The situation has only worsened with the devaluation of the dollar against the mark, and Arri price increases. Now, new 16SRII camera packages easily push $60,000 (and with the introduction of the 16SR3 the cost of putting together a new Arri set up surpasses $100,000).

In 1989, this is what I wrote about the Aaton vs. the 16SR:

Only the Aaton camera is in the 16SR's class, and the argument over which is better has gone on for years. It generally goes something like this: in favor of the Aaton - its video tap system has been designed in, rather than added on, which makes it smaller and far less time consuming to install; it can be switched to shoot Super-16 quickly and easily making it two cameras in one, the viewfinder is considerably brighter and more magnified; it is a far simpler camera with less moving parts (it should therefore be more rugged and reliable). It also has the capability of using Aaton's superb CTR time code.

In favor of the SR - it is the heart of a true filming system, and all accessories from matte boxes to speed controls work simply and easily (it can be quite a struggle to put a zoom motor or follow focus on an Aaton, for example, and it usually involves the use of an Arri sliding base plate); shooting Super 16 is almost always a rare and special production, and there is a Super 16SR available; Arri is a world standard, and the owner has many choices possible for rental and service (Aaton is not as common); the 16SR has undergone very few changes since its introduction, so that all accessories and related equipment fit virtually all the cameras; the 16SR is extremely rugged and reliable even though it is more complex.

Other than these points, the cameras are functionally identical. They both have 400' quick change coax mags, 180 degree rotating mirror shutters, extensions finders, 12 volt Arri on-board batteries, the ability to use all the same zoom and prime lenses (the Aaton will accept some 35mm still camera primes with an adapter - the SR won't) and both machines cost about the same.

Most people who buy the Aaton do so because they feel they are getting a greater value (because of the Super-16 changability) and because they believe it to be somewhat more advanced than the Arri. Most people who buy the SR do so because they feel that Arri equipment is more rugged and reliable, they know that they are buying into a complete system, and because they like the idea of being able to rent accessories and get their machine repaired in many more places, which gives them the ability to shop around for these services.

Now, in 1993, more factors have come into play when comparing the Aaton to the 16SR.

First, which Aaton are we talking about? In 1984, Aaton introduced the XTR camera, which is far more reliable and less costly to maintain than the older LTR cameras. About this time, film manufacturers introduced sharper, faster, and less grainy stocks that were, unfortunately, softer. They were far more prone to scratching, and Aaton had to redesign their magazines to handle these more delicate stocks when shooting super 16. What this means is that LTR mags (the ones with what is called the **non-reverse light trap**) shouldn't be used for super 16 - they'll scratch. If you have an LTR, you have to use XTR mags, and certain modifications have to be done to you camera, to shoot super 16. So, you can't really say that a standard LTR can shoot super 16 anymore.

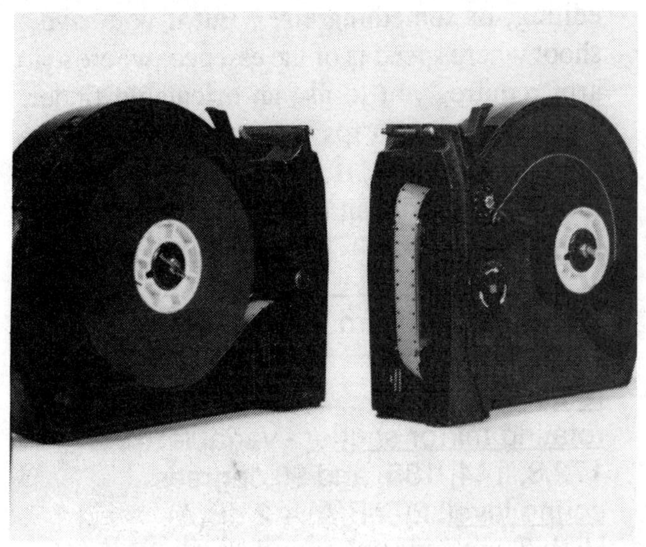

16SR Threading

Denz, a German company, has just introduced a standard/super16 conversion for 16SR I and II cameras that has a PL mount and allows the user to shoot in both formats (changeover from standard to super 16 can be done in the field). The cost is about $10,000, which sounds exorbitant, but not when you compare this to the cost of fitting an expensive-to-maintain LTR with three XTR mags and a body modification for super 16, which in any case would not include that very strong, very universal PL mount.

There are those who say that by the time you get through updating an old LTR to perform like an XTR you might as well buy an XTR. You'd also save money (quite a large amount of money, from what repair technicians tell me) in the long run due to reduced maintenance.

It might make sense to buy an older 16SR and upgrade it with the Denz conversion. This might be the least expensive way to get reliable performance in a super 16 camera.

Do you really need this expensive, high tech machine to make your film? Absolutely not. A 16BL or and NPR or CP/R will also get the job done, but there's a catch. If your production is small, and the shooting simple, a 16SR won't really do anything extra for you. You might as well take the expensive rental money and spend it on set design, or sound editing, or something else. But if you have a shoot where speed is of the essence, where a jib arm requires you to use an orientable finder, where a 60 or 70 fps rate *and* 24 crystal are required - in short, if the shoot gets complex - the SR (or maybe an Aaton) is irreplaceable.

Arri 16SR3

reflex viewing
rotating mirror shutter - variable: 180, 172.8, 144, 135, and 90 degrees
sound level: 20 dB(A) + 2 dB(A)
High Speed model sound level: 27dB(A) + 2 dB(A)
fps: 5-75 crystal accurate to .001 fps
High Speed model fps range: 10-150 fps
pin registration
power: 24 volts DC
lens mount: single Arri PL type (54mm)
switchable from standard to super 16
temperature range: -20 to + 50 C
loading options: 400' external quick change co-axial magazines
accessories: extension finder, various speed controls, follow focus, power zoom motors, sliding base plate, various matte boxes, video tap: color or B+W with anti flicker processor, time code, viewing screens.

How would I change the 16SR? Here's my wish list:

I'd make the mags easier to load in the changing bag. It's too difficult to push film into the little window on the feed side when a full roll of film is placed on the core adapter, and mounting the load on the core adapter *after* pushing the film through is not much of a solution. Also, getting the film to catch correctly on that sprocketed roller is hard. Granted, with practice, you can accomplish all this easily, but why should I have to practice? I'd rather spend time thinking about the shot, or the scene, or the story.

The camera's carry handle is too small, and although I realize it is currently using up all the real estate between the swing over finder and the mag lock lever, something should be done to make me feel more secure when I have to carry the camera.

The handgrip is great, but the on-off switch in it hesitates sometimes and fails often, and of course Arri has over designed the switch so that repair is ridiculously expensive (Radio shack sells a nice replacement for $1.19 but you have to do some serious handle modification to make it fit). The tiny, fragile 4 pin connector on the end of the cable from the grip is stupid; an Arri original part, it breaks easily and can be repaired only with great difficulty that is warranted because a new cable/connector assembly costs over $125. Also, if you happen to switch the grip on and drag the connector plug over the jack while trying to connect it (the tiny holes are upside down), you can short out a circuit and blow a trace in the lightmeter circuit.

The 11 pin Fischer accessory jack is fine, but the red indicator dot that helps you align the plug and jack is upside down (why?) making it harder to orient the plug.

The battery adapter has never worked right. Arri should simply bow to Anton-Bauer and make a better bracket that uses their excellent video batteries.

Okay, okay! I hear you saying that these are minor problems, and they are. I'm willing to live with these shortcomings and make modifications myself where possible, because the 16SR is a really great camera. It runs forever, is as well made as anything on the planet, and produces excellent results. The only problem I really hate is the mag loading difficulty, and I'm willing to live with that.

Arri has finally updated the SR, and probably reluctantly so because not many people are buying new 16mm cameras anyway and because the camera was designed so well in the first place. The 16SR3 is merely a refinement of the I and II rather than an all out make-over.

The big changes from the SRI and II are that this camera can shoot standard and super 16, has a PL mount, runs on 24 volts, has 80 bit SMPTE RP 114 standard time code, and a variable shutter. It seems to me that Arri really got it right this time. These are just the right additions/changes that are needed to assure the cameras success in the HDTV-possible future.

The necessity of having a sixteen camera that can shoot standard and super 16 will, I believe, be more and more important as wide screen NTSC and then actual HDTV is introduced. During the slow advance of these new formats, D.P.s will be asked to shoot in both standard and super 16, and Arri claims the SR3 can be easily user field switchable.

Even if the PL mount didn't allow you to use lenses intended for 35mm (it does), it would still be a welcome addition because it is simply stronger and less troublesome (and probably makes the camera quieter) than the old Arri bayonet type.

The variable shutter is a nice touch, allowing users to do things like shoot TV screens both here and in Europe at 24 and 25 fps respectively and not get the "roll bar". Unlike the 35mm Arri 535, however, the shutter cannot be changed during a shot for those groovy time shift things that are all the rage right now (but which will probably fall into the gimmick pile right on top of "zoom in, dolly out"). Getting a 24 fps/144 degree shot in 16mm usually meant hunting down a modified CP 16R for the day and finding the appropriate lens adapter, but owning 16SR3 makes this history.

Now for my wish list:

The mags are virtually identical except that a nice raised ridge has been placed on both sides near the top which makes for a better grip when changing them. Unfortunately, the threading is exactly the same (not super easy like Aaton mags), but fortunately, the mags from 16SRII will fit (they are super 16 friendly, I've been told), so if you wanted to save money, you could just buy a 16SR3 body and find some good used II mags. Except that only the SR3 mags can be fitted with a time code module.

Since the time code module (the device that exposes time code on the film) is inside the mags, rather than the camera, there is a gap between the gate and the module. Since the loop (amount of slack film before and after the gate) can vary when the mags are loaded, a small loop size sensor in the base of the camera measures the loop each time the camera is loaded and adjusts the time code to compensate. Aaton placed their time code module in the gate itself to avoid all this complication. One might judge the Aaton system as better for its simplicity, but complications to Arri are not necessarily problems, because they make every piece and every part so well. It's a sure bet that although the SR3 has many more parts than an Aaton XTR or Xprod, reliabilty of the SR3 will be superb.

Arri has come up with a solution to the tiny carry handle problem: the SR3 handle is bigger and actually swivels out of the way (you push a small release button first) so you can take mags off the camera without banging your finger on the handle.

The handgrip on the SR3 has a much better, recessed on/off switch (no need to go to Radio Shack for replacement), and the cable that plugs into the camera from the grip has a much nicer, less expensive, and repairable Lemo type connector.

The camera has an LCD panel on the left side for counting feet or meters, changing speed, and displaying shutter angle, low battery warning, out of speed, end of film, and last but not least, time code user bits and sensitivity. Since this information cannot be displayed all at once, you must push a button to switch from one display to the next; state-of-the-art 16 cameras are, it seems, in a state of control-display infancy, just like those early VCRs that were so tedious to set (you'd end up taping Shop At

Home instead of Cheers).

The SR3 also has a variable pitch adjustment on the right side of the camera, just above where the handgrip mount is. This is a great feature. After loading the camera, and during roll-off for scratch testing, the cameraperson can adjust the pitch, or length of pulldown claw stroke until the camera is running at its quietest.

How does this work? Camera stocks vary, no matter how carefully they are manufactured. Temperature can affect the pitch, or distance between perforations, so that any given camera will not match this new distance. This can result in excess noise as the claw will not "grab" each perf as precisely as possible. With the variable pitch adjustment, however, the operator can set the claw stroke to match the film, resulting in a quieter camera. A special tool is used to make this adjustment, and also change the shutter angle. It is stored in the body of the camera, toward the rear and to the left.

The SR3 is an almost unbelievably well made piece of equipment. It should hold up as well as its predecessors, which is to say famously.

Cinema Products CP 16/R

<u>reflex viewing</u>
<u>rotating mirror shutter</u> - 156 degrees fixed; 170 and 144 available.
<u>length of exposure @ 24 fps</u>: 1/55.4 sec. (156 degrees); 1/50.8 sec. (170 degrees); 1/60th sec (144 degrees).
<u>flange/focal distance</u>: 1.500"
<u>fps</u>: 12, 16, 20, 24, 28, 32, 36, forward only.
<u>footage counter</u>: 0-9,999' additive, rear of camera
<u>frame counter</u>: none
<u>power</u>: 20 volts DC
<u>lens mount</u>: locking bayonet type CP
<u>matte box</u>: two stages; holds 1 4x4 and 1 4 1/2 round filter
<u>loading options</u>: 400' and 1200' external magazines only
<u>accessories</u>: orientable finder, extension finder, video tap (later models only); matte box, zoom motor and follow focus as part of special "Studio Rig"

This is Cinema Products final version of a camera that is based on the Bach Auricon 16mm sound-on-film cameras.

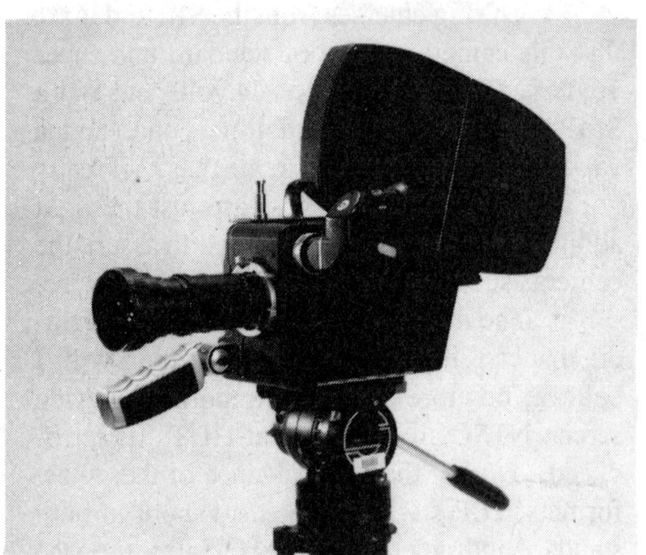

Cinema Products CP16R

Originally, CP began by converting Auricon Pro cameras to ones that would be far more functional in the field. They literally sawed off the top of the Auricon and installed a flat plate that would accept 400' and 1200' Mitchell magazines, then fitted the cameras with Angenieux 12-120 type A (built in viewfinder) zoom lenses. With the addition of 20 volt crystal motors and on-board batteries, the resulting machine was: a) reflex, b) crystal controlled, c) operated with lightweight on-board batteries, and d) capable of using interchangeable, large capacity mags. These cameras were referred to as CP/Auricon Conversions.

With the success of these machines, CP began building their own design, still based heavily on the Auricon, but with all their modifications built in, resulting in a sleek, lightweight camera that had a back-slanted mag well and a shortened, forward mounted viewfinder making the entire machine excellent to shoulder. These were called CP 16/A cameras, after the type A lenses that were affixed to them. A successful design, but far from ideal, especially in the area of the lens (see the chapter on lens mounts and lenses).

Finally, CP added a rotating mirror reflex shutter, and a new lens mount. Now camerapeople can interchange lenses on CP/Rs and any lens mounted in Arri Bayonet or Arri

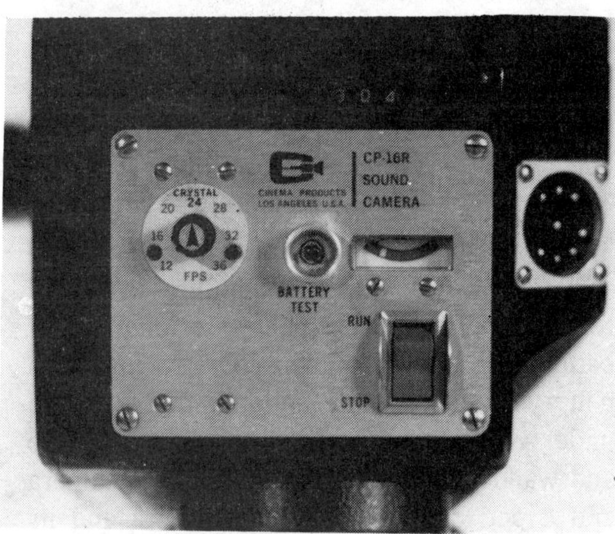

CP16R Rear Panel

Standard will fit as well as those with CP mounts (provided the proper adapter was available). A special *fiber optic viewing screen* takes the place of the ground glass found in other cameras, and this makes the finder brighter and sharper. The area around this screen has an L.E.D. in the shape of the letter S, which serves as an out-of-speed warning visible to the operator during the shot. CP built new magazines (PLC-4) out of Lexan, a light, high impact plastic. These mags have hinged doors for the feed and take-up compartments and are considerably quicker to load. This last machine was dubbed the CP 16/R, and along with the CP 16-A, became the most successful 16mm camera for TV newsgathering in the United States.

All in all, a camera with a large number of good features for shooting double system sound:

1) The camera is light, and great to hand hold. The use of the CP orientable finder makes it even more versatile, and comfortable to shoot with;

2) The on-board batteries are small, and lightweight, and free the operator from cumbersome battery belts and power cables;

3) The camera needs no blimp housing for lenses, and adapters are available to enable the cameraperson to affix virtually any rental lens to the camera;

4) The camera is *extremely* rugged, and quite cheap, as far as 16mm cameras go. Spare parts are easily had from CP in California, and it's a breeze to repair this machine.

Now for the bad:

1) The camera has no registration pin. Some would argue that this is a serious flaw, while others shoot with the camera and satisfied with the registration. CP's have good registration, and only a properly executed, critical test would show the difference between a CP and, say, the registration of an Arri SR.

2) It's a genuine drag to thread. Instead of snapping on a loaded mag in 5 seconds, as with the NPR, ACL, SR, or AATON, you are required to thread a complicated pathway through many guide rollers that usually takes several minutes - longer if you're in a cold environment. Not a good scene if you need to work fast - say, in a critical documentary situation. If you misthread this machine (run film *under* the mag guide rollers, rather than *over* them, for example), it will still run, and it may even sound and look fine at first glance, but it will also scratch the living daylights out of your film. Even though there is a detailed threading diagram printed on a plate inside every CP, some people misthread them and have their film ruined.

3) The camera can be noisy. So can any other camera, it's true, but older, worn CP's or those

that have received poor maintenance emit a high pitched wail that comes right out of the lens, into the scene. You can wrap up an old NPR or BL with a down jacket and sound blankets, but how do you stop CP noise that comes right out of the lens? Simple: get a large, clear filter - a series 9, or better yet, a 4 1/2 round, insert it in any holder, and wrap the neck of a heavy down jacket around it (you might have to tape it to the jacket carefully to keep it from slipping). Slide

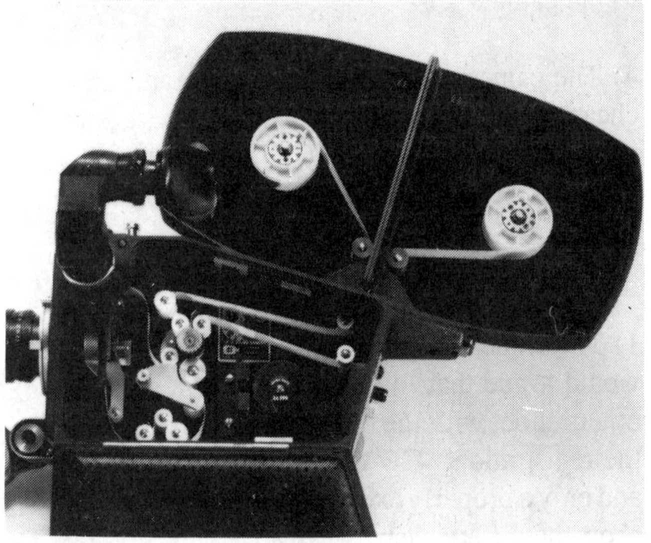

CP16 Threading

this over the lens and camera and have the Assistant Cameraperson hold the filter holder so that it makes *no contact* with the lens during the shot. This will dramatically reduce the noise emitted from even the oldest, crankiest CP. If this seems unreasonable, keep in mind that you'll only have to do this for interior shooting, and any other camera will have to be wrapped similarly (but without the clear filter) to be quiet enough - even a 16SR or and Aaton, despite what the manufacturer claims - to shoot smaller interiors.

4) You'll be hard pressed to find a matte box for this camera. Even though the manufacturer made them, rental houses won't stock them (rental houses generally rent SRs and Aatons exclusively). To get the benefits of a matte box, an Arri sliding base plate and matte box will probably have to be rented.

A few more things:

The on-board batteries are rated at 550 milliamp/hours, which means that they have approximately one-eighth the film driving capacity of a 4 amp/hour Cine-60 belt. The camera is very efficient, however, and the on-boards can be expected to drive 2000' of film. Expected, that is, if they are

a) New. Batteries loose their capacity with age, and over charging. Are yours fresh from Cinema Products, or old and tired?

b) Warm. Go out into the cold air with a CP (even on a day with temperatures in the mid forties) and you can expect a serious loss of battery capacity. To keep yours warm, get a battery extender cable and put the on-board under your jacket (don't forget that it's there and wander off for coffee, pulling the camera and tripod over!) Since the camera and its associated lubricants are colder, it will run less film in the cold than at room temperature, but if you keep the battery warm you can still count on enough running time to finish the shoot.

c) Charged. This almost goes without saying. To find out how charged your batteries are, see the section on batteries in the Test and Cleaning chapter.

All in all, count on considerably less from your CP on-boards - say, twelve to fifteen hundred feet per unit, and always carry at least two. Batteries can be rented, but 20 volts is something of an odd power requirement. The 16.8 volt output of certain Cine-60 belts will drive the camera, however.

A number of camerapeople have told me that the CP/R viewfinder is seriously inaccurate. They feel that this camera exposes a significantly greater part of the scene than the frame markings on the fiber screen indicate. I've seen a number of shots from several different productions that include such things as light stands, microphones and diffusion gels. Be careful! Test the framing thoroughly (see the Testing and Cleaning chapter).

You may (or may not) have trouble shooting certain black and white negative and reversal stocks with a CP/R. These films will often "chatter" in the gate excessively, and sometimes they won't run for more than a few seconds without the loop being lost. According to Derek Whitehouse of Whitehouse Audio Visual (and former head of Cinema Products Repair Department) this is because these stocks often have a short **pitch**, or distance between perforations, causing the claw to strike the upper edge of each perf rather than entering smoothly. Any film that is old should also be suspect because film shrinks with age. My experience has been that some of these cameras will happily run shorter pitch film, while others won't tolerate it. Be sure to run a good length of film through the camera to make sure that the camera will accommodate it.

An often seen problem with these machines is a tiny light leak that appears about one foot *before* the end of each shot (the flash frame). It seems that the velvet gasket (great name for a rock band, eh?) which sits between the camera and the mag gets mashed down with age, and allows a very small amount of light to strike the film. It is such a small leak that only when the camera is stopped - between takes - does the film get enough light to affect exposure. The leak appears as a thin streak across about 1/3 of just one frame. Generally speaking, this isn't much of a problem, because it only affects the very last foot of the take, and this section of film comes almost always *after* the director has yelled cut anyway. Still, many filmmakers are disappointed to see that this last bit of film is unusable. To keep this from happening, inspect the velvet and ask for a replacement if it is worn out. Also, be sure that the magazines seat tightly on the camera.

One nice feature of the CP is a built in speed checking function. The single inching knob has ridges on it that will appear to "freeze" when viewed under 60 Hz lighting (U.S. standard frequency) if the camera is set at 24 fps.

Cinema Products GSMO

reflex viewing
rotating mirror shutter - 180 degrees fixed
length of exposure: 1/48th sec. @ 24 fps
flange/focal distance: 1.500"
fps: 12, 16, 20, 24, 28, 32, 36 forward only.
footage counter: 0-9,999' additive
frame counter: none
power: 20 volts DC
lens mount: locking bayonet type CP
loading options: 400' and 100' external coaxial magazines only
accessories: orientable finder, extension finder, dual purpose finder, video tap

GSMO stands for *G*un *S*ight, *M*an *O*perated, according to the manufacturer, Cinema Products. It sounds as if this camera was intended to be the new, updated replacement for the old GSAP cameras which were mounted on military aircraft for filming bombing and strafing runs. Actually, the GSMO is Cinema Products' answer to the Aaton and 16SR. You can think of it basically as a CP which has been made smaller, lighter, and uses quick change, coaxial mags. It's also considerably cheaper than either the Aaton or 16SR. All this sounds like the 16mm camera buyer's holy grail: a quick, rugged, cheap camera with all the goodies - but the GSMO never caught on in a big way; there aren't too many in use today.

The one filmmaker I know of who owns one says this is because the camera just isn't slick or sexy or European enough, and this is certainly true - GSMOs are rather boxy affairs, and they're all painted gray. Others say that they can't believe that the magazines work well; they have a wild, loop-de-loop threading pattern that seems to have been adopted to give the 100' magazines a low profile. Still others think that Cinema Products just couldn't design a really good, really *quiet* camera. They expect the GSMO to be as loud as the CP/R. Finally, one has to question the marketing smarts of a company that would name a new, expensive, state of the art motion picture camera "gizmo".

The funny thing about these criticisms is that they usually come from people who have never seen the camera. By the time CP introduced the GSMO there were so many 16SRs and Aatons in rental houses and user's hands that no one wanted to get involved with another machine, even if it meant a savings of, at the time, nearly five thousand dollars. So few are in use - virtually none at rental houses - that no one wants to risk their production by using an unfamiliar camera. As for the criticism that the GSMO ought to be as loud as the CP/R because they're built by the same company, one has to question the logic here. Why was the CP/R so successful, if it is indeed so noisy? Why shouldn't the GSMO be as popular?

The reason may be this: an important shift in the nature of 16mm film production took place between the introduction of the CP/R and the GSMO. CP/R users were almost all entirely involved in shooting newsfilm for TV: color reversal with a magnetic sound stripe that could be developed quickly to make the 6 o'clock deadline. By the time the GSMO (and, for that matter, the Aaton, 16SR and, for the most part, ACL) was introduced, portable video rigs shooting videotape had walked away with the TV newsgathering business, and the CP/R users went with them. The group of camerapeople evaluating the GSMO were of an entirely different ilk: they were shooting *double system* documentaries, industrials and the occasional dramatic or comedic short. They had no loyalty to the CP/R and felt that this quick, light, handholdable machine designed principally for single system, sound on film work was too noisy and slow to load for their productions. The GSMO, they argued, should probably be the same.

Just how good or bad is the GSMO? The filmmaker I know of who uses one tested it against an Aaton when he purchased it; he said that footage from the two machines was identical when projected. He apparently found no objectionable problems with the threading or operation of the machine, because he did buy it, and was happy with his considerable savings over the Aaton. Aside from this, I can offer no advice, because I know of nobody else who uses one. They're such scarce machines that it's hard to find someone who has even seen one.

From the most recent sales catalogue - two and a half years old at the time of this writing - the GSMO offers several advantages over either the Aaton or 16SR. It has the unique capability to use tiny 100' mags, making for a really small shooting package when needed. There is an excellent dual purpose finder available that acts as an orientable finder with a built in extension. The lens mount is identical to the CP/R: rugged, well designed and compatible with CP mounted lenses and Arri Standard and Bayonet mounted lenses with an adapter. Finally, used, factory rebuilt GSMO packages can be had for well under $10,000 - easily half the price of a comparable 16SR.

Chances are, you'll only run into one of these cameras under very unusual circumstances. My only advice to you if this should happen and you are considering using or buying one is to take your time evaluating it and shoot a test if possible. You may find that for all its bad reputation, the GSMO is actually a good, slick and inexpensive machine.

Frezzolini FR-16

This camera is so identical in function to the CP 16/R that no discussion of it is needed, save this: it runs on 12 volts D.C. instead of 20, like the CP. This is an improvement, because 12 volt batteries can be had everywhere (especially since the introduction of home video cameras which generally run on 12 volts).

Other than voltage (and therefore batteries), the lens mounts, threading, mags, finders, footage counters - nearly everything - is the same for the FR-16 and CP/R (including framing and short pitch film problems). This means that lenses and mags are interchangeable, so if you intend to use a Frezzi, and need to rent something, you'll be better understood if you refer to it as a CP as most rental people are more familiar with the latter camera. Both machines are of identical manufacturing quality, too. (The LW-16 is the Frezzolini equivalent to the CP 16/A.)

Eclair NPR

reflex viewing
rotating mirror shutter - variable, 5 -180 degrees in five degree increments
flange/focal distance: 48 mm for Eclair (CA-1 mount) 17.5 mm for C mount
fps range: depends upon the capabilities of the many different motors available; generally 12 - 40 fps, and always forward only.
footage counter: 400-0', on magazine, subtractive; scales for both spool and core loads
frame counter: none
power: 12 volts DC
lens mount: two lens turret has 1 CA-1 mount and 1 C-mount; other combinations exist
matte box: two stages, first stage rotatable, holds two 2x2 filters
loading options: 400' loads in coaxial type mag.
accessories: orientable finder, crystal motor, compact Alcan crystal motor

This is nothing less than a milestone camera.

At the time of it's introduction in the early Sixties, motion picture cameras capable of sync shooting were heavy and cumbersome, and huge. For documentary shooting (some liked the term "Direct Cinema") the cameras were so obtrusive that "real life" - that is, the spontaneous action of subjects - was just not possible to record. People would act differently when they felt they were under the scrutiny of motion picture cameras, as well they should, since the environment around them was not the same - there was a film crew making a movie of them! (There are those that would argue that "real life" is never truly recorded anyway, because the medium itself always fundamentally alters the event). Before 1960, the best that most filmmakers could hope for was to build camouflage structures to hide their machines, like Alan Funt did for his TV show Candid Camera. Others "fabricated" documentaries, using actors and sets and scripting all the action.

Enter the Eclair NPR. Here was a camera that was *not* a box: it was designed principally to be rested on the shoulder, leaving the hands free to steady, focus and zoom. It had magazines of a completely new design: **coaxial.** This means that the feed and take-up compartments were stacked together, rather than separated like mouse ears, resulting in a more compact mag. But the most amazing thing about the NPR was that these same mags could be pre-loaded with film, and then snapped on and off the camera in less than ten seconds during the shoot.

To accomplish this, Eclair had to do something that was thought to be quite ridiculous from the standpoint of camera engineering at the time: they made the place of separation of mag and camera be the gate itself - that is, the aperture plate portion of the gate remained on the camera while the pressure plate stayed in the magazine. Any looseness or movement between mag and camera would, critics argued, destroy the focus of the film.

Incredibly enough, this is not a problem. The junction of mag and camera in the NPR is exceptionally strong and reliable (as it must be).

Other features of the NPR:

The camera sports a unique two lens turret that is usually mounted with a CA-1 mount (also called Cameflex, or simply Eclair mount) and a C-mount. The rotating mirror shutter has been specially "carved out" so that the short 17.5mm flange-focal distance of the C-mount is accommodated. The flange/focal distance of the CA-1 mount is 48mm, just 4mm short of Arriflex's 52mm - enough space so that an adapter can be placed either on the lens in question or the NPR, enabling the use of any Arri Standard or Bayonet lens.

In addition to this, a system is employed that enables the operator to vary the shutter angle from 5 to 180 degrees, in five degree increments. This can be quite handy in situations requiring shorter shutter angles, and for shooting TV monitors within sync scenes - at 145 degrees. Although 144 degrees is the ideal for this, the resulting image at 145 is quite acceptable, especially when you're faced with the prospect of renting a special camera for what often amounts to a single shot.

The motor forms the base of the camera and is easily detached, and several manufacturers other than Eclair have introduced aftermarket units. Initially these other motors were desireable because they were crystal controlled - the early Eclair motors being cable sync only - but eventually motors like the Alcan 54 (made by Aaton) combined several advantages: crystal speed control (24 and 25 fps), variable speed control, and compactness. Cameras with the Alcan are considered much more valuable because this small motor makes them far easier to hand hold.

Ultimately, the NPR affected not only the way documentaries could be shot, but the entire film industry, right up to Hollywood itself. With the addition of the Nagra, the camera crew could be quite unobtrusive, and silent, and best of all - mobile. The crew could follow the subject up or down stairs, and into buildings, capturing sync scenes virtually unobtainable beforehand. Filmmakers began producing films with a new kind of truth, changing viewers perceptions about what constitutes "reality" on film. These works had an infinitely more powerful realism than anything that could be "fabricated", or suggested up until that time, and this became a new filmic reference which Hollywood films (and TV, for that matter) had to grapple with.

Quite a lot of impact for one camera. It is true, of course, that faster lenses, sensitive films stocks and portable tape recorders such as the Nagra were equally involved (as well as the Arri 16BL and Auricon conversions and the impact of TV news gathering), but the NPR embodied all the new criteria for 16mm sync cameras - and it was the first.

At the time of this writing, the NPR is well past it's 30th birthday. Is it still a viable sync camera today?

That depends on who you ask. There are those who've always hated the NPR, saying that it is fragile and unreliable. Others still use them and see very little reason to shell out thirty grand (or more) for an Arri SR or an Aaton. They're particularly useful when you must have quick-change mag capability, and the money for rental of a 16SR or Aaton is not available. No other 16mm sync camera has the NPR's variable shutter (except the new and very expensive Arri 16SR3) and it's ability to shoot at 145 and 180 degrees without an expensive trip to the camera technician. Another plus is that C-mount prime lenses are often very good, and very cheap. The owner of an NPR can build quite a collection of high quality Switar primes, for example, at a small fraction of the cost of Zeiss or Angenieux lenses. The camera isn't bad to hand hold, especially with the small Alcan motor and an orientable finder (far better than the 16BL), but they're not all that good either - certainly not as good as a CP.

Eclair ACL

oscillating mirror+rotating blade shutter: 175 degrees fixed
length of exposure: 1/49.4 sec. @ 24 fps
flange/focal distance: 48mm CA-1 mount, 17.5mm C-mount.
fps range: 8 to 75 fps, forward only
footage counter: on magazines
frame counter: none
power: 12 volts DC.
lens mount: Arri Standard and Bayonet as well as C, CA-1 and Nikon available.
matte box: none
loading options: 400' and 200' external

magazines only
<u>accessories</u>: more powerful "multi-duty" motor, TTL metering system, handgrip, orientable finder

This is the successor to the NPR, and its engineers seem to have pulled out all the stops in an attempt to create the smallest, most compact professional 16mm sync camera ever. Some would contend that they accomplished their goal, while others see the ACL as a failure.

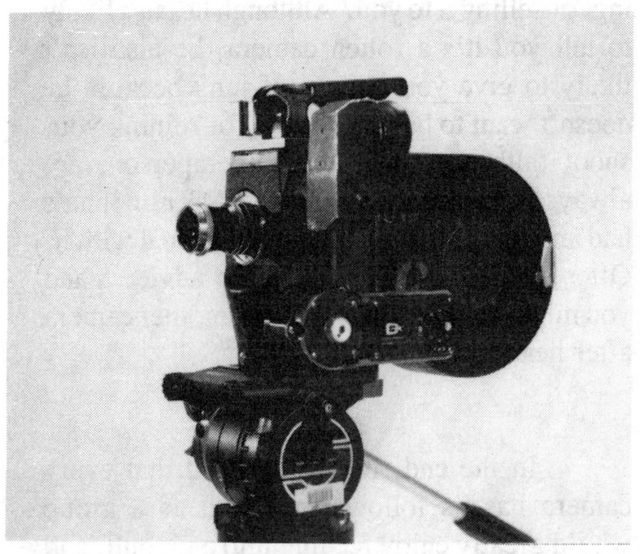

Eclair ACL, 10mm C-mount Prime, 200' Mag

Eclair engineers came up with a unique oscillating (rather than rotating) mirror reflex design that works in conjunction with a standard rotating blade type shutter. The mirror in this camera is mounted on a long shaft and bobs back and forth over the gate. The goal of this system was to allow for the use of C - mount lenses while having the camera housing itself be very small. Added to this was a tiny crystal motor (in comparison to those of the NPR or 16BL) and small magazines with a 200' capacity. The resulting overall design was quite small indeed.

Unfortunately, 200' of film was not enough. In certain situations, the size and weight reduction might be a viable trade-off for the shortened filming time, but for everyday working situations, 200', or about five and one-half minutes, was (and is) far too short. Using the camera with these mags means the cameraman must go into the changing bag more often, and experience the awful feeling of running out of film at a critical time during shooting twice as many times.

Eclair's answer was the introduction of a 400' magazine. These are so large and heavy in comparison to the 200' mags and the body of the camera itself that it is ludicrous. A new "multi purpose" motor had to be introduced to drive these big mags. There is no matte box for the ACL - an Arri or other type must be adapted.

The problems with this camera seem to fall into three categories: the mags, the mirror, and the loop.

The *mags* have been known to fall off the camera. That's right, fall off! The locking system on many is not reliable, especially in the case of the 400' mags, so many camerapeople resort to heavily gaffertaping the top of the mags to the body (incredible, eh?). There are certain 400' mags that have a very strange method of winding the film on the take-up side: the arm and roller arrangement that usually aligns the film on the core has been replaced by an arm fitted with large rubber wheels that are driven by a belt. They rest on the sprocket hole area of the film and literally force the film around the core by friction. The general consensus of most camera technicians is that this magazine does not work - period.

Since the *mirror* oscillates - that is, it stops and starts 24 times per second, rather than rotating smoothly - there is a slight associated vibration, and noise. Some technicians feel that this is an inherent flaw; this mirror will eventually wear out prematurely, or at the very least cause vibration problems leading to noise and an unsteady image in the finder, they argue. Eclair built the arm in such a way that it weighs only three grams - and the mirror actually seems to be quite durable. I know of one case where the arm became bent so that eye focus shifted depending on its position, but it should be kept in mind that rotating mirrors have their problems too, and sometimes (though rarely) need replacement.

The camera has a reputation for loosing

the loop. There are those who maintain that if the inching knob found on the motor is given a few twists before each loaded mag is started for the first time, the camera will not have any loop loosing problems, and will be, in fact, quite reliable (see Anton Wilson's book "Cinema Workshop", listed in the bibliography) but others think that this is just baloney.

Overall, a few things should be said for the ACL. It is a very compact camera, especially with the 200' mags in place. The lens mount system is superb: interchangeable adapters allow the cameraperson to attach Arri Standard, Arri Bayonet, Eclair and even Nikon lenses. Removal of these adapters reveals a C - mount permanently attached to the camera

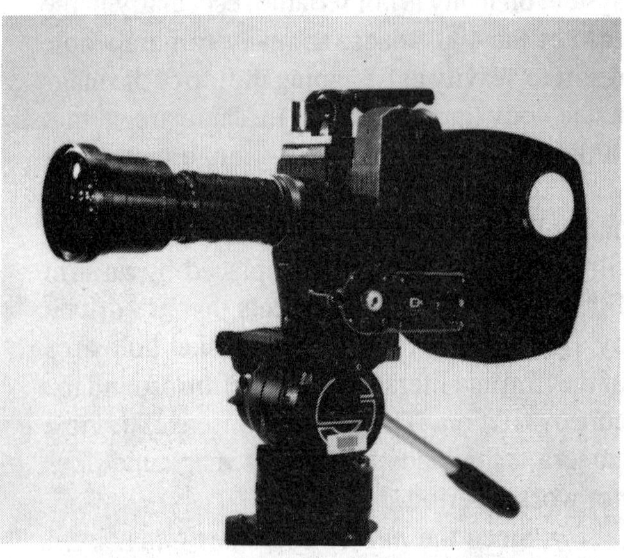

Eclair ACL, 9.5-95 Zoom, 400' Mag

body, enabling users to make use of even more lenses. The multi-duty motor has variable speed settings of 8, 12, 24 (or 25), 50 and 75 fps - quite a range, although most technicians discourage the high speed settings as they would with any sync camera (continued high speed use wears the machine prematurely, and makes it noisier as well.) Finally, there are camerapeople who have owned them for years and swear by them (and ostensibly pamper them) and think they're just great. The camera has all the quickness of loading of a 16SR or NPR with the addition of lightness and tininess. It's awfully good to hand hold too, and if you take one on a long hike, those small 200' mags rapidly become old friends.

Should you use one? To find out, make sure you give the camera a thorough going over. Besides doing all the standard tests (see the Test chapter) run a few 400' foot rolls of film through the camera, starting and stopping many times. Wiggle the mag to body connection. In short, try to make the thing mess up. If it has problems here, count on many more during the shoot. Then, talk to whoever is renting, loaning, or selling it to you. Although he isn't likely to tell you it's a rotten camera, he also isn't likely to give you a piece of junk because he doesn't want to be responsible for ruining your shoot (although you, the cameraperson, are always ultimately responsible). Ask him if he's had any trouble, and what he did to deal with it. Often, he'll have some valuable advice - and you might decide to get a hold of another camera after hearing it.

In the end, it must be said that every camera has its followers as well as a group who'd greatly enjoy feeding it to a pit bull, and this one is no exception. Even a 16SR can be the source of catastrophe if somebody mistreated it before you got your hands on it, so remember that with all movie cameras: approach with caution.

Lenses

Lens mounts. Before the subject of lenses is tackled, lens mounts must be discussed. No other area of motion picture camera technology is as confusing to the novice as lens mount compatibility. The reason for this is simple: the manufacturers of cameras have wildly different, and often incompatible ways of getting lenses and cameras to mesh.

Lenses are made by certain manufacturers: Angenieux, Zeiss, Cooke, etc. Cameras are made by others: Arriflex, Bolex, Aaton, etc. Some mechanical provision must be made to get the lenses affixed to the camera, and this device is called the lens mount. It is designed principally by the manufacturer of the *camera.* This is not to say that the lens designer is not aware of the uses to which his or her lens will be put; it simply means that any given lens mount is associated with a camera, not the lens.

For example - an Angenieux 12-120 is probably the most common zoom lens in 16mm, and it can be found in many different mounts: C, CP, Cameflex, Arri Bayonet, etc. A 12-120 in **Arri Bayonet** - that is, one that has the *lens half* of an Arri Bayonet mount affixed to it is identical to a 12-120 in **CP mount**. Same lens, different mount.

What is meant by lens half? Every lens mount has two halves: the part that is screwed down, locked on or machined into the camera, and the part that is screwed or locked to the lens. The line where these two halves meet is called the **flange**. The distance from this line to where the emulsion side of the film is held in the gate is called the **flange-focal distance** (a discussion of the flange-focal distance is found in the first chapter - The Camera).

For a given lens to work properly - that is, focus and zoom accurately, it must always be held at a precise distance from the emulsion at all times. This distance is measured from a place inside the lens called a nodal point, to the film plane, when the lens is focused on an object at infinity. For a given lens, this distance never changes. In the photo on the previous page, each Angenieux 12-120 zoom is affixed to a different lens mount, but the distance from the lens to the film plane *stays the same.* Although the flange-focal distances of each camera and mount are different, the nodal point/focal distance does not vary.

Why do the flange/focal distances vary? There are simple explanations, but to really understand what is going on, a short history of camera design is required.

The C mount camera - the one we said was either a Filmo or a Bolex - has a very short flange-focal distance: 17.5 mm. This mount is a screw-in type, 32 threads per inch, 1 inch in diameter. Of all the mounts used in 16mm, the C is possibly the oldest and easily the most ubiquitous. Sixteen millimeter was originally conceived as an amateur medium, and this tiny mount made it possible for home enthusiasts to have three prime lenses - wide, standard and telephoto - mounted on their camera all at the same time and still be reasonably compact. By rotating the lens **turret**, the filmmaker could select between these lenses. (No such thing as

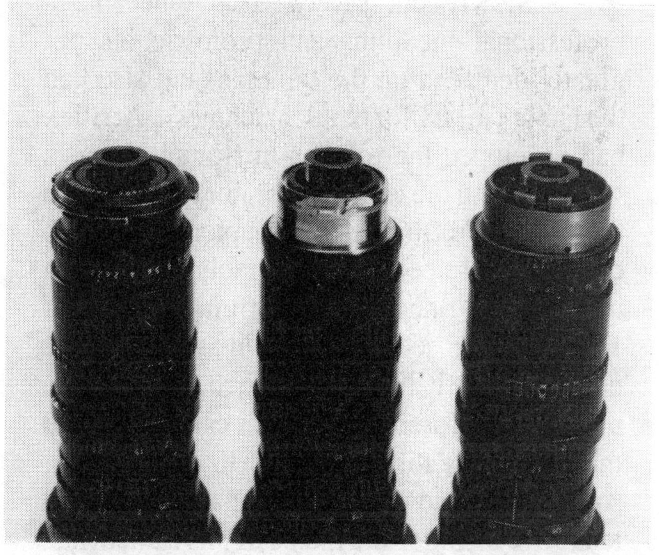

3 Angenieux 12-120s: CP, Arri Bayo, and Eclair Mount

a zoom, or variable focal length lens at this time.) The idea was to keep the camera light and compact, and have all the lenses available at the instant Aunt Ruth or little Billy did something worthy of filming.

There are problems with this approach, however. The lenses themselves - although capable of delivering high quality images - have extremely small rings for adjusting focus and iris. Most amateurs simply set them once, before the shot, but professionals often need to change focus during a take. Turning one of these rings to pull focus is a nightmare since the distance between say, the six and eight foot markings might only be an eighth of an inch. To make matters worse, the mount is a *screw in only* - no lock is used, and even a slight twist on the focus ring may also unscrew the lens, loosening it in the mount.

Slowly but surely, 16mm became a professional medium, and professionals put greater demands on the cameras (and also had the money to pay for better machines). Arriflex had developed the rotating mirror shutter as a way of letting the camera operator look through the lens while filming (see chapter one) and to do this, they needed considerably more room between the flange and the film. Instead of 17.5mm, Arri settled on 52mm as the distance necessary to fit its special mirror shutter into place on its professional 35mm camera. But at this time, there still was no such thing as a zoom, so it also had to design their machines with 3 lens turrets. Since the flange of this camera had to be changed to a new position up the barrel of the lens, the mount became wider. The mount itself - called **Arri Standard** - was a bayonet, or non-screw in type of mount, and it contained small locking levers, and a hook that kept the lens from turning in the mount when the focus ring was twisted. Most of the lens elements were actually inside the camera when the lens was mounted, and the two halves of the mount were coated very lightly with grease to facilitate the twisting action necessary to focus. When Arri entered the 16mm market, they used the same mount for their 16mm cameras as their 35's.

When the zoom did finally come along, it presented several problems. It was much longer and heavier than standard primes of the day. Because of the design requirements inherent in zooms, the tolerances of the flange/focal distance were far more critical than for primes. This means that zoom lenses must be held to the camera with far more precision than most primes. Arri Standard was not the ideal mount since it was machined from aluminum, a relatively soft metal that tended to "give" under the weight of the longer, heavier zooms, and since it was initially designed to work with primes that focused by a twisting action that eventually wore down the critical surfaces. The answer was a new mount: Arri Bayonet.

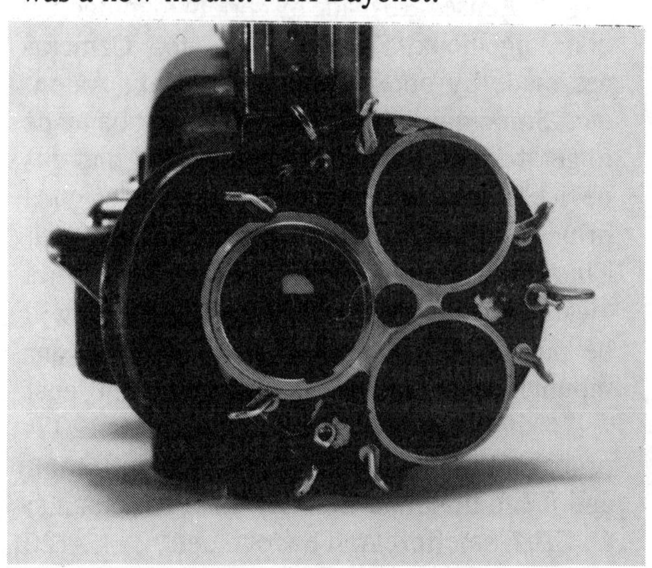

Arri 16SB: Two Standard and One Bayonet Mounts

This mount is made of stainless steel. The lens half has two small studs protruding from the barrel that fit into slots in the camera half. This done, the lens is then given a slight twist clockwise until a "click" is heard - and the mounting is complete. There is no need for twisting of lens half and camera half in relation to each other for focusing since zoom lenses focus either internally, or by movement of the front element. The Arri Bayonet mount holds the lens tight and secure, with tolerances down to at least half a hundredth of a millimeter. On top of all this, the Arri Bayonet mount was designed small enough so that it could replace just one of the three Arri Standard mounts on a three lens turret. It could also be used to mount any Arri Standard lens as well.

Quite a design achievement. The mount allowed for minimal camera modification - older cameras could have new Arri Bayonet equipped turrets to update them, and the mount itself could be used just like the Arri Standard, if need be. No obsolescence!

Ultimately, trying to make the mount serve so many different requirements led to problems. The fact that you must twist an Arri Bayonet mounted lens to seat it - thereby introducing stress to the lens itself - was a direct result of the mount having been built so small. And even though it is made of stainless steel, it is still not as strong as it could be if it were larger - like other mounts.

At this time (in general, the decade of the 1960's) there were other manufacturers who were keenly aware of the problems Arri encountered. Manufacturers were also aware that lenses mounted in either Arri Bayonet or Arri Standard were far and away the most common, so that any mount they designed had to allow the user to also mount Arri lenses - if they wanted their cameras to catch on and compete.

Eclair had several cameras on the market: the Cameflex and the NPR, to name the most popular, and each shared what is commonly called the **Eclair Mount** (also known as **Cameflex** and **CA-1**). This mount operates similarly to the Arri Bayonet - that is, the barrel of the mount on the lens is inserted into the lens port, seated, then given a fifteen or twenty degree twist clockwise. This mount has *no lock,* however. The lens is simply twisted until it feels snug. This can cause problems, because some people over-tighten the lens, and have trouble removing it, while others under-tighten and risk loosening the lens while twisting the zoom or focus controls during a shot. Still others forget to twist the lens *clockwise* when tightening and actually twist it counter-clockwise. This jams the lens in the mount, often resulting in a trip to the service technician for removal.

The Eclair mount's flange-focal distance is 48mm - shorter than Arri's 52mm. Why? The 4mm difference is just enough to fit an **adapter** between camera and lens which allows Arri Standard and Arri Bayonet mounted lenses to be used in Eclair cameras. Smart. This means that the NPR, for example, has the ability to use more lenses, and makes it more versatile. The NPR also has a special mirror shutter that, unlike the Arri, is carved out in such a way that even C-mount lenses, with their 17.5mm flange-focal distance, can be used! (to read more about this, see section on the NPR in the chapter on 16mm cameras). So the NPR is one of the most versatile mirror shutter cameras - in terms of lens compatibility - ever designed (the other is the Eclair ACL).

Cinema Products began making cameras that were conversions of an existing machine: the Bach Auricon 16mm sound camera. These conversions can be thought of as "hot rodding" - CP took the basic Auricon Pro 600 model, sawed off the top and replaced it with a flat base that allowed the use of removable 400' Mitchell magazines. It affixed Angenieux 12-120 type A lenses (these have built in viewfinders) to the front of the camera, and finished up the job by adding 20 volt, crystal controlled motors and on-board batteries. What it ended up with was a light, rugged, relatively inexpensive machine which was very popular in the days when TV news gathering footage was shot on magnetically striped color reversal.

The conversion cameras used C-mounts for holding the side-finder Angenieux 12-120 lenses - a precarious practice, since these lenses are quite long and heavy for such a tiny mount. Because of this, these lenses often shifted or twisted in the mount, and because the finder was attached to the lens, the unsuspecting cameraperson thought nothing was wrong. When the footage was screened, problems in framing such as un-level horizons and tilted scenes were the result. There were other drawbacks as well: since there was no mirror shutter and no viewing system at all save for the side-finder on the zoom, this lens became the only one that could be used unless the operator was willing to shoot "from the hip" - that is, generally point the camera without seeing any definite frame because there is no finder on the camera.

Even with these problems, CP was quite successful. It eventually began making their own cameras, rather than converting Auricons. This new machine, called the CP 16/A, was smaller and sleeker, and much better balanced on the shoulder - actually one of the best hand-holding designs ever made - but it still had one C-mount, with the same side-finder Angenieux lenses screwed into it. With the introduction of its last model, the CP 16 - R, CP solved the sidefinder problems: they incorporated a 156 degree rotating mirror shutter.

It also created a new mount for the CP/R, based on the flange lock design of the Mitchell BNC - the CP mount. It is quite superior to the Arri Bayonet mount because the locking aspect is a function of the mount, not the lens; one simply inserts the lens into the mount, and rotates a locking ring that encircles the mount to lock the lens secure. This mount type is also much stronger than the Arri Bayonet, and is capable of holding longer primes and zooms without need of support. It does, however, take up much more space on the front of a camera, so it cannot be used on a three lens turret. This is presumably why Arri did not opt for this type of mount when it designed the Arri Bayonet.

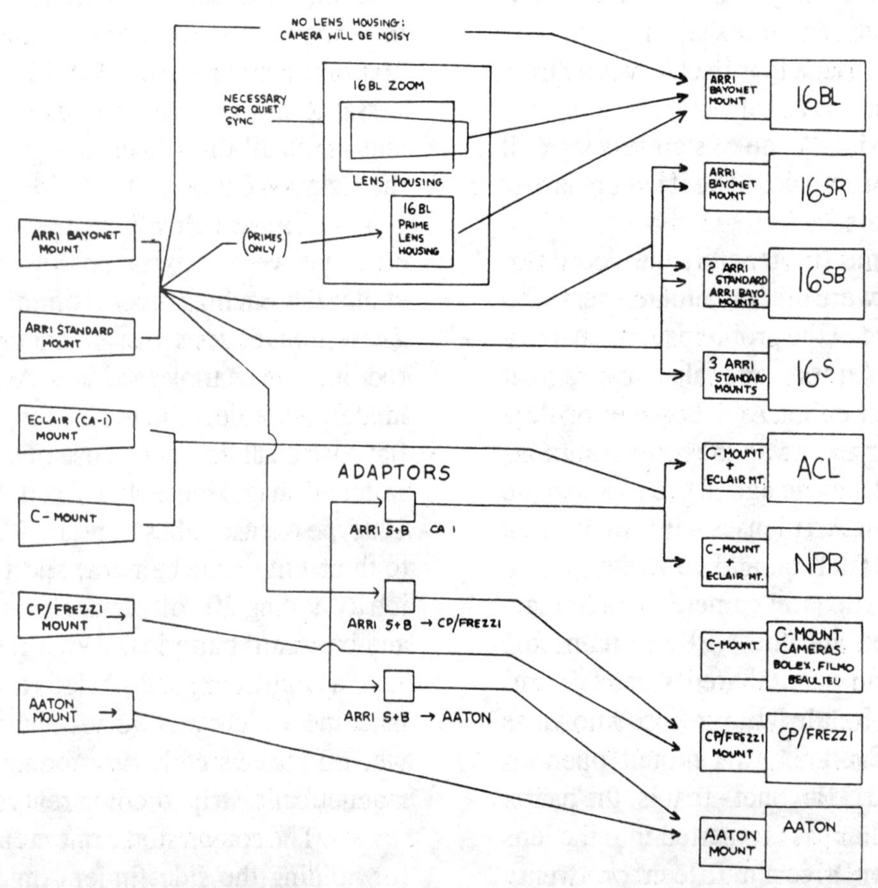

Eventually, three-lens turrets became extinct. The zoom lens allowed documentary and newsgathering camerapersons to quickly select different focal lengths without changing lenses, and those who use prime lenses today (primes still deliver the ultimate in sharpness and contrast) generally have the time to change lenses - for example, in Hollywood feature production, so only one lens mount is needed on the camera, whether the operator is using primes or a zoom.

One should also note that the **Frezzolini**

company had a camera manufacturing history that seems to have closely mirrored CP. It also produced cameras that are based on the Auricon movement: the Frezzolini LW-16 is very nearly identical to the CP16/A, and the Frezzolini FR-16 is very nearly identical to the CP16/R. So identical, in fact, that many critical parts such as pressure plates and guide rollers are interchangeable. Most important, however, is that the magazines (Mitchell 400'and CP PLC-4) and lens mounts are the very same for these two cameras. Flange-focal distances are both 1.500 inches (this is an American machine, remember!). So you can think of these different cameras as one in the same if you are renting lenses.

1.5 inches is 38.1 mm - once again, shorter than Arri's 52mm so that - you guessed it - adapters are available to enable you to put either Arri Standard or Arri Bayonet mounted lenses onto CP or Frezzolini cameras.

Bolex cameras had 3 C-mounts on a single flat turret for years, and there seems to be an endless supply of these machines resting silently in closets and attics everywhere. The newer Bolex Bayonet mount is the company's answer to the problems caused by the zoom lens; it is, like the CP mount, a small version of the Mitchell BNC, and very strong. The flange-focal distance here is 26.46mm, and there are adapters available for mounting Arri Bayonet, Arri Standard, the older C mounted lenses, and a host of others, including the excellent lenses manufactured for 35mm still use. A really good, and quite compact mount.

Aaton developed a mount similar to the CP and Frezzi, design-wise: they made a small version of the Mitchell BNC mount. The Aaton mount works and acts just like the CP/Frezzi - so much so, in fact, that they look almost identical at first glance. The Aaton flange-focal distance, however, is 40mm, and the two mounts are incompatible. But Arri Standard and Bayonet lenses will work with an adapter (of course!).

All **Arriflex** cameras have either Arri Standard or Arri Bayonet mounts (or both, as in Arri three lens turret cameras) - or one other: Arri PL (Positive Lock). This is Arri's best and latest mount, used on 35mm cameras and the new 16SR3, and it is identical in function to the CP and Aaton mount. Arri now supplies its 35mm cameras with this mount only; adapters are available to put Arri Standard and Arri Bayonet lenses onto these cameras. People prefer this mount for 35mm work because it is stronger and quicker, and they say that it actually makes the camera quieter. Quite a set of improvements.

The promise (threat?) of HDTV has actually caused the unthinkable: Arri and Aaton cameras now have a lens mount in common! Arri has introduced their 16SR3 with an Arri PL mount, the same one they use on their 35mm cameras, and Aaton is using the same mount on their X-Prod camera. This allows both cameras to make use of many 35mm lenses mounted in PL.

This brings us to the final section of our discussion of lens mounts, and that is **compatibility**. The chart on the previous page shows what is possible.

You'll see that lenses mounted in Arri Standard and Arri Bayonet will fit any other camera, while those in Aaton, CP/Frezzi, Eclair (also called Cameflex and abbreviated CA-1) and C will only fit cameras that have those respective mounts. This is why the overwhelming majority of rental lenses are mounted in Arri Standard or Arri Bayonet. With the right adapters, the rental technician knows he or she can rent lenses with these mounts to people with *any kind* of professional camera.

Adapters differ widely in means of locking/tightening as well as in materials and construction. Some are made of aluminum; others are brass and/or stainless steel. The very best are made by an English firm called Optical Textile, and by Chrosziel in Western Germany. These adapters are machined to very small tolerances and are made of stainless steel. Some have quick locking mechanisms.

Others are not so well made. Some require you to tighten screws into the barrel of the Arri Standard or Arri Bayonet mount which takes time and invariably causes some damage. Some are not made with high precision and can be satisfactory with primes, but disastrous with zooms.

If you decide to rent an expensive, hot zoom like the Zeiss 10-100 T2 or the Cooke 9-50, try to get a discount on the adapter - and make sure you get a good one. Ask if it is made by Optical Textile or Chrosziel. Bring your camera in when you pick up the lens, test both camera and lens as described in the first chapter of this book, and ask the rental personnel to test the rig on their collimator.

This might sound like overkill, but a large number of camera/lens related problems occur when you put one person's lens on another person's camera. Unscrupulous repair people will, for example, reset a lens' depth (flange/focal distance) to compensate for a problem in the camera that they are incapable of repairing. Many people have no idea that this has been done until they rent a lens which is maintained at *correct industry tolerances*. They get back the ruined footage and then they blame the rental house! A good test comparing tape and eye will, of course, catch such a problem, but small errors are hard to detect.

The rental people may agree to collimate your camera and their lens without charge or disagreement, or they may argue that their lens is correct, and any problem present is in your camera. They are far more likely to do the latter if you arrive at a busy time - any Friday afternoon, for example. Your powers of persuasion are put to the test here just as in any other aspect of filmmaking. Try to get to know these people as people, and often they'll cut you a deal, or turn you on to a good assistant who needs work (or perhaps recommend *you* to somebody else). You can return the favor by returning to them for future business and recommending their establishments to others.

T stops and F stops. F stops are numbers which are generated from a mathematical formula that compares the size of the iris hole in a given lens to the focal length. F stops are important for determining exposure: the larger the hole, the more light is let through the lens to the film. They also determine depth of field: the smaller the iris hole, the greater the depth of field. Lenses, however, have one additional factor that F stops don't account for: light loss due to diffraction, reflection, and absorption of the lens elements (glass) themselves. T stops take this into account. For example, a simple prime lens may have only a very few elements in it, and the resulting T stop (2.4) and F stop (2.3) may be nearly identical. Large zoom lenses with great focal length ranges, however, have many more elements. The difference in T and F stops may be 1/2 stop or more.

In most cases, however, the difference is minimal. When T stops are marked on a lens, use them; think of them as more accurate F stops. If only F stops are present, chances are the difference between them and the actual T stops (if engraved on the lens) is so slight that you have no worry - use the F stops. If you are using a lens that has both (many do), again, use the T stops, unless you need to do a very critical depth of field computation. In this case, the F stops are the ones to reference because they directly affect depth of field.

Coverage. You should know that many lenses can be used on both 16mm and 35mm cameras. A "normal" lens for 16mm motion picture photography is generally thought to be about 16mm, whereas a 35mm camera's normal lens is 32 to 40mm. A take shot with these two set ups - a 16mm lens on a 16mm camera and a 32mm lens on a 35mm camera - will look about the same when projected (providing that the 35mm is framed and projected 1.33). For example, if you shot your sister's car with these two rigs from the same distance, the car would be roughly the same size in both frames, 16mm and 35mm. (Actually, "normal" is a nebulous term; many feel that a normal focal length lens for 16mm cameras is about 25mm.)

Coverage, when talking about lenses for motion picture cameras, refers to the amount of area a given lens throws on the film plane. There are, for example, 25mm lenses that were designed for use on 16mm cameras that, if mounted on a 35, will not cover the entire 35mm frame. If you look through the viewfinder of the 35mm camera in this case, you would likely see the image only in a round area in the center of the frame - the outer edges would be dark. Replacing this 25mm with one that covers 35mm would result in a viewfinder that has no dark edges; the entire frame would have an image.

If a given lens covers 35mm and will fit on a 16mm camera, by all means, use it if you want to. If, on the other hand, you are shooting with a 35mm camera and are wondering if a certain lens will cover, mount it. You'll see in the viewfinder of any beam splitter or mirror shutter reflex camera whether the lens actually covers the frame.

The only other time coverage becomes an issue is when people want to shoot super-16. Some primes cover the enlarged frame nicely, while others won't. Some zooms will cover super-16 over very useful parts of their focal length range. Again, when in question, simply mount the lens and look at the ground glass or viewing screen. What you see is what you get.

Lenses - 16mm

Primes or zoom?

Generally speaking, documentary cinematographers will only use prime lenses under unusual conditions - super speed primes for low light levels, for example. Sometimes primes will be used for special situations, such as a telephoto shot of the moon or macro (extreme close-up) of a flower or insects. For workaday documentary situations - hand holding the camera and capturing the actions of people - a wide ranging zoom lens, such as the Angenieux 12-120 or the Zeiss 10-100 is thought of as a necessity. Zooms permit the operator to instantly change focal length, allowing him/her to select exactly that frame which tells the story without having to physically move toward the subject and risk disturbing the action. They also allow the operator to zoom during a shot, of course, which can be a valuable tool in maintaining a given frame (keeping subjects in a "medium" shot, while they are moving toward the camera, for example) or slowly revealing new information. Since the zoom is their primary lens, most documentary camerapeople insist on using the very best one they can get their hands on.

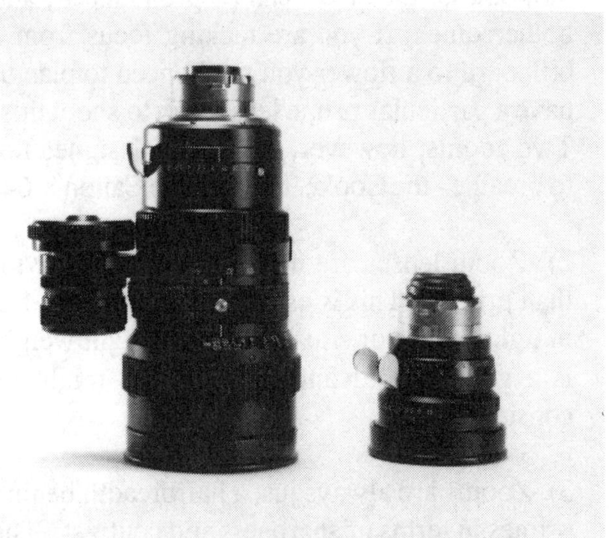

10-100 Zeiss Zoom and 25mm Zeiss Prime

Those engaged in non-documentary filmmaking have more of a choice, however, because they have the luxuries of time and script that the documentary cameraperson does not. To them, the quickness of the zoom may not be of such importance, so the question becomes one of optical quality: which will deliver the best overall image, primes or zooms?

The new zooms are superb. In terms of the sharpness and of the image they are virtually indistinguishable from prime lenses. Only a side-by-side comparison will reveal any benefit to be gained from primes, and it would be very slight. And only the very best primes will out perform these zooms. But zooms do have problems:

1) They generally **breathe** when the focus is racked, or changed during a shot. In other words, the lens will zoom slightly when the

focus ring is twisted. Ninety-five percent of the time, this is not a problem. If the subject is moving, or the camera is panning, tilting, dollying, or the lens is zooming, this breathing will go virtually unnoticed, because the audience will either be paying close attention to the moving subject, or the breathing will be incorporated into the changing frame. But if the shot is locked-off (that is, the camera/lens *isn't* doing any of the above) and the subject is motionless, the effect can be pronounced, and bothersome. If you are racking focus from a billboard to a flower you might need to plan to have a particular prime lens ready to shoot this. Two zooms, however, have been designed not to breathe - the Cooke 9-50 and the Canon 8-64.

2) Zoom lenses are much bigger and heavier than primes. This is usually not a problem, but in tight spaces or situations where light weight is a goal, the advantage of primes might be considerable.

3) Zooms are always just a hairbreadth behind primes in terms of sharpness and contrast. The reason for this is simple: it just isn't possible to make a lens with eight or nine (or more) glass elements as sharp as one with three or four.

All of the above problems are easily understood, and for the most part, quite easy to overcome, or at least easy to live with. The convenience that the cameraperson gains by using a zoom over primes - being able to select an unlimited number of focal lengths between say 12 and 120 millimeters - is such an advantage that few people shoot 16mm with primes anymore.

But it is this very same advantage that comprises the worst problem inherent in zoom lenses: they make you lazy.

Changing a focal length does more than allow you to get a wide shot without tearing down a wall or a close-up without moving the camera toward the subject. Different focal lengths have different aesthetic effects on the shot, and therefore evoke different emotional responses from the audience.

Endless discussions in cinema study texts and filmmaking books alike are devoted to the frame: mise-en-scene, composition, lighting. But very little exists about the importance of *focal length.* Most books do touch on the subject - they'll talk about how, for example, a telephoto lens collapses space: objects seem close together and actors running directly toward the lens seem to get nowhere (Dustin Hoffman at the end of *The Graduate* and Warren Beatty at the end of *The Parallax View*). They talk about how wide angle lenses can make objects and people look bulbous and distort straight lines. But these are extreme examples. The point here is this: the effects of focal length are very subtle. Often they lead the viewer to feel a certain way but be unable to define the source of the feeling. This is true of you the filmmaker as well as the viewer.

There may be an important difference between using a 32mm lens and a 50mm. Or an 85mm instead of a 100mm. For a given shot, taken out of context, the difference may not seem important, but for the whole - the sequence, the scene, the entire movie - using an 85mm instead of a 100mm (or vice versa) may mean the difference between a smooth, coherent visual statement which captures the drama of the script and a disjointed, almost-there-but-something's-not-right sequence.

Before the cameraperson looks through the finder, grabs the zoom ring and twists to decide the frame, he or she ought to ask him or herself this question: what is the goal of the shot? Is it supposed to evoke tension, or warmth? Should it seek to define the space occupied by the characters? How should it do this, by compressing it, or widening it? Should the audience get the feeling that the characters are caged by their surroundings, or lost in an emptiness? How does this shot fit into the scene? The completed film?

Using primes forces a discipline on the filmmaker that zooms do not. If you have to think about changing a lens to another focal length, or *moving the tripod* instead of zooming to a new focal length, or perhaps altering the shooting set to allow the use of a longer prime instead of simply zooming to a wider angle, you'll be forced to really think about the effects of focal length on your film.

So, we come back to the question: primes or zoom? In the end, it must be said that

a) primes still offer the ultimate in optical quality, although the difference is slight;

b) some zooms breathe when the focus is racked, but not all of them do this, and the problem is often negligible;

c) zooms are considerably quicker because they offer the filmmaker an infinite selection of focal lengths between a given range; and

d) zooms make filmmakers lazy whereas primes enforce a "focal length discipline".

Can you use a zoom and still make quality choices about focal length? Absolutely. If you understand the aesthetics of focal length and then impose this discipline on yourself, then the zoom becomes the better tool. You can think of it as a whole carload of individual prime lenses, and also use the unique zooming effect for certain shots as well.

Prime lenses - 16MM

Please note: what follows is by no means a complete list of all the 16mm lenses ever made on this particular globe. Instead, it is a gathering of the most common and most widely used lenses, ones you'll be likely to run into at rental houses and in most sales.

C-mount primes are plentiful and inexpensive, but they can only be used on cameras with C - mounts (no Arriflexes or CP16s) and they're really difficult to work with because the focus and iris rings are tiny and twisting them during a shot often causes the whole lens to unscrew from the mount. The very best are the Switars; these have superb sharpness and deliver very good contrast. You may run into c-mount primes with Rx engraved on them; these were made specifically for Bolex cameras with beam-splitter reflex systems and therefore have the footage scales altered. You can use these lenses on any c-mount camera, however. Just ignore the footage scales and focus by eye.

Kinoptik Tegea 5.7mm

Lens mount: Arri Standard
T stop range: T2.3-22
Minimum focus distance: fixed, 2'-inf. at T2
Filter size: 2x2
Tiffen adapter: none

This is the very widest prime lens you can use in 16mm photography without going to a "fisheye". If you lock the camera off, or move it very little, there will be surprisingly little distortion of the image (bending walls, floors, etc.), but if you pan around, or run with the camera, or have people put their noses up to the front element, things look wild. This lens is great fun to experiment with; all sorts of sequences come to mind: dream, panic, extreme motion, monster P.O.V. etc. Has a nifty means of filtering: a slot built into the lens allows you to slide 2x2 filters right in - a great time saver, and really a necessity since the front element is so huge and behind the lens filtering is out of the question because of the extremely short focal length.

Warning! Lenses which have extremely short focal lengths also have correspondingly short depths of focus. Make sure you have the depth of your camera (flange/focal distance) checked if you use the 5.7 Tegea. It also makes sense to have the lens collimated as well, although many rental houses do this as a matter of course whenever they rent this lens.

Angenieux 5.9mm

Lens mount: Arri Standard
T stop range: T2-22
Minimum focusing distance: fixed, 2' to inf. at T2
Filter sizes: 3x3, Series 9
Tiffen adapter: 75s9

This lens functions identically to the 5.7 Tegea with these exceptions: it is much more compact and is not filtered internally - you use a 3x3 square filter in a matte box (watch for vignetting!) or a Series 9 filter with an adapter. Also, see the Warning! at the end of the 5.7 Tegea description.

Kinoptik Tegea - 9.8mm

Lens mount: Arri Standard
T stop range: T2.3-22
Minimum focusing distance: 9"
Filter size: 2x2
Tiffen adapter: none

Although it can be used in 16mm, this lens was designed and built to be used for 35mm - it is the shortest focal length lens commonly used in this format. Chances are, you won't really be offered the opportunity to use this lens since smaller lenses designed for the 16mm format are available such as the 9mm Cooke and 8mm Zeiss Distagon, and the lens is somewhat in demand by 35 customers. It doesn't offer anything more in terms of sharpness or contrast than the Zeiss or Cooke.

Schneider (Arri Cine-Xenon Schneider Kreuznach) and Cooke primes

Lens mount: Arri Standard
Focal lengths from 9 to 150mm
T stop range: generally T2-22
Minimum focusing distance: 9" to 2 feet
Filter sizes: 2x2
Tiffen adapter: none

These lenses are mounted in Arri-standard are fairly common and deliver good images, but the older versions have crude mounts that must twist in relation to the camera and make it very difficult to pull focus. These same mounts often show wear that causes the image to shift or jerk when the focus ring is twisted. (Newer Schneiders have better lens mounts that focus internally and avoid both these troubles.) These lenses will open up to between T 2 and T 2.8, but if you need to shoot your film at these stops, you'd be better served by Zeiss primes - either the Distagons/Planars or the Superspeeds. Many lenses will be designed to be quite fast, but only perform well in the middle of their T - stop range, say between T - 4 and T - 11. Stops that are out of this range will often deliver usable images, especially in special situations like a close-up, where the apparent sharpness is enhanced by the closeness of the subject. But if you must shoot a large number of shots at very wide (T 1.3 to T 2.8/4) T stops, again, choose a lens that is designed for this. The 16BL may or may not work with Schneider or Cooke lenses that are 16mm or wider - they protrude too deep into the camera when mounted and the rear element can strike the rotating mirror shutter. To test: hold down the lens release button on the camera fully and attempt to seat the lens in question. If it won't fully seat (lens mount flanges won't come into contact) don't force it. The lens can't be used with the camera.

Zeiss primes - Distagons and Planars

focal length	T stop range	minimum focus
8mm	T2.4-16	less than 8"
16mm	T2.4-16	10"
24mm	T2.2-16	15"
32mm	T2.2-16	2'
50mm	T2.2-16	3'

Filter sizes: 2x2

Lens mount: Arri Standard
Tiffen adapters: none

These lenses are excellent optically and have the newer internally focusing type mounts. The mounts themselves are made of stainless steel rather than aluminum which makes them quite durable and resistant to the kind of wear that causes problems. Except for the 8mm Distagon, these lenses cover 35mm, so they're quite valuable and may be expensive to rent. Although 2x2 filters will cover, 3x3 are most often used because these lenses are generally mounted on cameras which utilize 3x3 matte boxes, like the Arri 16SR. Arri and Chroisziel make adapter rings, gears and/or studs that attach to these lenses which allows you to use their follow focus units. A note about the terminology: Distagon simply means wide angle; Planar means film or focal plane.

Zeiss Superspeeds

focal length	T stop range	min focus dist
9.5mm	T 1.3-16	10"
12mm	T 1.3-16	8"
16mm	T 1.3-16	10"
25mm	T 1.3-16	10"

Lens mount: Arri Bayonet
Filter sizes: 3x3, Series 9.
Tiffen adapter rings: 9.5/12 - 58m9; 16/25 - 70sslr9.

35mm coverage Superspeeds:

35mm	T 1.3-16	14"
50mm	T 1.3-16	28"
85mm	T 1.3-16	36"

Zeiss Superspeeds are thought to deliver the very best 16mm optical performance. They are super sharp even at T 1.3, and maintain this sharpness at other T stops as well. The 9.5, 12, 16 and 25mm Zeiss Superspeeds cover 16mm only; longer focal lengths cover 16mm and 35mm. Everybody and their uncle wants a set of these to shoot with, so don't expect to rent them cheaply. There are adapter rings made by Tiffen that allow you to affix Series 9 filters directly to these lenses: 70sslr9 for the 9.5 and 12, and 58m9 for the 16 and 25. The minimum square filter that will cover is 3x3. Arri and Chroisziel make adapter rings and studs that attach to these lenses to allow you to use their follow focus units. An accessory lens called an Aspheron fits over the front of the 9.5mm and 12mm lenses and converts them to super wide: 5 to 7mm! Newer versions of these lenses have been introduced by Zeiss that have integral focus gears for follow-focus use (the Arri follow-focus, not the Chroisziel, naturally) and larger barrels that have bigger, easier to read focus scales. Longer Zeiss Superspeeds exist (see above chart). These cover 35mm as well and are in even greater demand than the 16mm coverage Speeds.

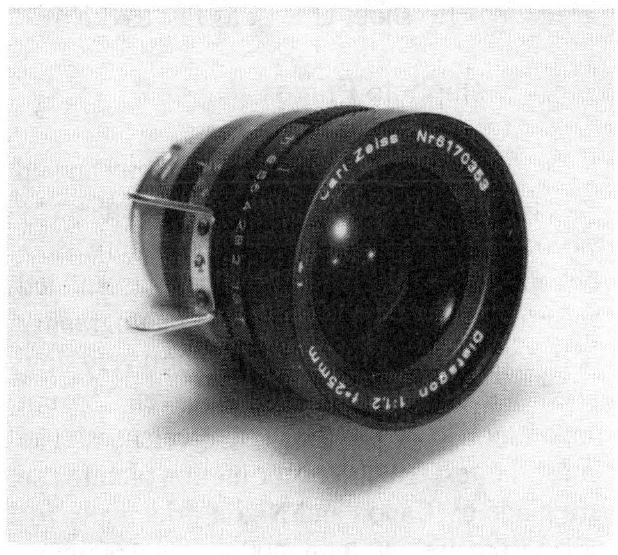

Zeiss 25mm T 1.3 Prime (Old Style)

Cinema Products Ultra-T

focal length	max. T stop
9mm	T 1.25
12.5mm	T 1.25
16mm	T 1.25
25mm	T 1.25

Filter sizes: 3x3, Series 9.

These lenses claim to operate all the way open to T 1.25. Many people feel they are quite good, but the general consensus among users and rental technicians is that they are no match for the Zeiss Superspeeds. They exhibit considerable flair at wider apertures which, all things considered, puts into question the very purpose of the lens (to shoot at least as fast as T1.4).

Telephoto Primes

Many telephoto primes - 150mm and up - are adapted from 35mm still photographers by various manufacturers for motion picture use - Nikon, Canon, etc. Others are assembled specifically for motion picture photography: Kilfitt, Century, Komura. Most sport very slow maximum apertures; T 4, 5.6 and even 7 are not uncommon, especially in the longer lenses. The latest, hottest telephotos for motion picture use are made by Canon and Nikon principally for still 35mm use: 300mm, 400mm, and 600mm. The 300, for example, boasts a maximum aperture of T2.8 and is exceptionally sharp and well made. These lenses cover 35mm movie apertures and are in great demand. Like other heavy lenses, they require the use of a support system such as a locking riser, support rods and sliding base plate (usually Arri) or they'll be damaged, and likewise damage the camera as well.

Zoom Lenses - 16mm

Angenieux

This company's lenses have come under disfavor from many camerapeople in recent years. The good and bad points of these lenses are discussed below. Although there are many different zooms made by Angenieux, they are all quite similar in many ways, and they can be partially discussed as a whole.

It should be stressed, however, that newer lenses - still mechanically identical to the 9.5-57, 12-120, and 10-150 - have been introduced with completely different element coatings. These are called Angenieux H.E.C. lenses (*H*igh *E*fficiency *C*oating), and they are dramatically superior to the older lenses. What follows is a discussion of the non-H.E.C., or older lenses.

Assets:

a) Wide ranges - a Angenieux 10-150, or a 9.5 to 95 possesses an excellent range of focal lengths. The long end of these zooms, as well as the 12 - 120, are often required as a matter of course in all kinds of filming - something to consider when you are thinking about renting a Cooke 9-50 or a Canon 8-64.

b) Ruggedness - Angenieux zooms have excellent mechanical designs. It is not uncommon to find twenty or even twenty-five year old zooms still functioning well. Many survive an occasional drop and need only a new front element or rear mount to continue service.

c) Compatibility - it's very easy to get adapter rings, zoom motor gears and sunshades for Angenieux lenses because they are the industry standard.

d) Low cost - an Angenieux lens will sometimes be included in a rental package price, whereas a Cook or Zeiss lens will incur added expense. If you are in the market to buy, you'll find excellent deals - good 12 - 120s often can be had for as little as $800.00. Repairing a damaged Angenieux is facilitated by the large number of technicians and companies who sell and service the lenses, and by the relatively inexpensive - and available - replacement parts.

e) Optical performance. Angenieux zooms deliver a softer, less contrasty look which should be (but isn't) in great demand considering the number of people who shoot everything through Low Contrast, Fog, Net, and Dot filters.

Liabilities:

a) Breathing - Angenieux lenses focus by the twisting movement of their front element. If you rack focus during a shot, the lens will also "breathe", or zoom slightly (see the discussion of zooms versus primes). Since many camerapeople like to mount filters directly to the front of the lens via the use of adapter rings, this turning motion also turns filters, which is bad news when using Polaroid filters. A careless focus rack can also cancel the desired Polaroid effect. The Cooke 9-50 and the Canon 8-64 zooms focus internally and breathe only slightly; many camerapeople report that the 10-100 Zeiss T2 breathes more than the Angenieuxs, but it's front element does not turn when focusing; it merely moves in and out.

c) Slow speed - that is, the optimum T stop range in regard to optical performance. On almost all Angenieux lenses, the sharpest, most contrasty results are obtained between T4 and T11, with 5.6 and 8 being the best. A 12 - 120, for example, will open up to T2.5, but the resulting image will be soft compared to that of a Zeiss 10-100 T2 at that T stop. This is not the horrible handicap that many camerapeople make it out to be, however. Many make the combined mistake of underexposing while shooting wide open with an Angenieux, and are quite justifiably disappointed with the results. What they've done is misuse good equipment, rather than use bad equipment. An Angenieux used between T4 and T11 will deliver sharp results. Knowing this fact means you can expect less sharpness and contrast at T2.5 - so if you plan to shoot your film at this T-stop, get a different lens.

d) Minimum focusing distance. Most Angenieux zooms (the 9.5-57 is an exception) focus down to no less than 5 feet. Attaching a series 9 close-up filter will shorten this distance, but doing this takes time, and in documentary situations, this can be a problem - an important shot can be missed while the cameraperson fumbles with the adapter.

e) Optical performance. Angenieux lenses just aren't as sharp and contrasty as the Cook 9-50, Zeiss 10-100 T2 or the Canon 8-64, even when used in their optimum T stop range. Many camerapeople demand one of these sharper lenses for every project and then many of these same people hang low contrast or 1/2 fog filters over them to soften the image up, fearful that the lens performance coupled with the sharp new color negative stocks will make their work look like video. (Film versus video is an entire book in itself; it can be mentioned here, however, that film and video never look the same to trained eyes, and even untrained viewers are affected by the difference, and that "softness" is usually better achieved with lighting than a piece of glass over the lens.)

Angenieux 9.5-95

T stop range: 3-22
Minimum focusing distance: 2.5'
Filter sizes: 4x4 and 4 1/2 round
Tiffen adapter: 83ss 4 1/2

This is the poorest Angenieux lens in terms of optical performance, and also the heaviest intended for 16mm use save the 12 - 240 (for some reason, one always sees them attached to tiny Eclair ACLs). Even so, it is capable of delivering quite satisfactory images when closed down past T4.

Angenieux 12 - 120

T stop range: 2.5-22
Minimum focusing distance: 5'
Filter sizes: 3x3 and series 9
Tiffen adapter: 72m9

This is the workhorse 16mm zoom lens, and easily the most common. They can be very new, and in excellent condition, or extremely worn and deliver bad results - and the external cosmetics are no indication of performance. If you can get the lens you are about to use on a lens projector or a collimator, and compare it with other lenses (you'll absolutely need others for comparison), you'll be better able to evaluate it before the shoot. Other than this, nothing short of shooting a film test will tell you whether it is good or bad. Once again, don't go by how the lens looks cosmetically; a good lens can look pretty beat, and vice-versa.

Angenieux 10-150

T stop range: T2.3-22
Minimum focusing distance: 5' for 16mm projector aperture, 2' for TV safe
Filter sizes: 3x3, series 9
Tiffen adapter: 72m9

An interesting lens with an unparalleled range, it also focuses down to 2 feet, although a red line on the focusing barrel indicates that *between 2 and 5 feet the lens vignettes* into 16mm projected area - *but not into TV safe* (the final image as seen on video after a film to tape transfer). Slightly faster than the 12-120 at T2.3, this lens is quite popular. Many camerapeople choose it to compliment the Angenieux 9.5-57, Cooke 9-50 or Canon 8-64 to get longer (telephoto) shots.

Angenieux 9.5-57

T stop range: 1.9-22
Minimum focusing distance: 2'
Filter sizes: 3x3, series 9
Tiffen adapter: 65m9

Easily the "hottest" Angenieux zoom now in use because of its speed and size. At T1.9, this is one of the fastest zooms around, although you'll get much sharper results if you use this lens between T2.8 and T11. Many camerapeople feel that this is the sharpest of all the Angenieux lenses. It also focuses down to 2 feet, making it an excellent choice for documentary shooting. Caution: this lens changes it's maximum aperture over its focal length. It will deliver T1.9 only at wide angle settings between 9.5 and 12 mm. From this range the resulting T stop is reduced until it reaches 2.5 between 45 - 57. Setting the iris at T 2.5 obviates this problem; once set at this stop, the lens will deliver T 2.5 throughout its focal length range.

Angenieux 12.5-75

T stop range: 2.5-22
Minimum focusing distance: 4'
Filter sizes: 3x3, series 9
Adapter: 56m9

An extremely tiny zoom - half the length of a 9-50 Cooke, and it opens up to T2.5. Very few of these are seen, but they are very good lenses, and it is surprising that more people haven't opted for them in past years. A Tiffen 56m9 adapter is needed to use series 9 filters with this lens, although much smaller filters such as series 7 or eight will work as well (but no rental houses stock anything smaller than series 9). Size 3x3 is the minimum square filter for matte box work.

Angenieux 12-240

T stop range: 3.5-22
Minimum focusing distance: 5'
Filter sizes: 4x4, 4 1/2 round
Tiffen adapter: 99ss 4 1/2

A big, heavy zoom with a truly monstrous range, the 12-240 is used only as a special purpose lens: wildlife photography, surveillance, and for dramatic zoom effects. It is so large that most cameras will need a sliding base plate and zoom support to keep from damaging the camera's mount.

Angenieux 16-44

T stop range: 1.3-22
Minimum focusing distance: 5'
Filter sizes: 3x3, series 9
Tiffen adapter: 72m9

The superspeed zoom - opens up to T1.3. Unlike other Angenieux lenses, this one performs very well wide open - it was designed specifically to do so. This lens together with a 12mm superspeed can usually be all you'll need to shoot an entire film at wide apertures. It offers the added plus of infinite focal length selection between 16 and 44 mm, something you can't get with primes.

Cooke 9-50mm

T stop range: 2.5-22
Minimum focusing distance: 1.5'
Filter sizes: 3x3, 4 1/2 round
Tiffen adapter: 83sslr 4 1/2
Super 16 version: 10.4-52mm

If you've read through this chapter from the beginning you already know much about this remarkable lens. It has a number of features which until recently were unmatched by any zoom:

a) It focuses down to less than 1.5 feet with no vignetting, even on projector aperture - very useful in documentary situations where stopping to attach a close up filter would slow things down.

b) It has a very useful range. Many camerapeople find the widest focal length - 9mm - is extremely useful in cramped shooting situations. Although the longest setting is only 50mm, most find that this is quite adequate, and simply add inexpensive 75, 100 and 150mm primes to their lens case.

c) This lens breathes (zooms) only very slightly when the focus is changed. This feature is often of paramount importance for a particular shot (see the section on primes vs. zooms).

On top of all this, the Cooke 9-50 is extremely sharp - perhaps the sharpest zoom of all.

It does have certain drawbacks, not the least of which is its price. A daily rental (undiscounted) is in the neighborhood of $100 dollars - that's right, one day! Although this cost is usually the same for the Zeiss (and probably the Canon), Cookes are so much in demand that rental establishments are far less likely to discount them.

The lens is also extraordinarily complex, and although they are certainly rugged and reliable, they are far from being as robust as the Angenieuxs - which in a way is an unfair comparison because the Angenieuxs can't do what the Cooke can. Nevertheless, as an owner (if you can afford the nearly $12,000 they sell for at the time of this writing!) you may find that extra care is in order for this lens: taking it off the camera between shots if the set is in the hot sun, for example (or finding an umbrella). One problem that many develop is in the iris control. The activating lever is a spring loaded cam, and sometimes the spring will be unable to close the iris back down. This is either caused by a weakened spring or a sticky iris bearing and is easily corrected, but the problem is so common it warrants mentioning here.

The front element of this zoom does not turn or even move in and out, but it is very large and requires 4 1/2 round filters (a Tiffen 83sslr 4 1/2 adapter is needed) to cover. Oddly enough, 3x3 filters are the minimum required for matte box work.

Zeiss

has made two zooms for 16mm that sound like the same lens. The old lens is called the T3, because that is it's widest T stop; the newer lens is called the T2.

Zeiss 10-100 T3

T stop range: 3.1-22
Minimum focusing distance: 39"
Filter sizes: 3x3, series 9
Tiffen adapter: 75sslr9

The optical performance of this lens is considered by some to be somewhat better than the 12-120 Angenieux, its biggest rival. It offers a few advantages: 10mm is a very handy focal length for many shots (when you're shooting in small rooms, sometimes 12mm just isn't wide enough), the front element of this lens doesn't twist when you focus so it's easier to use Polaroid filters with adapter rings rather than matte boxes, and then lens is fairly short physically. It is, however, a slow lens at T3, and like the Angenieuxs it will deliver much sharper images if you stop down and use it between T4 and T 11.

Zeiss 10-100 T2

T stop range: 2-16
Minimum focusing distance: 5' projector aperture; 3' TV safe
Filter sizes: 3x3, series 9
Tiffen adapter: 80sslr9

Everything said about the T3 is true for the T2 with these exceptions:

a) It is one of the very sharpest zoom lenses available for 16mm.
b) It has very good contrast characteristics - scenes shot with this lens seem to "pop" in clarity compared to older zooms (including the 10-100 T3), as if some kind of fuzzy membrane had been peeled away.

c) It is sharp all the way open to T2.

d) It has a useful macro function that turns the lens into a 10mm prime which focuses all the way down to its front element!

The drawbacks to this lens are: it is quite big and heavy, although virtually identical to the 9-50 Cooke and the Canon 8-64; it only focuses down to 5 feet (between 2 and 5 feet this lens vignettes on projector aperture, but not into TV safe); and it "breathes" (zooms when the focus is changed) severely.

In the past, camerapeople have chosen this lens over the 9-50 Cooke because it has a longer range of focal lengths (you can't shoot at 85 or 90mm with the Cooke) and/or because this lens is considerably faster - T2 as opposed to T2.5 People have chosen the Cooke over the Zeiss because the they are planning a shot where the severe breathing of the Zeiss will be unacceptable, or because they are going to shoot in a documentary type situation where the minimum focus of the Zeiss for projector aperture - 5' - is not close enough.

Zeiss has recently improved the 10-100 T2, however, by enlarging the front element (these newer models require an 88 sslr 4 1/2 adapter and 4 1/2 filters) so it eliminates vignetting at certain focal lengths. This enables the lens to focus down to 2' for both TV *and* projector apertures. While some users will find that the larger filter requirement is something of a drawback, others are sure to be pleased with the changes (along with other internal mechanical improvements), and the state-of-the-art 16mm zoom war may heat up.

Canon 7-56

T stop range: 2.1-22
Minimum focusing distance: less than 2'
Filter sizes: 4x4
Adapter: special 4x4 on lens holder (no Tiffen adapter available).

Wider *and* longer in range than the 9-50 Cooke, this lens is also about a half stop faster - almost as fast as the 10-100 Zeiss T2. It is considerably cheaper to purchase than either of these two lenses (but rental establishments aren't liable to pass this on to you when you rent). On top of all this, it breathes only slightly when the focus is racked, like the Cooke 9-50. It's only drawback seems to be that being a new lens, it is untested in long term ruggedness and reliability. Users report that it is very sharp and contrasty. There aren't many of these around as Canon stopped producing them when it decided to redesign the lens as the 8-64, making it more ugged and able to cover super 16.

ZOOM LENSES FOR SUPER 16

Following are a list of the most popular zoom lenses designed for super 16. If the zoom you own or are considering using is not on this list, it doesn't mean that it won't cover super 16. Most zooms for standard 16 will have a portion of their focal length range (usually from 25mm to 120mm) that will cover super 16. To find out, simply mount the zoom in question and zoom through the entire range. If you see vignetting, or circular darkening at the frame edges at certain focal lengths and/or iris settings in the viewfinder (like just after Porky Pig said "Th-That's all, folks!"), you are witnessing the lens' changing coverage range. When the vignetting begins to move into the taking area of the ground glass or fiber screen, the coverage is insufficient for the super 16 frame. All these lenses can be used for standard 16 filming.

The lenses below have been specifically engineered to give full coverage to the super 16 frame throughout their range.

Zeiss 11-110 T2.2

T stop range: 2.2 - 16
Minimum focusing distance: 1.5 meters
Adapter size: 87mm
Filter size: 4x4, 4 1/2 round
Matte box: petroff 4x4 and 4x5.650, chrosziel 4x4 and 4x5.650

This latest Zeiss offering updates the popular 10-100 for super 16. Many users will want to get this lens in the available PL mount to use on the 16SR3, the Aaton X-Prod, or Denz conversion Arri SR's. Due to its sharpness and range - all the way to 110mm - it is sure to be a favorite of those who can afford it. List price, at the time of this writing, is nearly $15,000. Breathing, or zooming slightly during focusing, is still somewhat of a problem with this lens, however. It seems to be just slightly worse in this respect than the Canon 11.5-138.

Optex conversion Zeiss 12-120 T2.4

Optex, an English firm, converts the standard 10-100 T2 to a 12-120 T2.4 for use in super 16. This may be a good deal for those who already own the lens since it may still be used for standard 16 after conversion.

Canon 8-64

T stop minimum: 2.3
Minimum focusing distance:
Filter size 4x4, 4x5.650
matte box: Canon 4x4 clip on, Petroff 4x4 and 4x5.650, Chrosziel 4x4 and 4x5.650

This lens has become the all around favorite of those shooting super 16. It breathes (zooms when focus is changed) almost not at all, is fast at T 2.3, and has the unmatched ability to gather images at 8 millimeters. Many people consider the wide angle capability of this lens to be a necessity in this day of low budgets, when set walls can't be torn apart for wide shots, or when funky wide shots are requested.

Canon 11.5-138

T stop minimum: T2.5
Minimum focusing distance:
Adapter size:
Filter size: 4 1/2 round (must be used with wide angle shade), 4x4, 4x5.650
Matte box: Canon 4x4 clip on, Petroff 4x4 and 4x5.650, Chrosziel 4x4 and 4x5.650

This very new lens is quickly catching on due to its great range - all the way to 138mm! - and excellent performance. Has some breathing, but not quite as much as the Zeiss zooms. Probably will be the new favorite for super 16 filming.

Filters

The subject of filters is fairly complex, and this complexity is compounded by the fact that different manufacturers have different "systems" and nomenclature even when describing similar products. *Tiffen* publishes information sheets and a catalogue for its filters; these can be had direct from Tiffen or at rental houses. *Harrison* has a publication called *The Mystery of Filters II* that tells all about its products. Finally, the *American Cinematographer Manual* contains an excellent section on filters and their use, and about lighting and exposure in cinematography in general (see bibliography). Although these sources of information are indispensable for anyone using filters extensively, several filters are basic to motion picture photography, and can be discussed here.

Neutral Density. These work like the lenses in sunglasses: darkened glass that cuts down the volume of light entering the lens. Unlike the lenses in sunglasses, however, they do not affect the transmission of color - that is, in addition to reducing light, they *do not* give the scene a bluish or greenish tint. They simply reduce light.

They are described this way: a Neutral Density 0.3 (called a ND 3 in movie jargon) cuts down 1/2 the light, or one F stop. A ND 0.6 cuts two stops, a 0.9 three, and a 1.2 cuts out four. You should know that it is possible to stack two or even three ND filters, so if you get a ND 0.3 and a 0.6, you actually have three filters: a ND 0.3, 0.6, and a value of 0.9 when the 0.3 and 0.6 are stacked.

What are ND filters used for? Say you are shooting outside, in the bright sun, and you've chosen a film that has an ASA of 200. You take a meter reading, and find that for your film and length of exposure (let's say it's an Arri 16S which has a 180 degree shutter, and you're going to shoot at 24 fps, so the length of exposure is 1/48th of a second) you find that you need to close the lens down to F 32! The lens you have only goes to F 22. The answer is simple: put a ND 0.6 over the lens. Since this filter cuts out 2 stops of light, the new iris setting will be F 16.

There are other, more subtle reasons for using ND filters. Imagine that you are shooting a love scene: two people, walking in a city park,

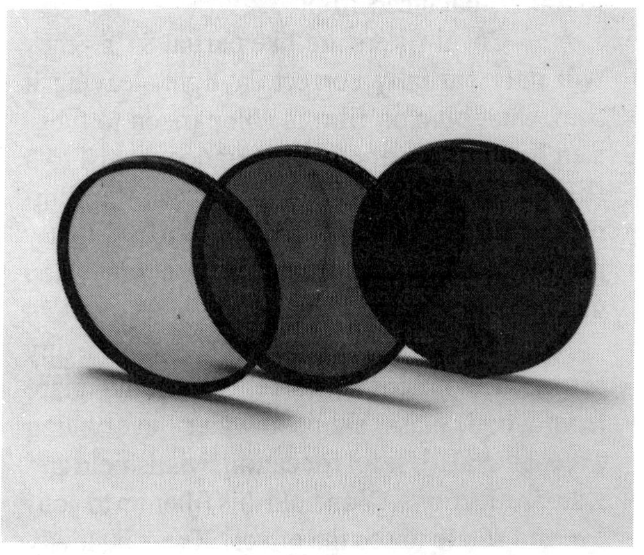

Series 9 ND Filters: 0.3, 0.6, 0.9

embrace and kiss. You've strategically placed a street performer and a hot dog vendor in the background to add color to the scene, but when you view the action through the viewfinder, you realize that a customer chewing on a hot dog with sauerkraut is just too distracting from the kiss. In fact, you're worried that people might laugh at the most important moment. The answer - aside from getting rid of your background people - is to use a ND filter. If you took a reading of the scene with a light meter, and found that F 11 was indicated, your depth of field would be too great, and the background would be in focus. But by placing a ND 0.6 over the lens, you could shoot an F 5.6, shrinking the depth of field, throwing the hot dog vendor and customer and the street performer out of focus, and directing the audience's attention to the kiss.

Neutral Density filters are often used to maintain a given F stop for an entire production so that the look of the film (as it is affected by the iris) will be continuous.

85. This is an orange filter used to convert daylight to tungsten. Color negative film stocks are (for the most part) balanced for light that is 3200 degrees Kelvin. Daylight is about 5600 degrees Kelvin (during midday) and is much bluer. The 85 filter "warms up" the daylight and enables you to shoot using tungsten (3200 K) balanced film.

Coral filters are like partial 85's - they will only partially correct daylight, leaving it somewhat blue on film in comparison to tungsten light. They are usually graded from 1 to 5 (light to heavy) and are useful when the filmmaker wants to let daylight be seen as slightly blue or when shooting at sunrise or sunset when daylight is closer to tungsten.

Polarizing. This filter is like a tiny screen which eliminates reflection and glare from wood, glass, skin and water - everything except metal. Useful for cutting windshield and water reflections. You hold this filter up to your eye and rotate to see the effect. Twist it slowly until you see glare disappear. Any degree of rotation may be used for light or heavy glare reduction - or you can rotate the filter *during* a shot to reveal something behind reflections. This filter also works as a Neutral Density filter because it cuts approximately 2 stops but doesn't affect color.

Close-up. Listed in the Lenses chapter of this book are the minimum focusing distances for most 16mm lenses. If you want to reduce this distance - get the subject closer to the film plane - you have several options. You can close the iris down three or four stops to increase depth of field, but chances are that this won't be very acceptable because you'll probably have to drastically alter your lighting set up. You can loosen the lens from its mount and move it out slightly toward the subject, but this is risky because a) the lens mount may leak light to the film, b) the lens is in danger of falling out or moving during the shot, and c) the footage marks on the lens will be inaccurate - you'll be forced to go by the image on the ground glass. The last way is the best: use a close-up filter.

These are actually not filters, but lenses of varying power that fit into adapter rings (just like filters) and reduce the minimum focusing distance. Although the use of a CU filter also renders the footage scale of the lens meaningless, the lens stays securely in the mount. CU filters come in values of +1/2, +1, +2, and +3. A CU +1 filter over an Angenieux 12-120 lens, for example, will reduce the minimum focus distance from five to about three feet. A CU +2 will reduce it further to about 2 feet. The CU +3 is perhaps too strong; it will degrade the image somewhat. You can stack these filters by putting the stronger values on the lens last (the convex side of the filter faces the subject). Although they're only widely available in Series 9 and 4 1/2 round, 3x3 square CU filters do exist.

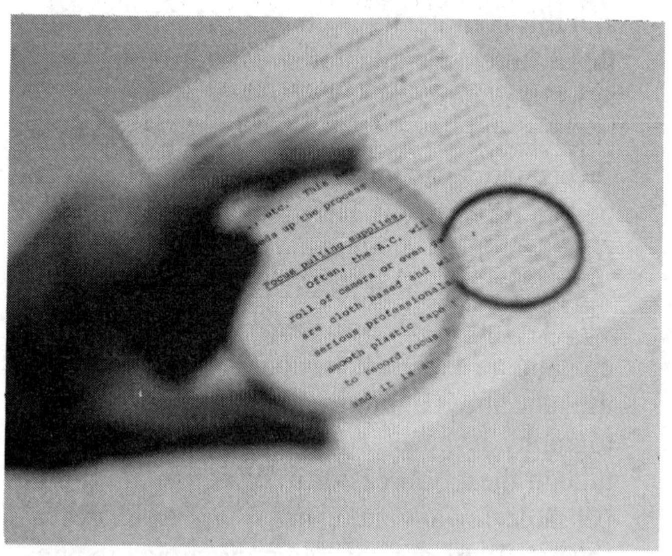

Series 9 CU +1 Filter

3x4 Graduated. These rectangular filters are half clear and half 85, or Neutral Density, etc. Example: 3x4 ND 0.6 grad - this filter would be useful for darkening only the sky or perhaps a bright building, but not the rest of the scene. The cameraperson can mount this filter into an Arri 16SR matte box slide (which will accommodate both 3x3 and 3x4 filters), then slide *and* rotate the filter until the dividing line between the ND 0.6 and clear areas is positioned correctly (on the horizon, or at the edge of the building, to continue with the examples).

Some filters of this type have a hard transition between one half and the other, while others are graduated, or change value slowly. Soft denotes a slow change, hard a quick one. For example, a 3x4 red with a soft grad means that the filter is red and uses the entire length of the 4" dimension to change from red to clear. A 3x4 red with a hard grad is one that has a distinct change from red to clear in the *center* of the filter.

These filters are usually quite costly, both to rent and to own. You may find that inexpensive **filter gels** can be substituted. Gels are made of thin plastic that can be cut with scissors to match the dividing line in a given shot, and its close proximity to the lens when it is placed in the matte box will throw it into soft focus and effectively "graduate" the change from the filtered and unfiltered side of the frame.

There are other filters that can accomplish the same effects (and probably some wilder ones too) than expensive glass filters from Tiffen or Harrison. These are the *plastic filters* which are manufactured and sold for use in 35mm still photography. They're inexpensive, optically excellent, and readily available. Their main drawback is their vulnerability to damage; the soft plastic used in their construction is easily scratched. With extra care, however, they can be the solution to the expensive filter dilemma.

Effect filters. Test the following by holding them up to your eye and by *shooting film tests* before the actual production.

Low Contrast filters are made of clear glass which has very slight surface irregularity and makes the overall image less contrasty. Other Low Cons are made of black or white mesh fabric (like nylon stocking material) or have tiny black dots embedded in the glass.

Fog - glass filters that give the scene a hazy or foggy look and flare lights and bright spots. They're usually graded from 1/2 to 5 (5 is heaviest) and they can create a very convincing fog atmosphere.

Double Fog. A combination of Low Con and Fog, these can produce heavy fog effects but with less loss of detail than using the number 4 or 5 Fogs.

There are many more filters (including effect) than mentioned above - again, consult the manufacturers publications and the Cinematographer Manual.

You can also make your own filters - here are some ideas:

Low Con - nylon stocking material makes excellent low contrast effects. Take a coat hanger, bend it into the shape of the filter desired (round for series 9, square for 3x3, etc.), then stretch the net material over a board or table. You can then glue or sew the net to the wire shape. Other people cut out cardboard rings or squares and then simply staple the nets to them. Try sheer black net for a slight lowering of contrast; double it for greater effect. White net will flare lights and gives a light haze to the scene; other colors can be used for wilder results. Remember that wide shots will need less lowering of contrast (as perceived sharpness is less) than medium and close-ups. You can make an entire set of nets (from very light to extra heavy, in all sorts of colors) that will cover all your needs for very little cash, and the results are every bit as good as those that can be had from expensive glass filters - plus, you can create your own unique effects, and always have your set of filters with you in case you have to match a shot from one shooting period to the next.

Star - these filters have small lines etched in them that diffract light and give highlights in the scene starbursts. You'll see this effect most often in schmaltzy game shows, beauty pageants and sporting events (like pro wrestling) on TV. Producers think this effect adds glamour (or something) to their shows. You can rent these filters, and they are described in to ways: by number of points, and in millimeters. For example, you might ask for a 6 point, 3mm star filter in series 9. This means there are three sets of parallel lines etched in the glass, and the lines are spaced at 3mm intervals. When these lines intersect, they form stars which have 6 points. The more points, and the closer they are to each other, the more stars there are in the grid, and the softer and more diffused the overall image will be, since the glass filter is, in effect, scratched up more. Wide angle lenses with their irises closed down will often have sufficient depth of field to see the lines in the filter, so be careful.

To make a complicated star filter like the one mentioned above would be very difficult, but you can make a filter that has one or two stars by buying a piece of clear acrylic plastic and using a sharp knife or razor blade and a straight edge to scratch it. You can then place this single star in exactly the right part of your scene to get the desired effect.

Color Filters - Exact color filters, such as an 85 or Red number 6 can only be had by purchasing them from manufacturers like Tiffen, Harrison or Kodak. But if you want to experiment with unusual colors, try your local plastics store. These shops usually sell special purpose plastics and laminates such as Lexan and ABS, but the majority of their business is selling clear and colored acrylic and acrylic related products. Most of the time, you'll find a scrap bin filled with all sorts of colored acrylic pieces that can be turned into filters simply by sawing them into shape. This technique can be especially interesting when used in making color filters for use in black and white photography, or when trying for weird, otherworldly sci-fi effects (either dramatic or comedic) in color shooting.

Fog - A piece of clear acrylic sanded with very fine sandpaper (600 grit) on one side will give you a strong fog effect. This can then be reduced by polishing it back with a rubbing and/or polishing compound (not wax or cleaner) made for auto finishes. An entire set of fogs from light to very strong can be made in this way. You can also get excellent effects by smearing petroleum jelly (Vaseline) onto a clear filter (NOT onto the lens!) A heavy layer can be wiped around the perimeter of the filter, leaving the center clear, giving a "dream" effect to the shot.

When using fog filters in 16mm, keep this in mind: since the format is much smaller than 35mm it is very intolerant of effects like low contrast and fog that degrade the image. If you plan to use fog, use a lot of it - enough so that viewers understand that it was intentional. A light fog or low contrast effect makes people think you were just too dumb to focus your lens properly!

Last but certainly not least, check out the high quality, inexpensive glass filters made for still photography. Many motion picture camera people are discouraged to find that still photo stores don't stock series 9 or 4 1/2 round. But they often stock 3x3 or 3x4 (as mentioned above) and many effect filters can be simply taped over lenses when they don't fit exactly.

Mounting

The easiest and least expensive way to mount a filter for photography is to simply attach it to the front of the lens with an **adapter ring**. This is a machined aluminum ring that either slips or screws on to the front of the lens and holds a round filter. This adapter will permit the use of a sunshade as well. The most common in 16mm are made by Tiffen, and hold **series 9 filters**. This filter is just slightly over 3 inches in diameter and is used to cover larger primes and almost all 16mm zoom lenses.

A Tiffen 72m9 adapter, for example, has 72mm threads which screw into the lens (Angenieux 12-120, 10-150) on one side, and a space which will hold a series 9 filter on the other. A **retaining ring** screws into the adapter and locks the filter into place, and provides another space in itself for a series 9 filter, or a sunshade. By stacking retaining rings one after another, multiple filters can be used - an 85 and a Polarizing, for example. A sunshade also provides a space to hold a filter, and can be screwed either into a retaining ring, or into the adapter itself.

The advantages to filtering with adapter rings are many: they are lightweight and compact, both on the lens and in the camera case or

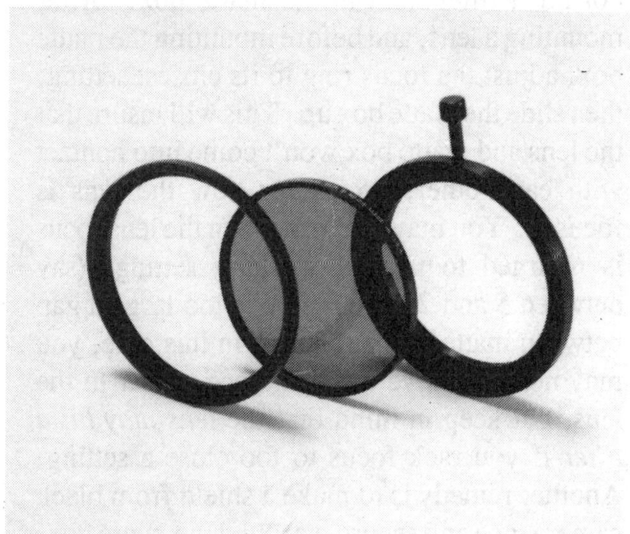

Series 9 Retaining Ring, Series 9 Filter, 72m9 Adapter

bag, and the cost is quite reasonable - an adapter, two retaining rings and a collapsible rubber sunshade from Tiffen costs as little as $75. If you are renting a zoom lens, the rental establishment will usually include the appropriate adapter, one retaining ring and a sunshade in the deal. The entire unit - adapter, retaining ring and shade - can be rotated as a whole by loosening it from the lens to allow for Polarizing functions.

The disadvantages are also many: changing filters is usually slow and tedious, since the threads on the various parts are small and easily cross-threaded (screwed together incorrectly), especially in cold weather when fingers get numb. This problem can be minimized greatly by using the slip on type of adapters (denoted by the letters "lr" in the Tiffen nomenclature, as in 80sslr9) and buying several adapter/sunshade combinations and pre-loading different filters for quick change - but all this tends to get costly, and bulky. Also, only certain zooms - the 9-50 Cooke and 10-100 Zeiss T2 and T3 - have slip on filter rings available for them by Tiffen.

Effect filters such as 3/4 grads can't be used with adapter rings, and since the entire filter set up will rotate if the front of the lens you happen to use rotates when focusing (most of them do), it can be difficult if not impossible to maintain a Polarizing effect when pulling focus during a shot.

Finally, you'll find it impossible to get adapter rings for many small primes - in this situation you'll be forced to use a matte box, or, for simple one time shots, taping a gel or glass filter directly onto the lens.

The **matte box** is the second way of holding filters, and it offers these advantages: filters are mounted in slides that are easily positioned in the matte box, and these can be pre-loaded beforehand for quick changes dur-

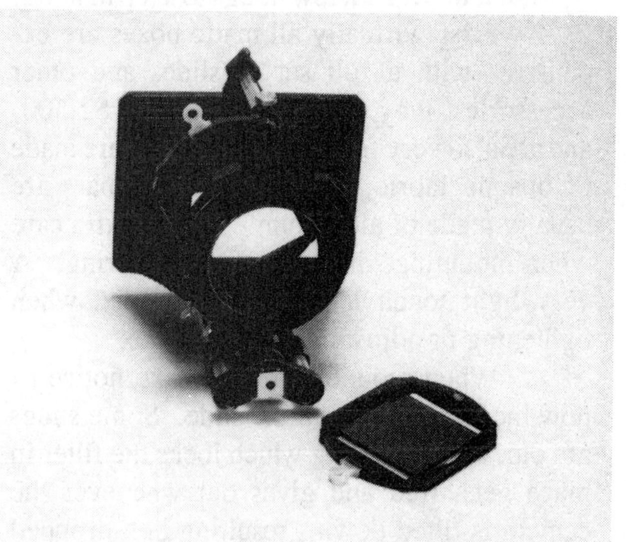

Arri 16SR 3x3 Matte Box and Slide

ing the shoot; effect slides such as Polarizing and 3x4s can be rotated and slid back and forth (or up and down) independent of lens focusing; and the matte box itself offers increased protection against the effects of light hitting the lens and producing flair or "fog".

To expose film, light must enter the lens, of course, but if strong light from an unwanted source - a grid mounted backlight, or sunshine, for example - strikes the front element of the lens directly, the result will often be a fogging, or dulling of the image. If the light is strong enough, it will cause the lens to flair -

bright spots of light (usually shaped like the iris of the lens) will appear on the film. By carefully adjusting the bellows portion of the matte box until no direct light (only light reflected from the scene) strikes the lens, these effects can be reduced, and often eliminated.

Conversely, the effect of flair is sometimes desired as an enhancement to the beauty or drama of the scene. This is often the case in documentaries (where it also adds realism or verite to the shot) and in music videos. You'll find many cinematographers and directors who are staunchly against this effect, saying it is an error similar to wind noise in a microphone, but others like it, and won't hesitate to use it if they feel it is appropriate.

Using a matte box is fairly straightforward, but there are a few things to keep in mind.

First, virtually all matte boxes are expensive (with a full set of slides and other accessories, they can cost upwards of $2,500) and are also very fragile. The bellows are made of opaque fabric, and the rods and bars are usually made of aluminum - so take extra care when mounting, dismounting and storing. A very light touch is all that is needed when tightening or adjusting any matte box.

When mounting filters, take notice of how the filter is held in the slide. Some slides are old, and the spring which locks the filter in place gets tired and gives out whenever the camera is tilted down - resulting in a dropped and probably damaged filter. Test the holder after the filter is in place by shaking it over a changing bag or jacket. If the filter pops out of the holder, secure it with a small piece of tape. The best time to clean a filter is *after* it is in the slide, since it's often impossible to mount a filter without leaving dirt and fingerprints on it.

Another type of ring - usually referred to as a donut - is needed to eliminate **kickback.** This is a problem that develops when light enters the rear of the matte box, strikes the filter inside, and gives a fog effect to the image. To keep this from happening, the outside edge of the front of the lens must be snug with the rear of the matte box, and since lenses vary greatly in diameter, **donuts** made of plastic, or sometimes of foam, are used to fill the gap.

Since the front element of almost all lenses will move away from the film plane (toward the matte box) when focusing on near subjects, care must be taken so that the lens does not hit a filter held in the matte box. After mounting a lens, and before mounting the matte box, adjust the focus ring to its closest setting, then slide the matte box up. This will insure that the lens and matte box won't come into contact with each other, no matter how the lens is focused. You may find that when the lens focus is returned to normal working settings (say between 5 and 20 feet) there is too large a gap between matte box and lens - in this case, you may need to move the matte box closer to the lens, but keep in mind that the *lens may hit a filter* if you rack focus to too close a setting. Another remedy is to make a shield from black camera tape and secure it around the matte box, or cut out your own custom donuts from scrap foam.

The disadvantages of matte boxes have been touched upon somewhat: their expense (they often cost extra to rent) and fragile nature. You'll also find that they can be hazardous when shooting in crowds under documentary situations. It's easy for the operator to bang into someone (or something) when moving and shooting in heavy crowds, and an adapter ring and rubber sunshade is much less vulnerable than a bulky matte box and rod set-up. Also, some cameras (Cinema Products CP/R and Frezzolini) have no matte boxes readily available. These require the cameraperson to rent an Arri matte box and sliding base plate.

The last way to filter your shots is to use a **behind the lens filter**; that is, a filter that you either mount onto the back of the lens or slide into the camera between the lens and the film plane. Since there is usually very little space between lens and film plane, **gels** must be used. These are made of thin (approximately .10 mm) flexible plastic (gelatin).

A CP 16R, for example, has a small metal slide - just slightly larger than a frame of

16mm film - which holds a gel and fits into a slot behind the lens of the camera. Gels are usually sold in 3x3 size and provided with special paper that protects them on both sides when they are cut into small pieces (with scissors) to fit the slide in question. Other cameras that have behind the lens filter slides are Eclair ACL, Bolex, Bell and Howell Filmo, Frezzolini, and early Arriflex 16SR I cameras (discontinued on later 16SR models, the slides themselves are extremely hard to find).

The advantages to filtering this way are many:

A) Gels are inexpensive. If you call around and price the rental of a set of 138mm round filters for a large zoom or telephoto, you'll soon see the benefit of simply buying the same set in 3x3 gels.

B) This same set of gels is, of course, far more compact and lightweight than the 138mm set (or series 9 and 3x3 glass filters, for that matter) and this could be quite important if you need to travel light.

C) If you are using a very dark filter, such as a ND 0.9, you'll be spared the trouble of trying to focus and frame through it because the filter is not in the path of the viewing system - it only affects the light just before it strikes the film.

The disadvantages to using behind the lens gel filters are:

A) You can't see the effect of the filter during the shot. As previously said, the filter sits just in front of the film plane, behind the lens, so that the light path of the reflex viewing system (usually incorporating a rotating mirror shutter) of the motion picture camera does not pass through the filter. For standard filters such as 85 and Neutral Density this is not important. But if you want to see the effect of a fog, low contrast or other effect filter, you have to pull the filter slide before the shot and preview the scene through it. Polarizing filters must be rotated until the desired effect is achieved - something that is very difficult to do because you have to keep pulling and inserting the behind the lens slide over and over again. For revelation shots with Polarizing filtration *during* a take (the filter is rotated, cutting the glare from a car window and revealing the antagonist, for example), the technique of behind the lens filtering is useless.

B) Gels are very fragile. Since they're made of soft plastic, they can be easily scratched or bent to the point of unusability. Although many small pieces may be cut to fit a behind the lens slide from just one 3x3 gel, extra care must be taken when handling them.

C) They can quickly degrade and/or ruin your image if they get dirty. Behind the lens gels sit right in front of the film plane, so the tiniest speck of dust will show up as a fairly well focused shadow on your film. Being plastic, they also attract dust, so you have to continuously check them. A blower brush and a can of air can help, but gels are very easy to damage in cleaning - it's usually best to toss a dirty gel and cut another.

D) They change the optical flange/focal distance by one-third their thickness. Bad news. What this means is that they are going to affect your focus, and in the worst way possible: what you see through your viewfinder is *not* what you are going to get on film.

If the average gel is .10 mm thick, and the refractive quality of the plastic alters the flange/focal distance by one third of this, you can count on an appreciable focus shift when using lenses wider than 25mm (in 16mm photography).

To see how this was arrived at, take a look at the chart below. It displays the **depth of focus** of lenses from 10 to 100 mm at F2. The area between the dotted lines represents acceptably sharp focus. At 25mm, for example, there is enough depth of focus so that even if the film plane was moved by .03mm from the ideal (.00mm) the image would still be sharp at F2. At F4 and 25mm, the image could be as much as .05mm away from the ideal. Because a .10mm gel will optically change the flange focal distance by about 1/3 its thickness (.03mm), only lenses longer than 25mm will have sufficient depth of focus - at F2 - to enable the use of behind the lens filter gels.

If you use a behind the lens filter for shorter lenses, both the ground glass (because it doesn't "see" the filter) and the footage marks on the lens (because these were set for a flange/ focal distance *not* altered by a gel) will be unreliable when focusing the camera. If you are shooting with lenses longer than 25mm, how-

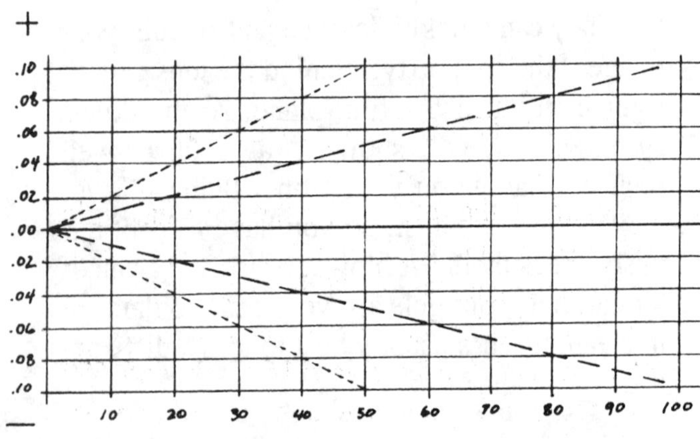

– – – – – F2 -------- F4

FOCAL LENGTH IN MM

ever, or if you can close down the iris for a particular shot (using the chart in as your guide), behind the lens filter gels are certainly viable.

E) Neutral Density gels are made in such a way as to seriously affect the sharpness of the image when used behind the lens. The darkening material is carbon black, rather than the dye used in optical glass filters, and this will affect the image (source: Richter Cine Equipment - see Resource List).

Filter Mounting Summary

Use an adapter ring/retainer ring/sunshade set up when simple filtering is needed, where a matte box is not provided for in the budget, and in situations where a matte box is too bulky or cumbersome. A large, fragile matte box with its protruding rods can be a real problem when shooting in crowds - at a parade, or a rowdy party or other event.

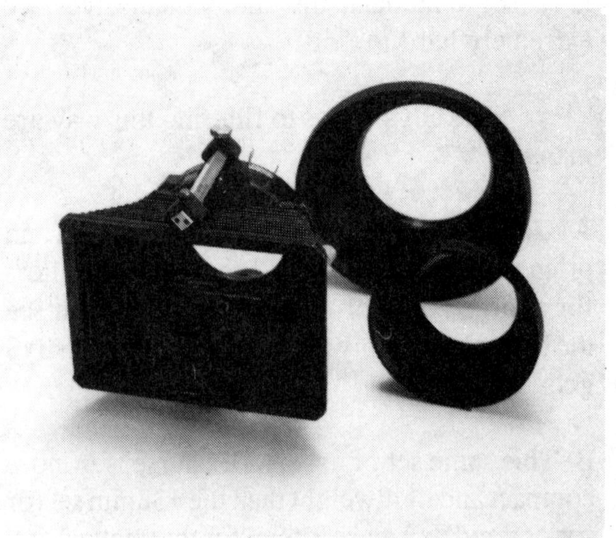

Arri 3x3 Matte Box, 4 1/2 Shade, Ser. 9 Shade

Use a matte box for complex filtering jobs - graduated filters, rotating Polaroids, etc., and when speed in changing filters is essential.

Use behind the lens gels for filtering lenses that are difficult to front-filter: large telephoto primes - or for situations where the density of the filter will make viewing difficult (remember, only the film "sees" the filter - you don't). Don't use behind the lens filters for lenses wider than 25mm at wide iris settings.

Sizes of in front of the lens filters:

Square and Rectangular Filters necessitate the use of the appropriate matte box (but in emergency situations, they can be carefully taped to the front of the lens).

2x2 - these are square filters with a measurement of 2" by 2". They'll cover the front element of small primes only; zooms and many wide angle lenses will require larger filters. The Arri 16S and Eclair NPR matte boxes hold this size of filter, and interestingly enough, both matte boxes are functionally identical, and both use the same exact type of filter holder (also called a filter slide).

3x3 - 3" by 3" square, these filters cover wide angle primes, such as the Zeiss 9.5mm and 12mm superspeed, and also most 16mm zooms.

3x4 - 3" by 4", these rectangular filters are usually either slowly graduated, or half and half with a hard transition (a graduated ND 0.6, for example, would be half ND 0.6 and half clear.

4x4 - 4" by 4", these filters are used to cover larger zooms and primes.

4x5.650 - 4" by 5.650", this size is also referred to as Panavision size. Most often used in 16mm for coverage of zoom lenses principally designed for super 16.

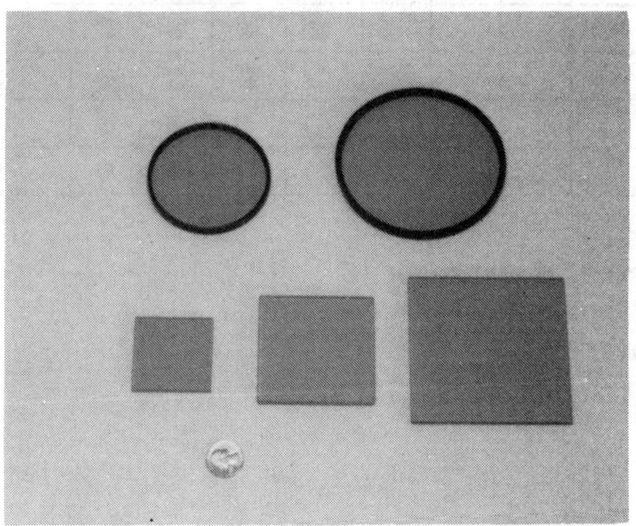

Clockwise From Top Left: Series 9, 4 1/2 Round, 4x4, 3x3, and 2z2 Filters

6.6x6.6 - 6.6" by 6.6", this size is used principally in 35mm, but many large telephotos used in 16mm will require this size if they cannot be rear-filtered via built in filter slots.

Round filters are generally mounted between a adapter and retainer ring (or between the adapter and sunshade) that attaches to the front of the lens.

Series 9 - about 78mm in diameter, or 3 inches. This is the standard filter size for most adapter/retainer ring set ups. Lenses will small diameter front elements are "stepped up" to Series 9 with the adapter so that many different lenses can work with the same set of Series 9 filters.

4 1/2 - about 114mm in diameter, or 4 1/2 inches, these filters are used to cover lenses like the 9-50 Cooke which have front elements too large for Series 9.

138mm - Very large round filters for covering lenses like the Angenieux 25-250 which are normally used in 35mm photography but also work in 16mm.

FILTERS FOR SUPER 16

The chart on the following page, painstakingly compiled by Ian McCausland at Abel Cinetech, tells which matte box or filter holder will cover the lenses indicated. It would seem that for future super 16 and standard 16 work, 4x5.650 may become the new standard, since it covers all but the most wide-angle lenses.

	11.5-138 Canon	11.5-138 Angenieux	8-64 Canon	12-120 Zeiss	5.9 Ang.	Zeiss Primes: 8	9.5	12	16	25	50
Chrosziel 6.6x6.6 Matte Box	●	●	●	●			●	●	●	●	●
Chrosziel 4x5.650 Matte Box	●	●	●	●			●	●	●	●	●
Chrosziel 4x4 Matte Box				●		○	●	●	●	●	●
Chros. 4x4 Video Matte Box				●		○	●	●	●	●	●
Chros. 4x4 Clamp On Matte Box	●		●			○	●	○	●	●	●
Chros. 4x4 Clamp On Shade	●					○	●	●	●		
Canon 4x4 Clamp On Matte Box	●		●							●	
Petroff 4x4 Matte Box						○	●	●	●	●	
4 1/2 Round + Wide Angle Shade		○	○			○	●	●	●	●	
4 1/2 Round + Univ. Shade		○	○				○	●	●	●	
Ser. 9 + Wide Angle Shade							○	●	●	●	
Ser. 9 + Univ. Shade							○	●	●	●	

● - will cover standard and super 16

○ - will cover standard 16 only

blank - does not cover

Accessories

Viewfinders

16mm motion picture cameras come with one viewfinder or eyepiece standard. But how a specific finder will function varies from camera to camera because all viewfinders are not created equal.

Fixed viewfinders are the simplest of the lot. They are usually attached to the rear of the camera (the 16S is a good example) but if they're mounted nearer the lens they can make the camera easier to hand hold because the operator can rest a large part of the weight of the machine on his or her shoulder when shooting. This kind of finder does not swivel or flip or rotate but it may be possible to attach a **periscope finder** to it. Arriflex makes this device for use on the Arri 16S and 16SB (and some of their 35mm cameras as well) and it rotates so that, for example, you don't have to lay down on the floor to look through the camera for a low shot. The main problem with this accessory is that as the operator rotates the finder, the ground glass image rotates as well, so if you look straight down into the eyepiece you see the scene sideways! It takes quite a bit of concentration and practice to use the periscope finder for anything other than locked-off or simple pan shots.

Rotatable finders work just like fixed ones with the periscope function built in - they rotate to allow the operator to find a more comfortable shooting position. Some can also swivel towards or away from the camera (examples: Kinoptik finder for the NPR and the standard finder for the 16BL) - this can be helpful to left-eyed operators and directors. Like a fixed finder with a periscope attachment, the image will rotate when the finder rotates.

Orientable finders rotate, but the image stays upright! Once you start using a camera with one, you won't want to go back, because you'll never even think about compromising operator comfort for camera position - you won't have to. If the camera is low or high, it doesn't matter - you just flip the finder to the most comfortable viewing position and shoot.

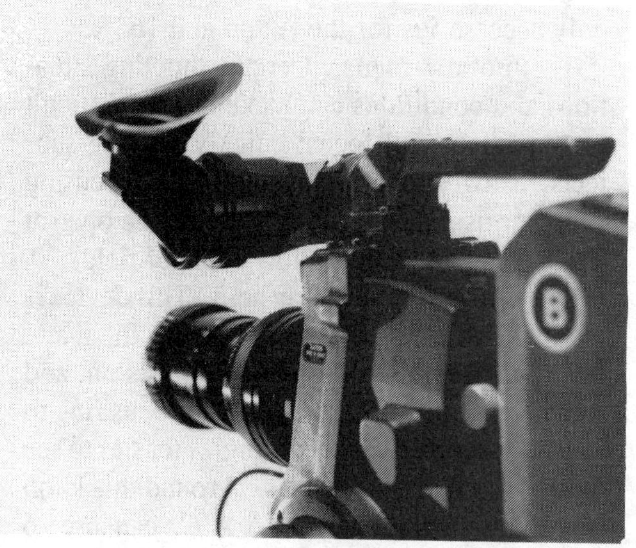

Aaton LTR Orientable Finder

Sometimes, the camera will have to be very high or very low in relation to the operator for long periods of time; high over-the-shoulder shots with the actors standing and knee level low shots are examples of this, and often the camera operator will ask for a **viewfinder extension**. This is used in conjunction with an orientable finder only, and makes operation in these situations easier because the eyepiece can be swung up or down through a much larger range.

The Arri 16BL has a unique accessory available called the **offset finder**. This is an optical elbow of sorts that moves the eyepiece up and forward so that the camera can move down and backward, and rest (partially) on the operator's shoulder for easier hand-holding.

Can you ask for an orientable finder for your rental camera? Well, if it's an Aaton or and Arri 16SR, you won't have to ask; orientable finders are standard on these cameras. The Eclair NPR, Cinema Products CP/R and Frezzi FR - 16 all have the capability of using, oddly enough, the exact same orientable finder, made by Angenieux. In addition, Cinema Products made a really good orientable finder for the CP and GSMO which folds *over itself* and puts the camera in better on-the-shoulder balance (Angenieux also redesigned their finder to work like this). It will also fit the NPR and Frezzi, but you'll have a hard time finding one - remember, almost all rental establishments have only accessories for the Aaton and 16SR.

Follow-focus. Certain shooting situations and conditions can make it very difficult to accurately pull focus: quickly moving subjects, using prime lenses with small focusing rings, or using superspeed primes wide open at T 1.3 (resulting in a shallow depth of field). A follow-focus accessory can help. This device is mounted on the same accessory rods the matte box (and possibly a zoom motor) rests on, and it transfers the motion of the small focus ring to a large knob placed at right angles (easier to see during shooting) to the lens. Around this knob is a larger white flange the A.C. can use to record individual footage marks with a grease pencil or *non*-indelible marker.

There are just two models in wide use for 16mm: Chroisziel and Arri. Both fit the 16SR double rods. The Chroisziel uses a continuous cable and ring/stud activator while the Arri is a gear drive set up. Either can be used on the Aaton or 16SR; a special version of the 16SR double support rods made by Chroisziel must be employed on the Aaton. Cinema Products made, at one time, a follow-focus unit for their 16mm cameras, but you will be hard pressed to find one at any rental house.

Do you need a follow-focus? Unless you are using small primes, superspeeds or the movement of your subjects will be fast and hard to follow, you really don't. Most zooms have very large focus rings to begin with, and these are very easy to tape, mark, and pull. In addition, the follow focus/support rod combination costs a fair amount of money to rent, and it slows down the changing of lenses (and therefore any hairchecks you need to do) considerably.

Zoom motors. When you need to have an ultra slow and/or ultra smooth zoom during a shot, you need a zoom motor. Many zoom activator rings are damped with a fair amount of grease, and there are **fluid zoom** drives made for many popular zoom lenses that operate like tiny fluid heads for the lens, and many camerapeople are quite skilled at making use of these to produce smooth manual zooms, but nothing will replace the results possible with a zoom motor.

There are several on the market. The most popular are Cinema Products J series (Numbers 4, 5, and 6) and the Micro Force zoom motor. Arri also makes a zoom for the 16SR, but it is not adaptable to other cameras as are the CP and Micro Force. The actual driving motor can be mounted on the lens itself (J5 and Micro Force) or swung from an Arri sliding base plate via a special arm (CP J4). The motor is controlled by a lever or trigger that moves it forward or reverse, and by a knob that controls the actual speed of the zoom. In addition, newer zoom drives have special circuitry that will quickly return the zoom ring on the lens back to a chosen starting point. This can be a real time saver when practicing long, slow zooms before a take.

Zoom motors have drawbacks, however, when compared to using fluid drives or zooming manually. They're bulky, expensive to rent, and may be difficult to mount to your camera if it isn't an Aaton or 16SR. The control unit often has to be gaffer taped or clamped to the pan arm of the tripod, and although some will draw power from the camera's 12V source, others have their own battery unit which requires extra charging and testing. Chances are the only time you *must* use a zoom motor is when you are shooting a product shot (cornflakes, shampoo, etc.) where the camera is locked off and nothing else is moving in the frame, and for very long, slow zooms. Fast zooms and ones that follow people and objects are usually easier and faster when done by hand.

Video Taps are available for the 16SR, Aaton, GSMO and later model CP/R cameras.

Once again, you'll probably only find taps for the 16SR and Aaton in stock at rental houses.

The 16SR tap configuration uses a fairly large Phillips video camera and a T shaped accessory viewfinder that replaces the standard elbow and negates the flipover function (the finder remains fully orientable, however). It is quite time consuming and somewhat complicated to install the tap and finder because a small ring which many people think is knurled (meant to be screwed and unscrewed by hand) is actually a gear that engages a small worm gear shaft and locking ring arrangement in the side of the camera. A hex wrench and special Arri tool are needed here. The Aaton tap is much smaller and quicker to install in its built in accessory port on the right side of the camera.

Both these taps require 12 vdc power, and it is wise to get separate block batteries or belts to run them (or 120 VAC battery eliminators where AC is available) as they require a large amount of power. Monitors of various sizes are available, and takes can be recorded on VCRs and played back on larger monitors for review. The image is poor quality, though: black and white with flicker (at 24 fps) and fiber optic screen markings. Better color cameras are becoming available, but for most people, the black and white tap cameras deliver satisfactory results, since the images are only used in production - not in the final product.

Video taps can be very useful. For example, when shooting in a moving car, the director can crouch down in the back seat with the monitor and judge the performance without being seen in the shot. Several people can watch a take at once: art directors, producers and, of course, the director, and everyone can see exactly what is happening - no surprises when the dailies are screened the next evening. The instant image is a good reference of communication for the entire crew.

But video taps also have many drawbacks. They actually can cost more to rent than the camera and lenses once all the accessories (batteries, monitors, cables) are included in the bill. They add bulk and immobilizing cables and wires to the camera rig, and another crewperson will be necessary if playback (with a VCR) is needed. They slow down the entire shoot - everyone wants to stop and look at the take, which has to be rewound and cued on the VCR. They are also somewhat problematic, so a qualified video operator is required to hook up and operate the system. Lastly, they take everyone's attention from what is happening in the actual scene and place it on a (usually) small, poor quality video image.

Once you've shot a film and finished it, you'll know how an actor or set will look when their images are transferred to film simply by looking at them - not at a video monitor. You'll know whether a performance is working or not, and if it isn't, you'll need to change it by talking to the performer, not the video screen. If you do talk to the talent while looking at the monitor, you've removed yourself from the scene and the real possibilities involved - and you've distanced yourself from the performers themselves. The tap can become an encumbrance rather than a creative tool.

Chances are, you'll only consider using a video tap for difficult shots or when clients expect or demand one. In this last case, put a nice large monitor and sound feed into a comfortable room away from the set, and man it with someone who's only job is to keep the clients happy, and *away from the action.* You'll be able to get done the work you've been paid to do with less interruption, and the client will feel important - this is where the video tap shines.

French flag. This is a device that can be used with a matte box or an adapter and shade, or all by itself. The arm is bent or adjusted so that the flag keeps stray light from hitting the lens, just like the matte box or sun shade. Unlike these, however, the flag can be placed to block light from a specific angle only, and does not interfere with mounting or dismounting of the lens or filter changing.

Until recently, most french flags were of a single type: a heavy, ball and socket arm attached with a crude screw clamp on one end and a wing nut affair on the other for securing the flag. These units seem rugged in and of themselves, but they have serious drawbacks. The worst is that the crude screw clamp gouges camera handles and eventually falls off. For

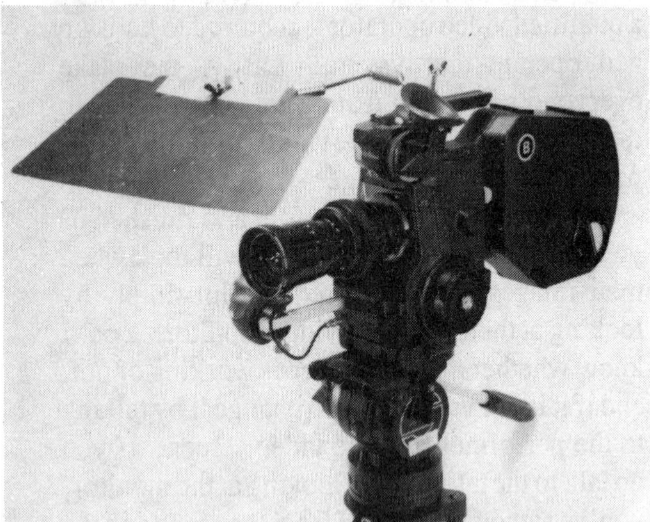

Aaton With Old Type French Flag

years, A.C.s wrapped the handles with camera tape, but this was a poor solution as the clamp loosened and fell off. Some had special adapters made, but the chief problem with this design is in the clamp itself.

Media Logic has introduced a better, and lighter french flag. The Logic Flag has a segmented plastic arm that pops apart and can be lengthened or shortened as needed by adding or subtracting segments. The arm is secured to an anodized aluminum mounting block that uses a 3/8-16 mounting screw to secure the whole affair neatly and easily to camera handles. The flag itself is made of an ultra light expanded black plastic.

The Logic Flag's only drawback is that the arm can move if you plan on really jerking the camera around, such as when running with the camera or during whip pans. In these situations, it's best to shorten the arm up, or pop the flag off. But what's great about the Logic Flag is that it has no "creep". Once its set, it won't slowly droop into the shot. The arm itself sees to this, and the flag can be moved around with the slightest touch.

Speed Controls:

See the Speeds and Angles chapter.

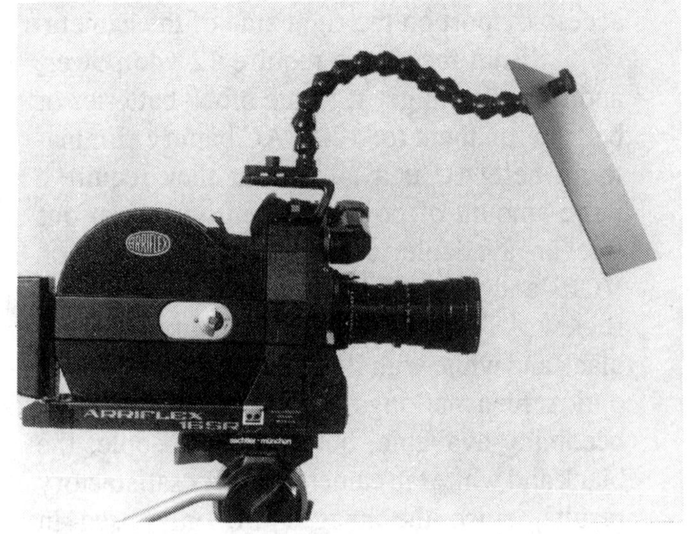

The Logic Flag From Media Logic

Tripods and Dollies

Tripods for motion picture cameras consist of three main parts: the head, the legs, and the spreader (also called the triangle).

The **head** is the heart of the tripod; it holds the camera securely and provides the essential camera movements of panning and tilting. These two motions are performed by completely separate mechanisms, each with its own **lock**. These locks are useful when you need to insure that the camera won't move - for instance, during a long telephoto shot, or for performing a registration test. The tilt lock has another important function: it keeps the camera from falling (tilting) when the tripod is unattended. Although tripods vary considerably in design, the tilt lock is almost always engaged by a small lever, and this is the very first thing to locate on an unfamiliar tripod. If you mount the camera and forget to secure the tilt lock fully, then walk away to move a case, or set a light, chances are that the camera will slowly tilt forward (zoom lenses usually make the camera front heavy) until the lens hits a tripod leg. At this point, the rig is almost always so front heavy that the entire tripod will come crashing to the floor, lens first. With a camera such as a 16SR or Aaton, this would invariably result in many thousands of dollars damage, and perhaps a completely destroyed lens. An Eclair NPR with its fragile body casting would likely be totalled. Make sure this doesn't happen to you: check the tilt lock and make it secure.

There are essentially three different types of tripod heads, and each category refers to how the pan and tilt movements are controlled mechanically. The first is a **friction head**, and this is the crudest and least desireable of the three. These heads attempt to smooth the pan and tilt motions by simple friction levers (usually located next to the pan and tilt locks, and often confused with them) that, once engaged, drag against an internal ring or flange. For all intents and purposes, this doesn't work. The resulting "smoothing" of motion actually results in a stiff, jerky binding that is completely unusable for anything except purposely poor pans and tilts. When you are offered a friction head, consider that you will only use it with no application of the friction controls - the pan and tilt will be free completely - or you'll use it for simple locked off (no pan or tilt) shots. An example of this type of machine is the old Mitchell Pro Junior head - a poorly functioning unit that was usually affixed to stiff, sturdy wooden legs. Because of the ruggedness and stiffness of this rig, it was actually quite useful for locked off shots: matte set ups, long telephoto shots, etc.

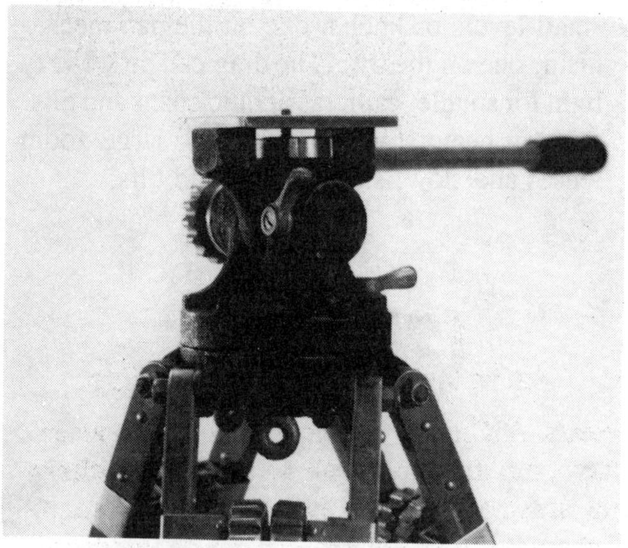

Mitchell Pro Junior Tripod Head

The second tripod head category is the **fluid head**. This type uses the resistance of an internal fluid, forced through a constrictive port, to smooth and dampen the motions of the pan and tilt. Another kind of head is in this same category: a viscous (heavy and sticky) grease is sandwiched between two (or more) flanges inside the head, and the resistance produced smooths the motion. Although a more accurate term for this latter type of unit might be "grease head", or "viscous head", you can imagine the marketing departments of various manufacturers cringing at the thought of having to put this in their advertising. This kind of head is always considered to be in the fluid head category by manufacturers, dealers and end users, and actually, most so called fluid heads work this way: Sachtler, ITE, Vinten, Universal, Ronford, Cartoni, and Miller. It is only the O'Connor that is a true fluid head.

The amount of **drag**, or dampening produced by the fluid head can be varied, usually via two small levers or knobs, one on the pan mechanism, one on the tilt. The drag can be set very light for smaller cameras or quick pans and tilts, or very heavy for big machines, large zoom lenses and slow, smooth pans and tilts.

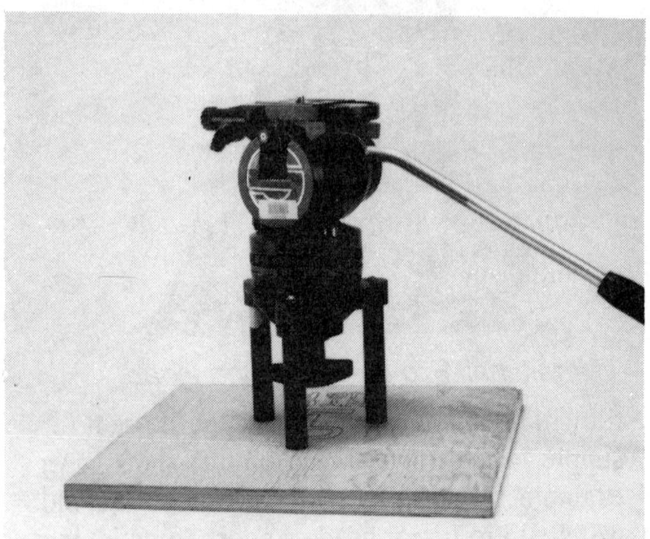

Sachtler Panorama Fluid Head

Fluid heads are thought to be essential in 16mm photography, and they are the industry standard tripod heads. No cameraperson would consider shooting anything but the most simple, locked off shot without one, unless he or she decided to do something fairly unusual in 16mm - use a **geared head**.

This head is very common in 35mm feature production, and in TV commercials which are also generally shot in 35mm. The motions of the tilt and pan are controlled by two large wheels (one for pan, one for tilt) that have knobs on them - imagine the control knob on the right side of a sewing machine with a small knob on it that makes it easier to turn. There are small **gear shifters** that alter the ratio of turns-to-degrees of tilt for each wheel, allowing, for example, fast pans in high gear, or long, slow ones in low. These heads produce extremely smooth results, but they are very expensive to rent, require massive tripods to support them (in comparison to standard 16mm fluid heads) because they are themselves so huge (they're designed for 35mm cameras) and take a fair amount of practice to master, because the knobs control everything. Operating a geared head is like drawing on an Etch-a-Sketch - seems simple, but isn't. Also, you can't zoom or change focus easily while using a geared head because you need both hands on the wheels. Most people would have a hard time telling footage shot with a geared head from that filmed with a fluid - for most work, the difference is undetectable. But geared heads offer one distinct advantage: you can stop and start them on a dime, and with great precision.

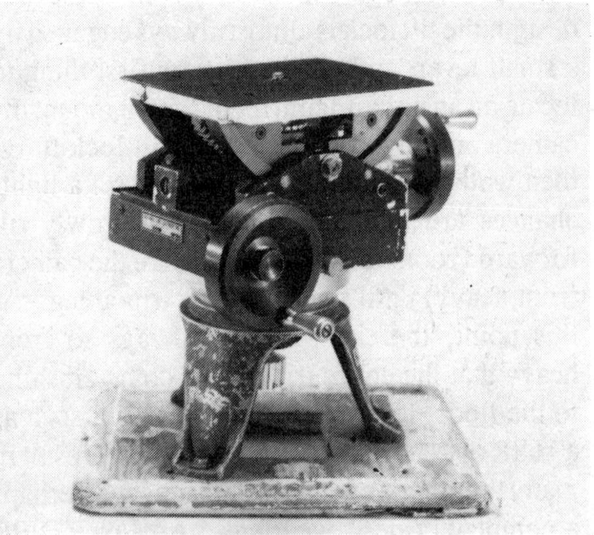

Geared Head

For example, say you need to pan from moving car to a sign that has important, plot advancing information (BRIDGE OUT, 2 MILES). The car is moving very fast, and you need to pan with it, then come to an immediate and specifically composed stop on the sign. With a fluid head, the camera will have a tendency to float past the sign, or perhaps stop before it, and when it does stop, the motion won't be precise. The geared head can go from a full, fast pan to a dead stop quickly and precisely, and you can practice before the shot and literally count off the exact number of turns of the pan wheel that will land the sign neatly (and aesthetically) in the right place in your frame.

Because of the size, weight, cost, and difficulty of operating a geared head, camerapeople seldom use them for 16mm. But if you have a specific shot that would benefit from one (like the example above) or want to practice for when you break in to 35mm, by all means, get one. One way many people practice using a geared head is to tape a narrow beam flashlight to the top and trace a wall chart with a figure eight drawn on it over and over again.

Since most people shooting 16mm will be using a fluid head, what follows is a description specific to this type. (The geared and friction heads are actually somewhat simpler, usually with less controls and functions.)

Mounting the camera on the head is done in one of two ways: directly to the head on a protruding screw, or via a quick release plate. The first refers to the simpler, older method: a screw on the head locks into the base of the camera, usually by turning a large knurled knob underneath the top plate of the head. Some tripods have small gears that transfer the turning motion of the screw to a lever that allows you to tighten the camera to the head better and easier. The standard screw size for 16mm cameras and tripods for 16mm use is 3/8-16. The first number refers to the diameter of the screw (3/8"), and the second the number of threads per inch - in this case, 16. 35mm cameras also use this size screw. Still, Super 8 and smaller 16mm cameras (Scoopic, Beaulieu, and some Bolex) use an accordingly smaller screw - 1/4-20. If you are using a smaller 16mm camera, you will probably have to find a tripod with a 1/4-20 screw, and this will likely be a smaller tripod as well.

Many people tighten the camera to the head this way: they mount the camera slightly crooked on the top plate - pointing 5 or 10 degrees left (counterclockwise) of what it should be. They tighten the mounting screw as much as they can with their fingers, then twist the entire camera to the right until it is straight on the head. This last bit of tightening makes the

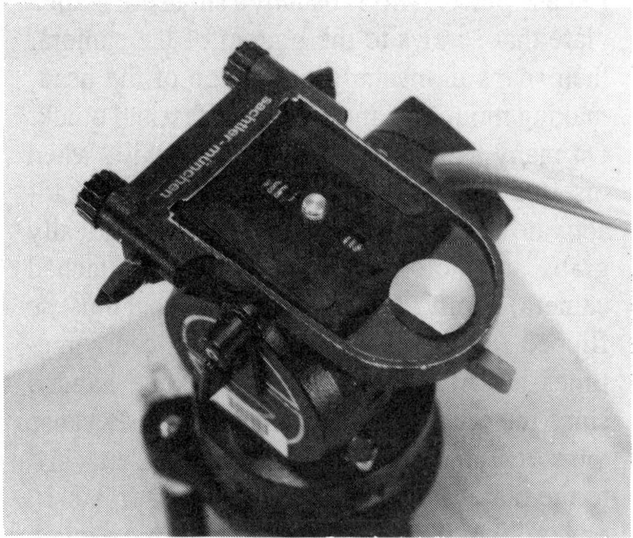

Sachtler Panorama Quick Release Plate

camera super-secure on the head, but it must be done carefully, because if it is over-tightened, the entire bottom mounting plate on the camera can rip out, or the threads can strip. Either is an expensive repair usually requiring the complete disassembly of the camera and cancellation of the day's shoot.

Getting the camera straight on the head - that is, the lens axis parallel to the tilt axis when mounting - is important for avoiding what I call the special Caesar Romero/Batman effect. On the TV series Batman, all the villains hideouts were shown with wildly un-level floors and un-vertical walls in relation to the frame. It was a great effect - funny and weird - and unless you get the camera on the head straight, it will likely be yours. A camera that is set crooked on the head will, instead of tilting straight up and down, tilt *and* swing, as if it were nodding yes and partially shaking no to some strange question. A pan attempted with an incorrectly mounted camera will result in a room that tilts, either at the head or tail of the shot. Most of the time, you'll want to avoid this, but if you want to experiment, by all means, give it a try. The results can be very effective for a number of situations (comedy, paranoia, the Riddler's P.O.V., etc.)

The second means of mounting the camera has all but eclipsed the first - the **quick release plate.** This is usually a small dovetailed plate that screws to the bottom of the camera, then snaps in instantly on the top of the head, making mounting and removing fast and quick. On many tripods, the camera plate will, when inserted correctly on the top of the head, activate a spring driven latch that automatically grabs and holds the plate (and the attached camera) firmly. Others have levers that must be flipped to tighten the plate, which can sometimes be difficult to accomplish one handed since the other is holding the camera. Because the screw that goes into the camera is attached to the plate, it can be changed to either 3/8-16 or 1/4-20 in seconds, so tripods that have quick release plates are more versatile. Instant mounting also carries with it the threat of too instant removal, and yes, if you are using this type of head and you turn the wrong lever, the *camera may fall off the head!* Most heads have safeties (just like on guns) that prevent this, but some are so prone to damage - as on the older Sachtler Panorama - that they may not be there at all, so be careful.

Another warning: if you lose the small, black anodized aluminum quick release plate, your shoot is dead. It will be virtually impossible to mount the camera to the head. A friend of mine tells the story of how he landed in Ireland for a documentary shoot, only to discover that the Sachtler quick release plate on the base of his Aaton was back in New York. It never made it out of the repair house he sent the camera to for a check up before the trip. He thought his shoot was dead until the machine shop of the factory he was there to document made him a new, functioning plate! I can't imagine anyone else being so lucky. It's very easy to forget to check that there is a quick release plate in with all the equipment - either on the camera or seated on the tripod head.

Leveling the head is important because if the base of the tripod head is not level, once again, you may be heading for the Caesar Romero/Batman effect. Almost all heads contain bubble levels built in, similar to those in a carpenter's level. You level the head in one of two ways: by adjusting the lengths of the legs (slow and tedious) or by adjusting the ball leveling device at the base of the head (quick and easy). The ball level has become standard on modern tripods. It's usually a 100mm hemisphere at the base of the head that seats in a 100mm cup at the top of the appropriate tripod. A threaded shaft with a tightening knob runs through the center of the ball, tightening the head to the tripod, and also allowing for leveling adjustment without changing the length of the legs.

To level a ball based head, you would proceed this way: first, find the final position and height of the tripod for the shot in question. There's no sense in leveling the head if you readjust the legs or drag the rig to the right three feet to get a better angle, as these will change everything and require you to re-level. Once this is done, mount the camera (if it isn't already on the head), lock the pan and tilt, then make sure any accessories, especially magazines, are tight and secure.. Grasp the top of the camera - often, this will be the mag, but sometimes it's the carrying handle - and loosen the ball lock knob. Swivel the camera *and* head together until the small bubble in the level is in the center of the indicator ring. Tighten the ball knob, and the camera is level. The reason you grab the top of the camera is that this makes the actual leveling much easier. If you grab the head itself, the tiniest movement changes ball in relation to the tripod cup greatly, whereas the same movement applied to the top of the camera will move the ball much less, giving you better control.

Leveling a non-ball based head - usually an old friction head with a flat base like Mitchell Junior - can only be accomplished by adjusting the length of the legs. This is a genuine pain, and will drive even the most patient A.C. crazy after a while.

A new device has been added to all the top of the line tripods sold today, and it really makes the head perform - *and* it makes it safer. It's called, for the most part, the **spring counterbalance**. If you've ever tilted a heavy 16BL or NPR down sharply, you know how difficult it can be to wrestle with the weight of the machine. If you slip or accidentally let go of the pan handle, or forget to set the tilt lock and walk away, wham! - down goes the whole rig. The spring counterbalance is simply an adjustable, internal spring in the head that, once set, counteracts the weight of the camera in question, and keeps this from happening. Once the camera is loaded and all the accessories, including lenses, matte boxes, etc. have been attached, you release the tilt lock and drag and find the balance - not the level - of the camera. Since most cameras are front heavy due to the weight of the lens, the camera will probably be tilted backward somewhat when it is balanced. At this point, you set the spring counterbalance, and voila, the camera will be balanced, and seemingly weightless on the head. If you let go of the pan handle, the camera will simply bob back and forth slightly, and if you set the drag first, the camera will probably stay wherever you tilt it, up or down.

I've just described the best case of a spring counterbalance at work - in actuality, if the camera is light, the spring may be too heavy and always be fighting you, pushing the camera back up to the level position. If the camera is too heavy or un-wieldy - usually NPRs are because they're so tall - the spring won't be strong enough, and the camera will tilt forward or backward even with the spring counterbalance on. For the most part, they work very well once you find the balance and set them correctly, and no one would should pay for any tripod (either as a rental or purchase) that doesn't have one.

Another option on many new heads is a **sliding top plate**. This allows you to pre-balance the camera rig before setting the spring counterbalance, and is especially useful when using big, heavy zooms, telephoto lenses, zoom motors or follow focus units that make a camera very front heavy. They are not, however, substitutes for spring counterbalances in any way, shape or form, but rather compliment them.

The second main part of the tripod as a whole is the **leg assembly**. The individual legs are made of wood on older tripods, and of aluminum, stainless steel (referred to as inox by some manufacturers) and carbon fiber on the newer ones. Wooden legs are actually very light and stiff, but the design is old and rarely incorporates a built in spreader (discussed next). Aluminum is light, cheap, and somewhat more flexible (not good) than the others. Stainless or inox is heaviest and most durable, quite stiff and somewhat expensive. Carbon fiber legs are the newest, hottest thing on the market. They're far and away the lightest legs, are extremely stiff, outrageously expensive and the most fragile of all. Carbon fiber legs should only be considered where every last ounce must be shaved from a camera package - for example, when shooting a movie about mountaineering that requires a lot of hand carrying of the equipment.

Legs generally come in three sizes: **standard, baby** and **high-hat**. Hi hats are usually not a set of legs at all, but a 100mm bowl mounted to a 14" (or thereabouts) square piece of plywood. Baby legs are generally half to two-thirds the length of standard legs, and are useful when lining up low shots. A fourth length is sometimes available: **long legs**. These may be necessitated by very tall leading actors or a large number of high angle shots in the storyboard. If you are on a limited budget and don't have an infinite amount of space in the equipment van, just rent standard legs and a hi-hat. The standard legs will take care of the bulk of your shooting including moderately low shots, while the high hat can be placed on the ground for very low shots and on a phone book or camera case for those in between. The high hat can also be clamped to a ladder (with ordinary woodworking C-clamps) for shots normally done with long legs, and window ledges, car hoods and pick-up truck beds for almost everything else.

Recently, **two stage tripod legs** have become the rage. Instead of having two sections of aluminum, steel or carbon fiber that slide in relation to each other to make the tripod go up or down, the two stage tripods have three (there are two locking knobs per leg). Having a set of two stage legs is like having a set of standard and baby legs at the same time. You save the extra carrying weight and time it takes to change from baby to standard legs. Of course, two stage legs are more expensive than standard legs.

It almost goes without saying that the top of the tripod must match the base of the head, and recently, manufactures have moved toward making this easier with an adaptation of the 100mm bowl as standard for heads intended to be used with 16mm cameras.

The last main part of a tripod is the **spreader**. This three armed device keeps the legs of the tripod from doing the splits and crashing the head and camera to the ground when the rig is set up on hard, shiny surfaces - linoleum, wood, etc. It is best removed when shooting on soft or very uneven surfaces, such as grass, gravel, steep slopes, etc. Here the sharp tips of the tripod can be spread out and dug in to the ground to give the tripod stability. Spreaders have the capability to extend, just like the tripod legs themselves, and it is a good idea to take advantage of this to get the legs spread out for each shot. The wider the spread of the legs, the more stabile the tripod will be, but maximum height will be lost. For the lowest shot possible, the spreader should be spread out all the way; reverse this for getting the tripod to its highest.

The latest thing in spreaders are those that fold up *with the tripod* for fast storage. The older, non folding spreaders are still cursed for the ridiculous amount of time and aggravation it takes to set and mount them on the legs.

The tripods themselves vary from one manufacturer to the next, but they're all getting slicker and faster and better. Aside from having a good, smooth functioning fluid head, you might think that all the rest of the tripod - the legs, spreader, mounting, counterbalance, etc. - is really not that important, but it is. In fact, I believe that the kind of tripod you use is often more important than the kind of camera.

A CP/R, for example, is only really a problem machine when you need to be able to change magazines instantly, because the threading of the camera body takes so long. Other than this, I have no qualms about using one even when compared to a 16SR or an Aaton. But give me an ancient Miller or an old Universal tripod head and legs, and I'll come very close to cancelling the shoot. The new tripods, especially the Sachtler, are so fast, so perfect in setting up and performing during a shot that you can actually get twice as many set ups done in a day in some cases. Thinking about doing a hi hat shot? If you are using a Sachtler, you can have the whole rig mounted on the hi hat faster than the time you spend agonizing over the thought of dismounting an old Universal and remounting it on the hi hat. Need to pop the camera off for a hand held shot? With a head that has a quick release, snap!, the camera is free - so fast, you will always want to get the shot, rather than decide against it because the removal and remounting will take too long.

Sachtler tripods are, in my opinion, simply the best. The fluid action is excellent, the head is extremely rugged and durable (they never die, only get rebuilt) and the entire system from the quick release plate to the counterbalance to the integral folding/quick removing spreader is unsurpassed. The only quarrel people have with them is that the standard legs for the Panorama models (these are the ones intended for 16mm use) are a little short. Die hard O'Connor fans insist that their wooden legs - especially those made by Peter Lisand - are stronger, stiffer and longer, but you can actually get Peter Lisand legs for your Sachtler head, and many people do. The only real criticism that Sachtler must face is that the cost of their tripods are outrageous: about $5000 at the time of this writing for a head, standard inox legs, heavy duty triangle and case.

Recently, Cartoni, Vinten, and Miller have introduced excellent, updated units that really do perform up to Sachtler standards. The Cartoni units especially are an excellent alternative to Sachtler, and the company has introduced innovations such as a head that has a Sachtler release plate on the bottom, allowing you to mount their Cartoni on another Cartoni or a Sachtler for really funky, "dutch" shots.

Take time to figure out just exactly how the tripod you are going to use functions, because if you don't, the result may be much worse than poor shots - you could wreck the camera. If you are on an extremely tight shooting schedule, and the crew is going to be small, try to get enough money to rent a good, fast tripod. The time you save will actually more than pay for the extra cost, and because you won't have to wrestle with the tripod so much, you'll have more time to think about the shots themselves. Good tripods take moving the camera from a chore to almost a pleasure - you'll find yourself changing the height or angle of the camera with no hesitation. Good tripods, in short, help you make better movies.

Dollies are those things with which you move the camera, either during or between the shots. There are several categories; the simplest and cheapest is the **3-wheel.** This dolly replaces the spreader on the tripod and allows you to move the camera over smooth surfaces only, because the wheels are usually small and made of hard rubber or plastic. Three-wheel dollies are generally thought to be of use just for moving the camera *between shots*, because it is very difficult for operators to frame and follow action and for the A.C.s to pull focus while pushing and walking behind cameras. Simple, short dolly shots can be accomplished with 3-wheels, though, and since they fold up neatly and compactly and are cheap, they can be quite handy, especially if you know that the floor or sidewalk you'll be shooting on is very smooth. Usually, though, you won't have a floor that is smooth enough for a 3 wheel.

Platform dollies comprise the next category. These usually consist of steerable, four wheel platforms on which you can place the tripod and have two people - the camera operator and A.C. - stand on as well. There are two main types: **Doorway** and **Western.** Doorway dollies look something like go-carts with the seats and engines removed. They have large pneumatic rubber wheels that need relatively smooth surfaces to run on to produce good dolly shots, although not as smooth as a 3-wheel requires. They are small enough to run through most doors (hence the name) and can be turned upside-down for added stability (but less ground clearance). They're light enough to be easily hauled up stairs by two or three people, and inexpensive to rent. They also make great equipment carts before and after the shoot. Western dollies are much larger and have big, near automobile sized wheels that can run over rougher surfaces. They can also be towed slowly behind cars. Matthews Corporation is the principle builder of these two dollies.

Column or **pedestal** dollies - the next category - are heavy, expensive and have a center stand built in that can be used to raise or lower the camera between shots. The column is very sturdy and obviates tripod legs; you attach a fluid or geared head directly to it. They also have built in, moveable seats for the operator and A.C. These are also "doorway" dollies in the sense that they are usually quite compact and can fit easily through doors and other obstacles. Most dollies of this type have the ability to crab: all four wheels can be made to turn at the same time by twisting a single wheel/shaft. This can be especially useful when working in very tight spaces. Column dollies can run either on smooth surfaces by attaching standard, non-pneumatic rubber wheels, or on special rounded track by using convex surfaced (bogey) wheels. Track comes in straight and curved sections, and by laying it out and leveling it over rough and uneven surfaces with wooden wedges and apple boxes (small wood crates), the smoothest dolly shots can be achieved. A **mini jib** may be attached to this kind of dolly;

these are devices that allow the camera to crane upward (as opposed to simply tilt upward) and use the weight and integrity of this type of heavy support. The mini jib is used for mounting the camera and camera accessories only; the jonathan jib is much larger and has two seats for the operator and A.C. Both work something like playground teeter-totters and require the use of special counterweights to be balanced. Column dollies usually are made available with Mitchell Standard and 100mm or 150mm bowl to fit any tripod. Elemack, Panther and Fisher make dollies in this category; Arri makes a jonathan style jib called a Cine-jib. Recently, small jib arms that mount on tripod legs have appeared, allowing you to get small crane moves without renting a camera dolly. The Losmandy Porta Jib, Cinekinetic Jib, and the Media Logic Jib fall into this category and can be very useful.

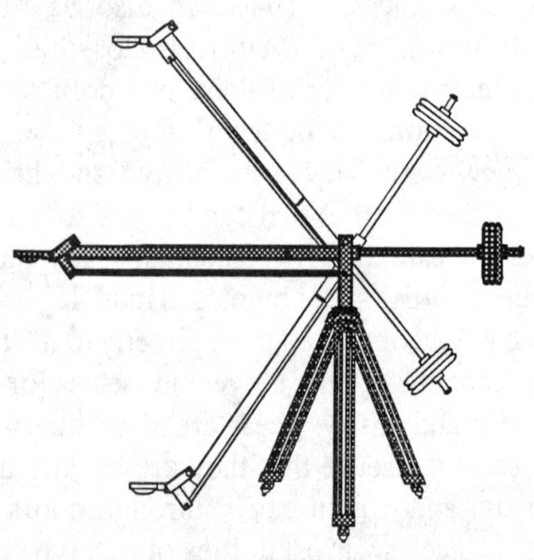

Media Logic Mini Jib

What kind of dolly do you need? It all depends on the complexity of the shot(s) in question and the amount of rental money available. It also depends on the *type* of dolly shot in question; some call for extremely smooth results while others could almost be done hand held.

For example, take this sequence written near the beginning of a feature length, dramatic script:

EXT. FOREST - LATE AFTERNOON

MAGGIE is on a dirt path at the entrance to a forest, stretching and getting ready for her training run. She shakes her arms and shoulders, takes a deep breath, then begins running through

THE FOREST - sunlight gleaming through the slowing passing trees. Maggie sees the beauty of this remote place, looks at peace as she runs.

Scripts are usually written like the above one: without specific camera moves indicated (no words like zoom, telephoto, or dolly). It is left up to the director and cinematographer (working within the budget and goals set by the producer) to decide the actual shots. The stretching/getting ready sequence, for example, could be done in one shot: she finishes an achilles stretch, ties her right shoe, and takes off. Or, it could be many: a close-up of her face, showing her concentration, then another on her training shoes as she tightens the laces on one, then the back of her muscular legs as she carefully stretches them, then a medium shot of her as she bursts into a run. The second set of shots may sound more exciting and visual than the first, but it may be that this type of sequence should only be shown later, in the heat of a competition. It all depends on the requirements of the script, and the sensibility of the director and cinematographer.

The second to the last line however, says unequivocally, dolly shot. There's no other way to show trees passing and sunlight shining through them without moving the camera. This kind of shot needs a smooth dolly because it will be wide and the background will be a major element. It won't do to have the background jerk or rock since this would make the audience aware of the camera and the film process, and generally look sloppy, drawing our attention away from the intended emotion of the script.

If the sequence were written this way however:

EXT. FOREST - LATE AFTERNOON

MAGGIE is on a dirt path at the entrance to a forest, stretching and getting ready for her training run. She shakes her arms and shoulders, takes a deep breath, then begins running through

THE FOREST - Shafts of light cross her determined face as she races through the woods.

- things would be very different. The shot of Maggie in motion is not a wide shot, but a close-up. The audience's reference for dolly smoothness will not be trees and landscape, but the actress playing Maggie herself, and she'll be running quickly, bobbing up and down. While the dolly shot in the first example may very well require an expensive column dolly resting on fifty feet of track, the second dolly shot could easily be done hand held - from the tailgate of a truck if the path is wide enough and not too steep. Or the operator could sit in a chair placed on a western or doorway dolly. The actress will be moving so much in this close-up that anyone skilled in hand-held shooting should be able to get a good take easily.

Script interpretation, then, dictates the kind of dolly used. After you become familiar with various dollies and their capabilities, you'll be able to read any script and know just exactly what kind of dolly is called for.

One thing you should keep in mind: when you use any of the dollies mentioned above in a production, you aren't just using a single piece of equipment that costs anywhere from thirty to one-hundred and fifty dollars a day to rent; you'll also need a station wagon, van or truck and several strong people, because this is what you'll need to transport, lift and operate it. It takes time to lay out and level metal track with wedges and apple boxes, slowing down any production considerably. If you add fifty or seventy five dollars a day to the dolly rental for the van, a similar amount for the rental of several lengths of track, and at the very least, food for the extra crew, you can see that dolly shots can be very expensive.

Recent developments in dolly design have brought some relief to this problem, however. Someone came up with the brilliant idea of using PVC pipe - (specifically 1/2" schedule 40 plumbing pipe) as "track". Long sections of this very light, flexible and inexpensive tubing can be laid out over rough surfaces, and a dolly such as the Media Logic Fast Track or Cinekinetic's Rolling Wonder can be run over it, producing superbly smooth results. These units can be stowed in the trunk of almost any car (the PVC pipe is strapped to the roof).

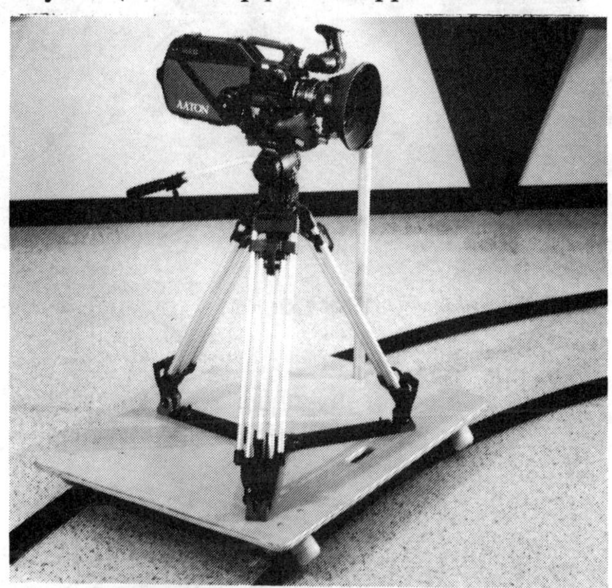

Media Logic Fast Track Dolly

The Fast Track has a 30"x40" deck, which can hold operator, assistant and tripod, yet it fits through most doorways. Media Logic also offers Track Locks, small expanding hardwood inserts that lock the track together, eliminating loose joints. They recommend cutting track down to just five feet in length for ease of transport and offer a heavy storage bag that holds the Track Locks, track, and an aluminum pushbar that comes with the dolly. Now, instead of renting a van, an expensive Elemack or Panther dolly, and the services of three strong people to lift the dolly, a single crewmember can carry the dolly in one hand (the Fast Track weighs about 25 pounds) and the carry bag with as much as 40 feet of track in the other. The Fast Track has wheel trucks that swivel, allowing it to go around curves, and Media Logic sells five foot sections of curved plastic pipe (standard 8' inside radius). Since the trucks on this dolly are placed at 24 1/2" centers, it will run on standard Matthews steel track if needed.

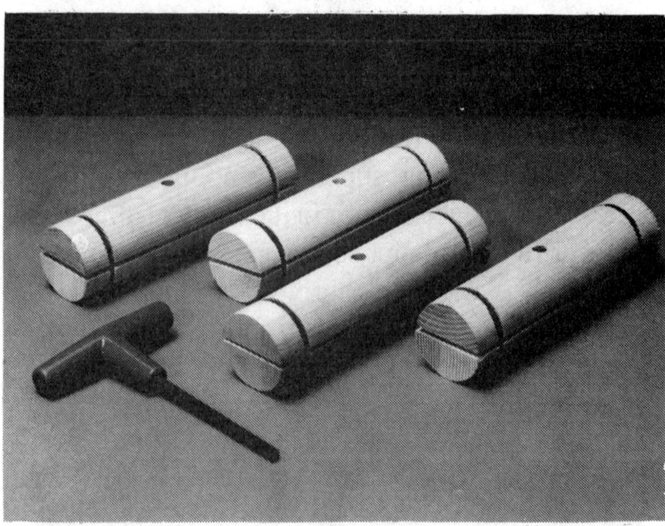

Track Locks

Media Logic offers this dolly two ways: fully assembled for just under $500, or as a kit that requires the purchaser buy, cut and drill his/her own plywood deck for $325.

A few tips when using this type of dolly:

- use WD 40 (a lubricating spray) or better yet, Pledge brand furniture polish (doesn't attract dirt and leaves no waxy buildup!) on the wheels or track to eliminate wheel squeak as needed. The latest word is that Pledge brand furniture polish is better since it doesn't attract dirt and lasts longer. Don't use silicon spray; it makes squeaks worse. Talcum or baby powder also works to stop noise.

- you can screw or bolt the wheel trucks of the Fast Track to a smaller plywood deck, or even to a hi hat to make a really tiny dolly. By using metal pipe or angle iron as track, you could "fly" a camera over a desk, under a truck, or through a car window for a really wild shot.

- ABS, another type of plumbing pipe, is better than PVC for track. It's black, instead of white, lighter, and much stronger. It may be a bit harder to find, but when you do, it should actually be cheaper than PVC, and is worth the trouble.

These dollies are seeing more and more use in low budget productions, and are sometime used in even high budget films because extremely long sections of pipe track can be laid out for very little money. Those who were previously faced with the expense of dolly moves are calling these pipe dollies fantastic.

The Matthews Corporation makes the **Briefcase Dolly**. Essentially a small platform unit that works very much like a doorway dolly, it folds up into a case for transport. It has the capability to run on either smooth surfaces, track, or pipe by changing wheels, and everything stores inside the case when it folds together. The overall package fits easily into most car trunks, and can be checked on airline flights. The major drawback is price - well over $2000 at the time of this writing.

While we're on the subject, don't forget **wheelchairs**. They might not roll so well over major sidewalk cracks, and old ones can be squeaky, but for many situations, they're just the ticket. In supermarkets, airports, hallways, and basketball and tennis courts - any smooth-surfaced location - they're great. The camera height that results from hand-held wheelchair shooting is often just right for the scene; if it's too low, you can adjust it by putting a phone book on the seat.

Other "dollies": **skateboards** for wild, low shots (the new ones are huge and work nicely), **cars** with the motor turned off for sync shooting (get lots of people to push), **shopping carts** when you can't find a wheelchair, and even **bicycles** and **roller skates**.

There's another way to move the camera that isn't really a dolly shot, but it is capable of producing unique and fantastic results: the **Shakeycam.** As far as I know, a 21 year old director by the name of Sam Rami first used this device in a low dollar horror film called "The Evil Dead". It is extremely primitive; it consists of a board, usually 6 or 8 feet long, with the camera mounted at right angles to the length, in the center. There are two operators who hold the board at each end and walk or (better yet) run with it. The length of the board acts to smooth the camera. The Shakeycam can produce shots obtainable in no other way; they're much smoother than running hand-held shots, and the operators can fly the camera up and over cars, people, and other obstacles for startling results (see the feature film "Raising Arizona").

The **Steadicam** is a device which provides dolly-like smoothness without the dolly - the camera is essentially hand-held. A special gimbal (swivel) is attached to an articulated, spring loaded arm, which is in turn attached to a torso brace that the operator wears. The camera is mounted above the gimbal (or sometimes below it - this is called "low mode") and the arm and gimbal compensate for any jerkiness that the operator generates, say, by walking. Since the camera must be isolated from the operator, a video tap is connected to the camera, and a small high intensity on-board monitor (TV screen) serves as the viewfinder.

Many people who see a Steadicam demonstrated for the first time - and see the fantastic footage that results - come to believe that this machine is the end-all and be-all in camera movement. No dolly track need be laid; the operator can climb or descend stairs, step on and off cranes and trucks, and walk over obstacles that can then be actually in the succeeding part of the shot. Nearly all the mobility that is possible with the hand-held camera is possible with the Steadicam but without the accompanying unsteadiness. The resulting shots can be excellent P.O.V.s of people, animals, supernatural creatures, etc. Before the Steadicam, directors wanting these kinds of shots had to settle for hand-held shots that just didn't look like a character's P.O.V.; the shakiness always implicated the camera and the camera operator in the shot, and made the viewer aware of the filmmaking process. Finally, the Steadicam allows the audience to feel in the scene and "with" the characters more than possibly any other device or technique can.

Unfortunately, there are serious drawbacks to the Steadicam. It is a considerably complex device that requires its operators to be extremely skilled. You cannot rent one, practice for a few hours and hope to get good results. Rare is the rental house that will let them out to anyone other than a Steadicam specialist who has taken a special course in its operation. Using the Steadicam is also dangerous; a sync camera loaded and mounted on the rig can weigh as much as 60 pounds, and any slight trip or stumble can end in disaster, both for operator and camera. Although the torso packs have emergency quick releases, many operators will charge double to shoot on docks or in boats, and some will simply refuse to shoot near water altogether. The wear and tear on back muscles and spinal column is horrendous; many operators see chiropractors as much as several times a week. Shots involving climbing stairs can cost double.

Since the camera must be isolated from direct human contact, all zooming (rarely done), irising and focusing must be done by remote control, either through a very light cable, or by radio. The latter is the method of choice because of maneuverability, but the resulting rig is even more complex and delicate. Cameras used on Steadicams often must have special magazines and power supplies (the batteries must be small on-boards) and they have to be carefully balanced on the rig for good results.

What this all means is that renting a Steadicam also means renting: a) a special camera fitted for the rig, b) the accompanying focus (and possibly zoom or iris) drive motors and radio controls, c) a video tap, d) several special batteries and chargers and most importantly, e) the services of two highly skilled people - the operator and his/her assistant. All this can cost anywhere from $500 to $2000 and up per day (this usually includes the camera and rig rental), depending on the complexity of the shot and other factors.

You should consider the Steadicam to be a tool capable of fantastic results that is, unfortunately, a problem budget-wise. You might, however, find someone to do your Steadicam work who is just starting out, and can give you a break in exchange for the chance to gain experience. It is also not unheard of for Steadicam veterans to donate their services to students and independents, if they feel they are making an important contribution to the film that would otherwise be unobtainable.

Many people (myself included) see the Steadicam for the first time assume that it operates with internal gyroscopes. Gyros are simply devices that spin and create a resistant force along a specific axis. In fact, anything that spins - a bicycle wheel, toy top, or figure skater - works as a gyro. At certain times, Steadicam operators use gyros to help stabilize shots, especially long takes that must be level and straight over great distances. But there are no gyros in the Steadicam.

Steadicams work to smooth shots in three ways: the spring action of the arm, the gymbal, and the fact that the operator does not have to look through the camera, because he or she can view the take on a small, high intensity video screen. Interestingly enough, you can get as much as eighty percent of the effect of a Steadicam with what the Geo Film Group calls their **Pogocam**. Imagine you are holding a ski pole. Above the grip and just above your hand is a film camera. On the bottom of the pole, where the sharp point would be is the camera battery, and some weights. Mounted to the side of the film camera is a small video camera that is aimed so that it sees almost exactly what the film camera sees, and on top of it all is a monitor that gets its image from the video camera.

When you use the Pogocam, your arm is functioning like the arm of a Steadicam, and your hand is the gymbal. You don't have to keep your eye to the camera because you can look at the video monitor, just as you would with a Steadicam.

People are using Pogocams more and more, startled by how well they work and pleased that the cost is so low. You can run with them, carry them up stairs or ladders for imitation crane shots, or even pass them from operator to operator during a take. They're smaller overall than a Steadicam and can squeeze into really tight places.

Most people use them for action sequences instead of hand holding the camera; at this time, there doesn't seem to be a sync version of the Pogocam (the principal cameras are 35mm Eyemos and 16mm Filmos). Other drawbacks are the fact that the viewing system isn't reflex, a maximum of 100' of film can be used and that your arm can get really tired after only a few takes. Still, the Pogocam really is, as the manufacturer says, "the simple alternative".

The **HID**, which stands for Helmet Integrated Display, was created by Mike Cameron, of Camair. It is a special helmet with a built in video monitor the places an image in front of the wearer's eye (right or left) as if it was floating in space at a distance of about eight feet. When connected to the video camera of a Pogocam or the video tap of a Steadicam, it allows the operator to do such things as shoot backward, but walk or run forward to avoid hitting obstacles. Using one takes some practice, which is fun, and just wearing one makes you look like some kind of robot mutant from the next century. The HID could prove invaluable for certain situations.

LIGHTMETERS

It should be clear by now that the scope of this book does not include lighting or cinematography. There are many who are far more qualified than I to tackle this topic, and many have. However, a considerable number of readers have told me they wished this book contained the same sort of evaluation of light meters as it does cameras. Toward that end, I'll attempt a short discussion of cinematography as it relates to the use of the specific light meters presented. For those of you who are either confused by the brevity or disgusted by the simplicity of the following, kindly high tail it to the bibliography for further reading.

A director of photography who learned his trade in the 1930's once said that he felt the two worst things that ever happened to cinematography were the zoom lens and the light meter. Although it doesn't take much thought to understand his feelings on zoom lenses (goofy zoom shots were the bane of the 1960's and seem to be making a strong comeback in vacuous music videos), the light meter is another matter.

What's wrong with light meters? Nothing really, unless you began shooting for movies before they came into wide use, before the 1950's. It's hard to imagine, but before this time, cameramen would simply stare at a scene, perhaps squint a bit, then call out F 5.6, or maybe F8, and start shooting. Years of experience in sets and on location enabled them to do nothing more than look at a shot to determine proper exposure.

They also had another advantage: 35mm black and white negative. Chances are, this was the stock that they were exposing. This negative was quite forgiving of over or under exposure. Was the iris opened up a bit too much on that close up so that the actress looks too bright? The negative, then, received too much light, causing it to be "thick", or dark, (hence, the "negative" of the light that struck it) so that when light was shined through it to the unexposed print stock, very little was allowed to pass, making it "thin", or clear (print stock is also negative), so that too much light from the projector, striking the final print, was picked up by the projector lens and thrown on the screen, making the actress look too bright. Instead of re-shooting the shot, the lab was simply asked to "print down" the footage, or shine more light through the thick, overexposed negative so that the final print wouldn't be so bright.

Much of the time, this compensation was done by the lab automatically; it's hard to say how many cameramen had no idea just how far off their exposures really were, but lab **timers**, or those who's responsibility it was to shine more or less light through the negative - a.k.a *timing the print* - certainly knew. At any rate, the director of photography mentioned earlier clearly felt that the light meter was a crutch for those who either were too inexperienced or too lazy to really see light.

There is no doubt that if we all shot for years with, say, large carbon arc lights placed at certain distances with certain unvarying films stocks under unchanging circumstances, light meters would be unnecessary. But for modern shooting, that is, filming under quartz lighting for one scene, then fluorescent mixed with daylight for the next, followed by a scene lit with HMIs or even practical neons, and *not* shooting day in and day out under constant circumstances (shooting jobs, for many cameramen, are often few and far between), a light meter is becomes very important. Add to this the problems presented by the less forgiving nature of color negative stocks, and further still by the 16mm gauge (more contrast and grain, and less sharpness than 35mm), it becomes clear that a device that can tell us how to set our camera is indispensable.

There are five factors of exposure - that is, things you, as a cameraperson, must decide upon (or existentially decide not to decide upon - groovy) to get an exposure. For the purposes of this introduction to light meters, exposure will be simplified to mean "how dark or light the scene or something in the scene is when it ends up on the screen". The first factor is

1 - Film Sensitivity.

Film comes from the manufacturer in a box with a rating printed or stamped on it that tells you how sensitive it is to light. This rating is a number with a alphabetic prefix, usually one of the following: DIN, ASA, ISO, or EI. The first three are abbreviations for standards organizations; the last, EI, stands for Exposure Index. I'm quite sure that in another five years, there'll be a new abbreviation (because things just *have* to change) so I'm putting in my vote for OOPS, or maybe UGH, or something else that photographers say when they get their film back from the lab. At any rate, ASA, ISO, and EI are all the same, and are prevalent in the U.S.

This rating system of film sensitivity works like this: a roll of film might have an ASA/ISO/EI of 200. This film is twice as sensitive to light (according to the manufacturer) as a roll marked ASA/ISO/EI 100 which is twice as sensitive to light as a roll labelled ASA/ISO/EI 50. So, if we decide to photograph a nice man in a derby seated on a park bench, and we are told that the roll of ASA/ISO/EI 200 film needs a certain amount of light for it to reproduce a normal exposure, then the roll of ASA 100 film (I'm tired of typing ASA/ISO/EI, so from now on I'm just going to type ASA, which is what I first learned) needs twice as much light for a normal exposure, and the roll of ASA 50 film needs twice as much as the roll of ASA 100, or four times as much as the roll of ASA 200. How much light is that? This brings us to our second factor of exposure:

2 - Light.

This factor can be broken down into two categories: **quantity** as in "Boy, them new fog lights on my monster truck sure are brighter than those factory jobs" and **quality**, as in "Now that I've got this sweater out of the store and into the parking lot, it looks bluer than I thought". Quantity refers to the *amount* of light. You can measure light quantity in a number of ways, but cinematographers generally stick to **footcandles**. A footcandle is remarkably easy to understand: it's the amount of light, shining on your face, that comes from a lighted candle held one foot from your nose. One foot - candle. Was that a really big candle you say, or just a little votive thing, or what? How long was the wick? I suppose an ordinary, kitchen drawer type candle is what footcandles are based upon, and if that's not good enough for you, then feel free to look up the scientific definition. But for everyone else, the candle-one-foot-from-your-nose definition should do. Please note that if you hold that candle at arm's length, say two and a half feet, you'll have less light striking your nose, and conversely, if you hold the candle less than a foot, your face will be brighter because more light will be striking it (and also get warm maybe - watch out for the hot wax). So the amount of light that falls on a given object from a given source is dependent on the **distance** between the two.

Quality of light is defined in **degrees Kelvin**. Kelvin is the temperature scale that has as zero not the freezing point of water (Celsius) or thirty two degrees below the freezing point of water (Fahrenheit) but the freezing point of matter; that is, when there is no movement of any sub-atomic particles. How does this relate to my sweater looking different in the parking lot?

If you take a lump of steel and hold a welding torch to it, it will get hot, then glow. The first color the lump of steel will glow is a dark red; as it gets hotter, the color will change to orange, then yellow, and finally white hot just about the time it turns into a puddle. If it could get any hotter it would actually turn greenish, then blue (following the colors of the rainbow) then indigo and violet. But long before blue it would probably vaporize. At any rate, you could describe the color of the light by measuring the temperature of the lump of steel, and that's just what goes on with **color temperature**, measured in degrees Kelvin. Instead of using a real piece of steel, scientists use a hypothetical black body; this way, they don't have to worry about getting burned by welding torches, and they can define the color of light given off from a lump of matter that might actually be vapor.

The color of light given off by a standard light bulb (the one in your fridge or in your desk lamp) is described as somewhere around 2800 degrees Kelvin. The light from the sun at midday is 5600 degrees Kelvin. The light from a candle is something like 2000 degrees Kelvin. Strange as it may seem, the more orange the light, the cooler (in terms of color temperature or degrees Kelvin) it is. This goes against much of our experience since cool things like the ocean or dense ice are blue and hot things like fire and chili peppers are red. So if someone asks you to cool some lights down on a set, it probably means put some blue plastic over them (gels) rather than orange (it might even mean that you are supposed to turn them off since light fixtures get physically hot), but you should find out just to be sure. Getting back to the sweater: it looks bluer in the parking lot than it did in the store because outside the light is bluer. Inside, the store was attractively lit with those tiny, expensive, chic quartz lights that have become popular lately. These are 3200 degrees Kelvin. Outside it was three in the afternoon an the color temperature from the sun was about 5000 degrees Kelvin. The next factor of exposure is the

3 - Iris

Inside the lens on your camera is an adjustable hole called the iris. If you want to change the amount of light passing through the lens, you twist a ring on the barrel of the lens and the iris opens up or closes down. The size of this hole in relation to the focal length is described by a number called an F stop. Standard F stops (those engraved on the barrels of lenses) usually start with some strange number that indicates the very widest the iris can open, like 1.7, then continue like this: 2, 2.8, 4, 5.6, 8, 11, 16, 22. The smaller the number, the larger the iris opening, and each of these standard F stops has a specific and pretty simple relationship to all the others. For example, F 2.8 describes an iris opening that lets in twice as much light at F 4, which in turn lets in twice as much light as F 5.6. You may run into lenses marked in T stops. These are stops that take into account that the amount of light a lens transmits to the film is based on more than a mathematical relationship between the size of the iris and the focal length of the lens. Lenses have glass in them, and even the best glass scatters and diffuses some light. Light loss due to the glass elements in a lens and their coatings is factored into F stops, and the result is T stops. So, always use T stops (when they're engraved on the lens) for determining exposure; use F stops for calculating depth of field. The next factor of exposure is

4 - Length of Exposure

Each frame of film must be exposed to light for a very precise amount of time, and in movie cameras, unlike still cameras, this amount of time is dependent on two things: the speed of the camera (in frames per second) and the shutter angle (in degrees). Nearly all 16mm and 35mm movie cameras have rotating shutters, that is, a shutter that is a disc with a section cut out, and this disc is placed between the lens and the film and rotates in time with the pulldown claw and the moving film (see chapter one). Since both the speed of the camera and the size of the angle of the cut out part of the shutter will determine the length of exposure of each frame of film, a formula for determining exposure time must include both variables:

$$\frac{\text{shutter}\angle}{360} \times \frac{1}{\text{fps}} = \text{length of exposure}$$

A 180 degree shutter (Arri 16S and 16SR) running at 24 frames per second will cover the gate half the time, and uncover it the other half, so that each frame receives 1/48th of a second of light from the lens. The last factor of exposure is

5 - You

What is a "normal" exposure? There really isn't any such thing. You have to decide whether you want the audience to think that the scene is outside at night, or beneath a descending alien ship, or on the beach at Coney Island. What's normal for each of these shots? What you *want* the scene to look like is correct, not some predetermined value.

Knowing all these factors - Film sensitivity, Light, Iris, Length of Exposure and You (what you want) - enables you to get a correct exposure. The light meter helps you determine these variables.

For example, say you need to get a shot of a bad guy waiting outside a building at night. In the shot, the bad guy stares up at a window, takes a puff on a cigarette, and checks his watch. You have very little money for your film, so you hope that there is enough light under a certain streetlight to get the shot without either running a power cord to some nearby establishment or renting a generator for additional lights. You pick up your light meter and stand under the street light in question at nine p.m. What it tells you is this: there are eight footcandles falling on your face. Now you can turn the little knobs and dials and scales on the back of the meter to convert this information into F-stops, but let's do that here, using this scale:

ASA 100 film/170 degree shutter/24fps

F	1.4	2	2.8	4	5.6	8
fc	25	50	100	200	400	800

Bad news for our bad guy. The street light is putting out less than one third the amount of light you need to photograph him with even the most expensive lens (a Zeiss Superspeed that opens up to T 1.3). Solutions? Find a brighter streetlight (not likely as most public street lights put out less than eight footcandles), rent a light and put it up high on a stand to *motivate* it (make it look like it is coming) from the angle of the street light and plug it into a rented/borrowed generator or someone's home, or use a faster stock (you might also try undercranking, or slowing down your camera - see this same example in the Speeds and Angles chapter).

Given your no budget circumstances, getting a faster stock sounds like the best idea. If the chart is expanded to include films with faster ASAs -

170 degree shutter/24fps:

ASA	1.4	2	2.8	4	5.6
100	25	50	100	200	400
200	13	25	50	100	200
400	6	13	25	50	100

- you see that an ASA 400 film would give us a normal exposure if we set our iris between F1.4 and 2 (closer to F1.4). This is a fine solution, except that the ASA 400 stock might a) not look as good as the 100, and therefore b) cause a visual "jump" when you try to cut the two together. Why wouldn't the stock look very good? Generally, the faster the film stock, the more "grainy" and contrasty it is, because the manufacturer must make each grain of light sensitive material in the emulsion larger to make the film more sensitive (or faster). Actually, I think this might just be a sham designed to make us spend money on lights, because each and every year, film manufacturers come out with new stocks that are faster, sharper, and less grainy than before - but only marginally. Maybe they're holding back.

Anyway, the ASA 200 stock may be the best compromise. Looking at the chart, you'll see that you can shoot at T1.3 with our Zeiss Superspeed at eight footcandles with the ASA 200 stock and get an "underexposed" shot of the bad guy. But remember - "normal" isn't important here; what *you want* is. If you shoot at eight footcandles/T 1.3 and let the lab know that it was your intention that the bad guy be somewhat dark, because that's what you want, the shot might be just fine. What's normal for a bad guy under a street light at night is quite different than normal for a downhill skier hitting the moguls on a sunny day. So having the bad guy standing under a dim light might be just the ticket.

Or maybe not. Perhaps you find that the grainy, gritty look of the ASA 400 stock is exactly right for your film (an urban crime drama) and after shooting a test, you decide that the whole film should be shot this way. Then again, you might decide that even though the grain might add something to the film, the audience might perceive the look as cheap. Decisions . . .

Up until this point, the light meter you've used was an **incident meter**. This meter measures the amount of light falling on the scene, and displays it in footcandles. Meters of this sort have a white plastic dome that gathers light and (in general) mimics the curve of the human face. To use one, you hold the meter up to the subject but point the dome towards the camera. In other words, the dome is *standing in for the face of the subject*. Incident meters also come with a flat disc that you can use instead of the dome to find out just how much light is coming from a particular fixture (light) on the set. Glance through a couple of magazines like American Cinematographer and you'll undoubtedly see directors of photography holding their incident meters up, shielding the dome or disc so that the meter only "sees" light from one fixture. This enables them to pin point the intensity and direction of all the light on the set, while looking like highly paid craftspeople in a glamour industry (usually they wear leather jackets, too). The disc is easier to use for this function because unlike the dome, it does not gather light from such a wide angle, but most cameramen use the dome for everything because it's too much bother to switch domes and discs all the time.

The other type of meter (there are only two) measures the amount of light reflecting off the scene. These are called **reflective meters**. Instead of holding these up near the face of the subject and letting light strike the dome, you point these *at* the subject. They work like this: after you've pointed the meter at the subject, you press a button, then do whatever the owner's manual tells you to do to find out the F stop. Usually this involves entering or setting ASA and length of exposure (often called shutter speed) into or onto the meter, then turning dials or pressing buttons until an F stop is displayed. You then set your camera's lens to this F stop, and when the film returns from the lab, whatever it was that you pointed the meter at to take a reading comes back represented on screen as 18% gray. Well, not exactly. The meter *assumed* that whatever you pointed it at was 18% gray, so it gave you an F stop that would expose the film in such a way that the resulting gray on the screen, within the total light to dark range of the projected image, would make the object look correct.

What is 18% gray? I've heard that grass (nice, average, not too burned or lush) is 18% gray - that is, it reflects 18% of the light that falls on it. Caucasian faces are supposed to be somewhere around 35% gray; black faces about 19%. Of course, everybody has a different complexion, so if you go around pointing a reflectance meter at all the *talent* in your film (a hip word for actors, actresses, and trained animals) without doing a bit of thinking first, your exposures will be all over the place. Since an exact 18% gray patch isn't tattooed to everyone's forehead at birth, companies sell carefully printed cards that are 18% gray. You simply angle this gray card half way between the lights and the camera and take a reflectance reading from it. Or, forget the reflectance meter and the gray card and take a reading with your incidence meter.

Which type of meter - incidence or reflectance - is better? Actually, the question should be "which meter do I use for situation x?" because each meter has its own advantages.

Use an incidence meter for

A) all around shooting when you have the time and ability to walk around the set.

B) when you want to know how much light is coming from, for example, the back light as opposed to the key (the main front) light.

Use a reflectance meter when

A) you don't have time to walk around the set. On many documentary and low budget shoots, you may be operating the camera and setting up lights (or just shooting with available light) and only have time to point a **spot meter** (a pistol-like reflectance meter that you can use to take readings from far away) at the subject.

B) you can't get to the scene. If you have to shoot clouds, or the top of the Empire State Building, or the President, use a reflectance meter (preferably a spot meter) because there may be obstacles to getting near the subject (testy Secret Service agents, for example).

C) you want to compare brightness levels of two objects within a shot or scene. If the script calls for you to shoot a sign by the side of the road that says "BRIDGE OUT, 2 MILES" but you think that the art department has painted the sign too dark, you can check with your reflectance meter. By pointing the meter at the sign, then at the background, you can compare the two. If the meter says that the sign needs F 4 for a normal exposure and the background needs F 4, you may be in trouble. This means that both the sign and the background are reflecting the same amount of light. If the sign is orange and the background is green and you are shooting color negative, you may be alright, but if you are shooting black and white film, the audience might not notice the sign because it will blend in to its surroundings. Solutions? Shine more light on the sign (might look silly), darken the background (could be difficult), or repaint the sign (might take too long). Perhaps it would be best to do the shot where the background is naturally darker. At any rate, an incident meter would only tell you how much light to shine on the scene to get a normal exposure; it wouldn't tell you that, in this case, the sign and the background are going to appear to blend together in the final print. Many cinematographers use a spot meter to check various parts of a scene after they've set the general reading with an incident meter. This way they can, for example, make sure that the walls are bright for a comedy script, or that the light stand that they absolutely cannot move will be so dark that the audience won't recognize it.

THOSE KNOBS, BUTTONS, AND WHEELS

Here lies the real confusion.

Almost every light meter, save for those that are extremely simple (like the Spectra Candela), have some sort of internal or external calculator for turning a light meter reading (sometimes expressed in footcandles) into an F stop. Older meters usually have a dial or a series of dials that slide around and give up this information; newer ones are likely to have little buttons and small LCD screens that do the same, plus a few more things. Don't be worried. No matter how fancy or funky, all do this: they take the factors of exposure listed above and, together with the reading that you take (either by incidence or reflectance) give you a F stop.

For instance, the good old, trusty (and inexpensive) Sekonic L 398 is primarily an incidence meter. You hold the meter up to the subject, point the "Lumi Dome" toward the camera, then press the button. The needle under the clear cover rests on a number, from zero to 1.25M, or 1250. These are footcandles. At this point you can put the meter down, go to the chart in this chapter, and find out what F stop will give you a normal exposure for that footcandle reading in conjunction with the length of exposure and film rating (in ASA/ISO/EI). Or, you can a) turn the little center thumbwheel on the L398 until the correct ASA for the film you are using appears, then b) rotate the larger, outer ring until the "L" lines up with the footcandle reading on the scale above it that is a duplicate of the scale under the clear cover (the one with the needle in it), then c) find the applicable fps rate on the tiny red cine scale on the bottom of the larger disk and see which F stop is closest to the red line that doesn't say it but actually is 24 fps. Whew. Writing all this out is, of course, more difficult than actually doing it, especially once you've practiced the procedure a few times. Still, the chart is easier. You can make one up with a typewriter, then reduce it with a photocopier and stick it on your meter case or even on the meter, and you'll never use those twirly rings again.

Most light meters are designed for use in still photography. A few have added functions that make them useful in cinematography. The important difference between the metering requirements for still and movie use is that motion picture cameras rarely have lengths of exposure at 24 fps that correspond exactly to "shutter speeds" of still cameras. The shutter speeds of still cameras have been pretty much standardized over the years. They usually start with B, which means that as long as you hold down the shutter button, the shutter stays open, then proceed to 1 for 1 second, 2 for 1/2 second, 4 for 1/4 second, then 8, then 15 (not quite half as much light as 1/8th of a second, but close) 30, 60, 125 (again, not quite half as much as 1/60th), 250, 500, 1000, and if it's a hot new model, 2000 and maybe even 4000. Some cameras have shutter speeds of 2 seconds, 4 seconds, and even longer. Motion picture camera "shutter speeds", or lengths of exposure, are based on the speed of the camera (in fps) together with the shutter angle (see chapter one). This combination rarely ends in, say 1/30th or 1/60th of a second at 24 fps, but generally falls between the two. A camera with a 180 degree shutter running at 24 fps has a shutter speed, or length of exposure, of 1/48th of a second. A CP with a 156 degree shutter and 24 fps has a 1/55.4 of a second length of exposure.

A few meters try to accommodate movie use by having cine scales that read not in shutter speeds, but in frames per second. This makes things much simpler, but it is important for you to find out just exactly what shutter angle these fps rates are based on. The Sekonic L398 has a cine scale that assumes you are using a camera with a 170 degree shutter. I don't know of any 16mm camera in much use these days that has a shutter angle of 170 degrees (save the Eclair NPR that has an adjustable shutter, or maybe one of the very few, later model CP 16R cameras). So, cine scales are usually closer to most camera's actual length of exposure than still camera shutter speeds, but not quite.

What to do? Most cinematographers use 24 fps on the cine scale or 1/60th of a second on the shutter speed scale, then keep in mind that there is a slight error in their exposure, compensate, and shoot. As long as they are consistent in setting their F stop, their results will be consistent.

There is another answer. Light in footcandles. Instead of letting the meter dictate your F stop based on close-but-not-quite exposure times, you can simply use - as described above - the footcandle reading and the charts listed in this chapter (also supplied by film manufacturers) and ignore all the buttons, knobs and wheels on your light meter. Many cinematographers work this way because it is extremely precise. The difference between 20 and 23 footcandles might be less than one twentieth of an F stop, and therefore impossible to set on a lens, but it is, nevertheless, 3 footcandles: a difference that might be important on screen.

By setting a single F stop for an entire scene, the careful cinematographer can then adjust his/her lights by footcandles to achieve the desired results in an extremely controlled manner.

The refrigerator in the shot, for example, might be allowed to have 35 footcandles falling on it, whereas the lead actress at the table only 26. Or maybe 27. Her bowl of cereal might have just 10. The shot overall would be filmed at, say F 4 so that the fridge would be lighter, the table darker, and the actress in between. A meter that accurately reads footcandles can give you the ability to light each part of a scene with accuracy that cannot be matched when you allow the meter to simply dictate an F stop.

Manufacturers usually print footcandle-to-F-stop charts based on 24 fps with a 170 degree shutter (like the one in this chapter), but you can, with a little math, make new charts based on the camera you are using.

SOME METERS

Please note that the following light meter critiques are made with the understanding that the meters will be used primarily for motion picture use. Many of the following meters are designed primarily for still photographers and will likely have features better suited to their needs (example: flash metering). Only the Spectra meters are actually targeted toward motion picture users. If a meter isn't highly recommended here, it doesn't mean it isn't an excellent meter for other uses.

EV

The only confusing rating on the following meter list is EV, which stands for Exposure Value. For some reason, this "system" is incorporated into practically every light meter. On newer meters like the Sekonic L328, you can set the meter to read out in F stops or EV numbers, and on the Pentax Digital Spot meter, you must convert EV numbers to F stops because the meter displays EV numbers only. Funny thing is, I've never met anyone who uses EV numbers.

The Exposure Value System seems to have been invented as a means to simplify the use of meters and cameras. The idea is this: you take a light meter reading, then transfer the EV number displayed on the meter to an EV knob or ring or whatever on the camera, and shoot. No hassle.

But what exactly is EV? After searching through at least 20 books on technical photography, I finally found just one that explained, to a certain extent, what EV is all about. Only one other even mentioned it. Some system.

An EV number represents a combination of F stop and shutter speed that allows a constant amount of light to reach the film. An EV 2, for example, represents a combination of F 2 and 1 second. Or, it can represent F2.8 and 2 seconds. Both these combinations allow for the same exposure (the same amount of light will strike the film). EV 2 is also F 5.6 and 8 seconds.

The reason no one uses EV numbers is because anyone who is inclined to use a light meter is also the sort of person who wants to understand what *separate* effect exposure time and F stop have on the creative process, rather than having them lumped together. For example, if you are using a still camera, the meter might tell you to set your camera on EV 8 for a given shot. EV 8 can be F 2 and 1/60th of a second, but it can also be F 2.8 and 1/30th of a second. If you set your camera to EV 8, will the shutter speed be 1/30 or 1/60? If you plan on hand holding the camera, you'd better find out as most experts will tell you that the shot might be blurry if you hand hold at less than 1/60th of a second. Or, you might want to set your F stop at F 16 to obtain a greater depth of field, but if the camera has just an EV control, it may decide to shoot at F 5.6 instead.

There are purportedly still cameras with EV controls that, once set, will maintain a constant EV value even when the shutter or iris is changed. They do this by changing one for the other. For example, if you decide to change the iris to increase depth of field, the shutter will automatically change to a slower speed to compensate, thereby maintaining a constant EV.

It seems that meter manufacturers are hoping that EV will somehow become a universal system. Instead of saying that their light meter functions over a range of light from 1 to 20,000 footcandles, they say from EV 4 to 17 or some such range. It's left to you to figure out what this translates to into terms you commonly use.

From my experience, 6 footcandles is just about the minimum amount of light you can shoot sync movies under. I've reached this conclusion based on the fact that most 16mm cameras have 180 degree shutters, the widest iris found on Zeiss superspeed lenses is T1.3, and 24 fps is the speed at which most sync work is done (sometimes 29.97 or 30 fps is used for films that will be finished on tape). All these variables together with a film stock that has an ASA of 400 means I can work at a minimum of 6 footcandles when the situation calls for it (the script must lend itself to the look of a slightly grainier, contrasty film stock and the shallow depth of field produced by shooting with the iris "wide open"). The lightmeter I want should be able to work from say one or two footcandles to bright sunshine.

Kodak states that at for an ASA 100 film shot at F 2.8 and 1/50 of a second, 100 footcandles are needed for a normal exposure. The EV number for F 2.8 and 1/50 is just about 10. This means that the EV number for 6 footcandles used with ASA 100 film is close to EV 6. Three footcandles is EV 5, one and a half is EV 4. So, a meter that works down to EV 4 should be fine, although from personal experience, I can tell you that the Sekonic L 398 meter, which claims to have an EV 4 to 17 range, isn't easy to use under thirty footcandles (the lines are too close together and readings vary from meter to meter too much).

You'll note that to make this EV to footcandle conversion, a film sensitivity (ASA) must be used, although only some of the meters list the ASA along with their stated EV ranges. I suppose we are to assume that the EV ranges are always at ASA 100.

It is quite possible that you'll need to shoot under moonlight, running your camera at 2 fps to obtain a longer exposure time. If this is the case, you may want to opt for a meter like the Minolta Auto Meter IVF that claims to be workable down to minus 2 EV.

RUGGEDNESS - The best thing about the new digital meters are their inherent ruggedness. Since they have LCD displays rather than jeweled-movement needles, they'll generally take a drop or two and come back for more. The analog meters listed here will break very easily. An excellent combination might be the Spectra Pro as a main meter with the Sekonic L328 or Minolta Auto IVF as a back up.

INCIDENT METERS - ANALOG

Sekonic L-398

Measuring range: EV 4 to EV 17
Film speed range: ASA 6 to 12000
F stop range: F 1-90
Shutter speed range: 60 sec. to 1/2000 sec.
Cine scale: 8 to 128 fps
Power source: incident or reflected light; no battery needed

The best inexpensive meter. If you have less than $100, this is the one to buy. It is an analog meter (see the Spectra Pro), perhaps the last of a dying breed. Don't expect it to be rugged, though; one good drop and the case will shatter. Has cine scale. You might think that this is a superior design, because it needs no battery. Its selenium photocell converts light directly to an electrical signal that moves the readout needle, but the elegance of this arrangement suffers under low light situations (no good for less than 30 footcandles). If you can scrape up a bit more money, go for the L328.

Spectra Pro

Measuring range, fc: 2 to 250; 20 to 2,500 and 200 to 25,000
F stop range: 0.5 to 45
Film speed range: ASA .1 - 32000
Shutter speeds: calibrated for 1/50 sec.
Power source: none

The grandfather. This is the meter that started it all, and it really has but two drawbacks after all these years: it is fragile (uses a jeweled needle to indicate readings) and expensive. It's pluses are many: it is very accurate, even in low light; it is extremely easy to use - you can simply insert an ASA "slide", or punched metal plate, into the top, then read F stops directly, or read in footcandles; best of all, it is an *analog* meter. Wave the Spectra Pro through a scene and the needle moves back and forth depending on the amount of light striking the dome. Newer, digital/solid state meters take just one reading at a time and give a value in numbers. There is a reason why racing cars use analog gauges on their dashes: it is simply easier and quicker to understand them than to have to mentally convert numerical values into physical ones. This meter seems to be the most popular, even today, among cinematographers. People only buy the newer, solid state meters because they are less expensive and far more rugged. Everyone that uses this device as their main meter packs two of them for the time when the first one gets dropped and breaks in the middle of the shoot. All those famous D.P.s in American Cinematographer magazine pack the Spectra Pro.

Variations of this meter are the Spectra Candela 300 and the Candela 50, which read out in footcandles only. You might like one of these meters better; their scales are extremely simple and converting from footcandles to F stops is as easy as making a chart for whatever ASA film you are using. You might also run into a used Spectra Combi 500 or Universal. These are no longer made, but they work very much like the Pro and could be a bargain.

INCIDENT METERS - DIGITAL

Spectra Professional IV

F stop range: F0.5 to 90; .1 stop increments
Film speed range: ASA 3 to 8000
Shutter speeds: 1/8000 sec to 30 min
Cine scale: 2 to 360 fps including 25 and 30
Footcandles: 0.1 to 70,000
Lux: 1 to 100,000

Here's Spectra's entry into the solid state, digital LCD readout meter war. It looks like a winner, especially since it reads out in footcandles (from 0.1 to 70,000!) and lux as well as in F stops and has extra fps speeds of 25 and 30. Because it reads out in footcandles, it is probably the closest solid state/digital readout meter to the Spectra Pro.

Sekonic L-318B and L-328

Meas. range: EV 0 - EV 19.9 at ASA 100
Film speed range: ASA 3 - 8000
F stop range: F 1 - 90
Shutter speed range: 30 min. to 1/8000 sec.
Cine scale: 8 - 128 fps @170 degree shutter
Power source: 1 AA battery

This is a great meter. It is tiny (you can actually carry it in a shirt pocket comfortably), solid state, and uses a single AA battery rather than an exotic, expensive cell. It has a complete cine scale (fps rather than shutter speed) and does a little battery check thing each time you turn it on. Perhaps best of all, it displays both ASA and shutter speed/length of exposure or cine speeds (fps) on the LCD screen continuously, so you know what all your settings are all the time, at a glance. The display is excellent; the digital F stop display is accompanied by a dial-like analog readout for fractions of a stop that can be understood intuitively. Watch out for the L-318 (no B suffix); it does not have a cine scale. You might want to get this same model in the flash meter version - L-328 - if you do still photography. The current catalog indicates that you have to buy the more expensive L-328 to get the cine scale, but the L-318B I own does have it. It doesn't read out in footcandles, though, only in F stops.

Gossen Luna Star F

Meas. range: EV -2 to EV 18/23 @ ASA 100
Film speed range: ASA 3 - 8000
F stop range: F 1 - 90
Shutter speed range: 60 min. to 1/8000 sec.
Cine scale: 8 - 64 fps, also 25 and 30 fps
Power source: one 9V Alkaline battery

This meter seems to be, at first glance, a nearly identical twin to the Sekonic L318B. The layout, size, display - almost everything is just like the Sekonic. The Gossen, however, does have these advantages: it sports extra cine speeds of 25 and 30 fps, and it is more sensitive in low light - down to - 2 EV. Gossen meters have attained a loyal following due to their precision and quality construction.

Minolta Auto III

Meas. range: EV -2.4 to 19.1 @ ASA 100
F stop range: 0.7 to 64
Film speed range: ASA 12 - 6400
Shutter speeds: 30 min. to 1/2000 sec.
Cine scale: 1/50 sec. only
Power source: 6V bat. (ex: Eveready 537)

This is the solid state favorite of cinematographers. Many use this one because it was the first rugged, inexpensive incidence meter on the scene. Time tested, it is a good buy, but inferior to the Sekonic L318B, Minolta Auto IVF and Gossen Luna Star F because it uses an expensive, hard to find battery, is bulky, and doesn't have a cine scale (just 1/50 of a second way at the end of the shutter speed scale, after 30 minutes). Digital readings are in full F stops with decimal increments; the last digit (tenths of a stop) is reduced in size, which makes it easy to overlook. Also, it is very easy to hit a setting button by mistake, so you must continually switch between TIME and ASA modes to make sure that you're initial settings are correct, since both cannot be displayed simultaneously. There is an analog scale at the top of the display but it only reads out in half stop increments. Still, it does have a wider measuring range (low light down to minus 2.4 EV) than the Sekonic L-318B. The Auto IIIF adds flash metering for use in still photography.

Minolta Auto Meter IVF

Measuring range: EV - 2.0 to 19.9
F stop range: 1.0 to 90 + 0.9
Film speed range: ASA 3 to 8000
Shutter speeds: 1/8000 sec to 30 min
Cine scale: 8 to 128 fps
Power source: AA battery

This recent introduction into Minolta's meter line has been clearly designed to take over for the aging Auto III. Although not quite the same shape as the Sekonic L318 and the Gossen Luna Star F, the Auto Meter IVF has a nearly identical layout as these two meters; it seems that light meter design is converging. The Auto IVF is better than the Minolta III because it displays time, ASA and F stop simultaneously, is smaller, and uses a single, common AA battery for power. Minolta has become wise to the fact that on their previous meters, the control buttons protruded too far and were easily bumped by accident. The Auto IVF control buttons are deeply recessed. Everything you could want in a primarily incident meter that reads out in F stops.

Minolta Flash Meter IV

I mention this expensive, bulky meter only because it adds one nice feature over the Auto III/IIIF: it displays shutter speed, ASA, and F stops simultaneously, like the Sekonic L 318B. Has no cine scale, not even 1/50 sec. It seems to be principally designed for advanced still photographers who mix ambient and flash sources, and want a sophisticated and programmable meter. Buy this meter if this is you, or you want to appear to be sophisticatedly different on a movie set to those who don't know what the heck kinda Minolta meter that is.

REFLECTANCE METERS: SPOT

Many meters attempt to be both incident and reflectance meters by having extra attachments and scales. I feel, however, that the only good reflectance meter is a spot meter. You hold these up like a handgun, then look through an eyepiece and aim a little circle or dot at your subject. Most use only a 1 degree angle of acceptance. With a spot meter of this type, you could measure the difference in reflectance between an actor's nose and his cheek at ten feet. This is the kind of accuracy you need in a reflectance meter, not one that requires you to hold the receiving end less than one foot from the subject (no good for the top of the Empire State Building, clouds, or the President.)

Pentax Spot 5

Angle of acceptance: 1 degree
Measuring range: EV 1.0 to EV 19
F stop range: 1-128
Film speed range: ASA 6 to 6400
Shutter speed range: 4 min. to 1/4000 sec.
Cine scale: none
Power source: three 1.5V special batteries

The last of the analog spot meters. You must convert scale numbers to F stops via an external ring. Big, ugly, rugged, accurate, inexpensive. The batteries are not as easy to find as 1.5V AAs and they are not cheap. I owned this one for years and dropped it over and over again because it was too big to fit in any pocket and kept falling out. I tried hitching it to my belt, but it swung around and banged into light stands. I ended up charging its keep to assistant camerapeople, who probably resented it. To its credit, it kept on working with only minor repairs. This meter is also sold as the Spectra Cine Spot.

Pentax Digital Spot

Angle of acceptance: 1 degree
Meas. range: EV 1.0 to EV 20 at 100 ASA
F stop range: 1-128
Film speed range: ASA 6 to 6400
Shutter speed range: 4 min. to 1/4000 sec.
Cine scale: none
Power source: one 6V alkaline or silver oxide battery

Not inexpensive, accurate. The smallest spot meter around, and therefore very nice. Some users complain that the spot, or target, is sometimes difficult to see, and that you must convert the digital numbers (EV) in the viewfinder to F stops via an external lens ring after taking a reading, but still, an excellent meter. If it read out it F stops directly and used a less exotic battery it would be the perfect spot meter.

Minolta Spotmeter F

Angle of acceptance: 1 degree
Meas. range: EV 1.0 to EV 22.5 at ASA 100
F stop range: 0.7 to 90
Film speed range: ASA 12 to 6400
Shutter speed range: 30 min. to 1/8000 sec.
Cine scale: 1/50 sec. only
Power source: 1 AA battery

Expensive, accurate. Major drawbacks: just a little too large to slip into a pocket, and buttons are easily set (or upset) when doing so. After an initial setting, this meter automatically reads out in F stops in the viewfinder, which I find very helpful.

Sekonic Digit Spot model L-488

Angle of acceptance: 1 degree; 20 degrees
Measuring range: EV 1 to EV 20 at ASA 100
F stop range: F1 to F90 - 0.9AV
Film speed range: ASA 3 to 8000
Shutter speed range: 30 min. to 1/8000 sec.
Power source: 2 AA batteries

Expensive, accurate. Reads out in F stops in the finder like the Minolta, but may have better control placement (controls are less likely to bumped accidentally). Both this meter and the Minolta would be far better if they were smaller, like the Pentax Digital. You may find the switchable angle of acceptance feature useful.

Sekonic Dual Spot F model L-778

Angle of acceptance: 1 degree + 3 degrees
Meas. range: EV 1 to EV 20.9 at ASA 100
F stop range: F 0.5 to 128+0.9AV
Film speed range: ASA 1 to 12500
Shutter speed range: 30 min. to 1/8000 sec.
Cine scale: 8 to 128 fps inc. 25 and 30 fps
Power source: 2 AA batteries

This meter uses ordinary batteries, reads out angle of acceptance (either 1 or 3 degrees), F stop and shutter speed/cine scale in the viewfinder - but it's too big! Well, if you can get over the size of this meter, you'll find that it is really excellent. The controls are simple and logical and it appears to be very well made.

Gossen Ultra Spot

Angle of acceptance: 1 degree
Measuring range: EV 1 to EV 22 at ASA 100
F stop range: F 1 to 90 9/10
Shutter speed range: 1/8,000 sec to 60 min
Cine scale: 8 to 64 fps
Battery: 9 volt

I couldn't examine this meter before press time; certainly could be an excellent meter.

During the Shoot

Making Home Base

Whether your shoot will be on a closed set or mostly outdoors, it's a good idea to designate a "home base" for all the camera equipment. This will be where you'll load mags, clean equipment, charge batteries, prepare camera reports, tape and mark cans, make repairs, etc. The home base table is a place where no food or drink can be set down, where tape, pens, tools and anything else the camera dept. uses cannot be borrowed. It is a good idea to have someone guard the base, especially if the set is not closed. On big shoots, the guard is generally also the 2nd A.C. (whose job is principally loading mags), but on smaller productions, a P.A. can be designated. Should the table itself or any equipment need to be moved, the camera department must be notified first.

Often, finding and securing a camera home base is difficult to do. If you are spending much of your time outside, on the go, home base may be any flat, relatively clean surface, such as a picnic table or the tailgate of a pick up truck or station wagon. In a small apartment, you may find yourself struggling with the wardrobe and/or art department for space. In any case, a general warning is in order here, one aimed more at production managers than camerapeople: make space for the camera department's home base.

The reason for this is simple. If a sound recordist or boom operator makes an error, it will most likely be apparent on playback of the take. If the make-up, wardrobe or set department makes an error, it is usually caught before the scene is shot. Actors are monitored primarily by the director and continuity person, and secondarily by the camera operator and sound recordist. But if the Assistant Cameraperson makes an error, it can go unchecked until the dailies are screened. Scratches, fogged footage from light leaks, mistakes in the bag - all the hard work and money involved in the day's shoot can be for nothing. With a secure, separate base, the A.C. can maintain order and concentrate on his or her task.

The production manager usually insures that the camera department has a home base. If he/she doesn't, it then falls to the D.P. or cameraperson to insist that space be made, and that it be hands off to the rest of the crew.

Loading

Specific loading procedures vary from camera to camera; the best sources of information on threading patterns for professional 16mm cameras are the *Professional Cameraman's Handbook and Motion Picture Camera Data* (see bibliography). Aside from this, loading in general can be discussed.

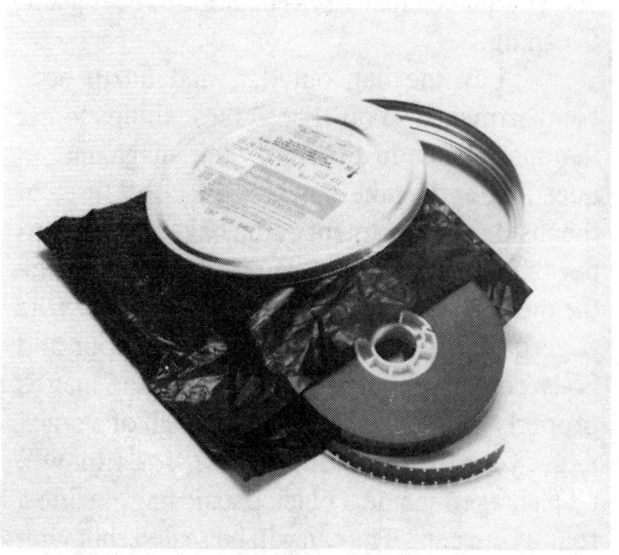

400' Core Load, Plastic Bag, and Can

Daylight spools make loading easier since no changing bag is needed, but they make plenty of noise, are short (usually 100') and aren't economical. Chances are you'll only use them for MOS shots: hand held exterior shooting with internal load capability cameras like the Arri S. Core loads will make up the majority of your camera original, and these need to be loaded in a darkroom, or what is more likely (and portable), a changing bag. Core loads are used in magazines only; cameras like the mentioned Arri S have their 100' internal capability designed only for daylight spools.

Before you get to the bag, make sure you have a secure home base - table, tailgate, etc. - as mentioned above. You should also assemble everything you need to complete the loading before going into the changing bag, and think through the entire procedure beforehand. You should let other crew-people know that once you have your hands in the changing bag, you may not, under any circumstances, be disturbed: no questions, conversation - nothing. One brief lapse of concentration while you are in the bag could end in disaster. It almost (but not quite) goes without saying that you should practice, practice, practice loading both the camera and mag in question. You will quite literally have to be good enough to load the magazines blindfolded. The bag and everything else should be clean - see chapter 8: Testing and Cleaning.

Lay the bag out flat, and unzip both compartments. You'll need these things to get the mag loaded: the film, the magazine in question, and a take-up core. Place all three in the inside compartment of the bag, and remember their locations, but before doing so, check the mag. Does it close correctly? What does the edge of the mag (the part where the door and body come together) feel like when the mag is properly closed? Is there just enough of a crack to get your fingernail in, or less? The film will be packaged inside a black plastic bag, inside a round film can. The can will be sealed shut with a strip of tape. Remove this before putting the can in the changing bag, but be careful that the can doesn't pop open before you slip it in. The plastic bag inside the film can is opaque and protects the film from light during this procedure.

Zip up the inner, then outer compartments, and fold the outer zipper underneath the changing bag so that light can't leak through. Put your arms through the sleeves of the changing bag, and pull the sleeves up over your elbows, so that the elastic is around your upper arm. Open the mag and swing the feed roll keeper arm (if there is one) out of the way. This done, open the can of film and place the top and bottom halves out of the way, into the corner of the bag. Unwrap the black plastic bag and pull out the film, then fold up the bag and place it in the open can. The magazine will have two core adapters, one for the take-up and one for the feed side of the mag. These devices allow you to use daylight spools in the mag when removed, or core loads when installed (cores have large diameter center holes; daylight spools small). Place the film flat on the bottom of the bag and carefully push the core adapter into the center of the core until it is full seated. The roll is now upside-down from what it needs to be when it is placed on the spindle in the mag, so make sure you've place the core into the right side of the roll of film for the mag in question.

This will vary from mag to mag. Some cameras, like the 16SR, load film on the feed side so that the film unwinds counterclockwise. Others, like the 16BL, feed clockwise. Still others, like the CP and NPR, can feed either way, as long as the emulsion always *faces the lens* in the gate. You will always get your film from the manufacturer loaded *emulsion in* (unless you ask for it otherwise). Specify B wind camera original. Once again, practice and study of the camera in question will tell you what side of the core load to push the adapter into.

To find out how the film will unwind before inserting the core adapter, however, you'll need to pull off a little film, and to do this, you need to remove the little piece of tape that manufacturers use to hold the end of the film down. Make sure you dispose of this piece of tape carefully; simply throwing it into the void of the bag can result in it finding its way into the mag, or worse: between the mag and mag door. You can end up **flashing** - exposing your film to room light - or jamming your mag. Stick this little piece of tape to the inside of the metal film can, and check for it when you leave the bag.

Under no circumstances should you use it to tape the film down to the take up core when loading the mag! It can end up stuck in the developing machine in the lab and cause real problems.

Now, with the film untaped and the core adapter inserted, resist the temptation to place the roll on the feed spindle, in the mag. A full 400' load of 16mm film will take up nearly all the space in the feed side and make it difficult for you to insert the film in the light trap of the mag. On some cameras, this is not much of a problem: the NPR and Aaton. But on others, you'll find it very difficult to thread the mag with a full load installed - the 16SR and CP, for example.

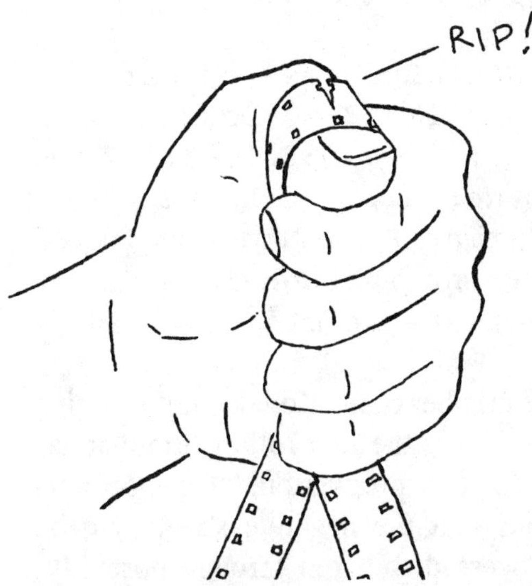

Breaking Film For Arri Cameras

At this point, you may have to do something special to get the film threaded into the mag. The 16BL and 16SR need to have the film broken across a set of perforations to get them to mesh correctly with sprockets in the mag. How do you find these holes in the bag, when you can't look at the film? Arri makes a special cutter that slices the film across the perfs, but you can easily do without one by wrapping the film, emulsion out, from your fist, over the front of your thumb (not your thumb knuckle) and back into your fist, and squeezing. The film will always break along its weakest point: a set of perfs. Other mags, like the CP PLC4-A and Mitchell, have felt light traps that only pass uncurled film. You'll have to carefully back-curl the film at the head of the roll to thread this type of mag, or crease the film. Creasing makes the film stiff and allows you to insert the film easily and quickly.

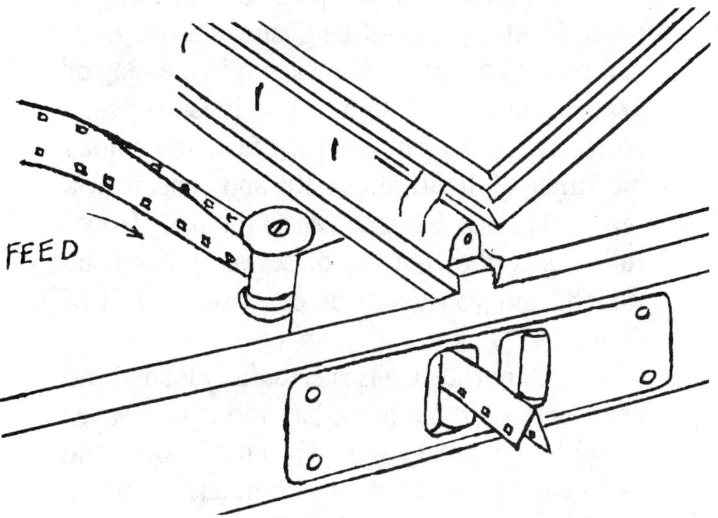

Creasing Film For CP and Mitchell Mags

Now all you may have to do is close the feed side door of the mag and come out of the bag: the mag could be of the **double compartment** type that need only the feed side loaded in the darkness of the changing bag. Or, you may have a **single compartment** mag such as on an Arri 16BL that requires you to pull film out of the feed to a mark (thereby setting the loop size) and thread up the take-up side of the mag before exiting the bag. In either case, once the threading is complete, and you've closed the door in question, stop - take time to feel the edge of the mag.

Earlier, before going into the bag, you closed the mag and felt the edge to see what it was like when it was fully closed. Now, before unzipping the bag, repeat this procedure. Some mags will actually close, but not completely (old Arri 16S mags are notorious for this). You pull the mag out of the bag and realize that something isn't right, when it's too late. By feeling around the edge of the mag, you can make sure it is fully closed *before* you expose it to light, and you accomplish one other thing:

you make sure that no part of the fabric of the inner changing bag is caught between the door and the body of the mag. This happens fairly often to beginners, and if it happens to you, you can't use that roll of film! It may be flashed, and you can't risk shooting 400' of film (possibly a day's work) and developing and printing it (over $100.) without being sure it's okay. If you do get part of the bag caught in the mag or expose the mag to light when it isn't closed correctly, go back into the bag fast, and unload the film. Pull off about 10' and send it in a separate plastic bag and can to the lab. Hopefully, only the first six or seven feet will be ruined, and you won't be out a whole roll of film.

Once the mag is successfully loaded and checked, pull it out of the bag and tape it. Old, funky looking mags should be taped around the perimeter of their doors completely, while 16SR mags just need a small piece of tape across the top (over both doors) or over their locks. In the first case, you are hoping that any small light leak in the mag will be caught by the tape. In the second, the mags never leak through the doors - the tape only serves as a reminder to you that the mag is loaded. Use a Sharpie or other indelible pen to mark the tape on the mag with this information: type of film loaded, length, roll # and date.

Attaching the film to the take up core may happen after you've loaded the camera and done a scratch test (double compartment mag) or in the bag (single compartment mag) but in any case, it's best done by double folding the film and carefully inserting it into the slot in the core. The core slot should be oriented so that it slants backward and grabs the film better. Make sure that the folded part of the film is entirely in the slot, because if it sticks out, it may cause the roll of film to have a bump in it that causes the take up roll arm to make noise. If the film isn't inserted in the slot straight it may wind off the core and cone out, jamming the camera or making noise.

Short ending means that you only shoot a portion of a roll; part is sent to the lab and the remainder is re-canned for later use. You'll more often than not be short ending every shooting day, so you need extra cans and plastic bags. A good rule is to get one extra can and bag for each roll (400') you plan on shooting. Labs give them out free for the asking. Always put your film in the plastic bag, fold it neatly, then place it in the can. After you open the bag, tape the can around the edge and use a Sharpie to mark the contents of the can. If you put your film either in the bag or the can alone, you are courting disaster. Cross out any old writing or labels on the can so there's no confusion.

The information on your can should contain the following: title, name of producer or director, type of film, footage, and instructions for developing. For example:

```
"The Silent Speeches of Harry
S. Truman" 11-18-93 Doug
Underdahl, 7248, 380' Roll 21 -
Develop Normal, One Light
Print, Print Roll Numbers in
Order, Print Through Edge Num-
bers, Release Negative
```

7248 is the number of the Kodak color negative in the can. This is the 21st roll of film that has been shot for this production. "Develop normal" means that the negative should not be pushed processed, but run through normally. "One light print" refers to the amount of compensation I want for my film when a print is made from the negative - in this case, I want none. "Print roll numbers in order" means that I want the lab to print this roll after 20 and before 22, so that things go easier for the person who has to synchronize the dailies.

Most camera rolls are 400' or less, because magazines that hold larger amounts of film (when available) make cameras unwieldy. Labs, however, like to print 16mm camera original onto rolls of camera stock that are 1200' long because it saves threading and handling time. Several different camera rolls, therefore, are usually printed on a single workpicture reel, and as long as the camera assistant and sound recordist remember to mark corresponding camera and sound rolls (1/4" audio tape) with the same number, the editor can easily sync sound and picture tracks. The 1/4" sound rolls will be assembled in order and transferred to 16mm magnetic film, and the order of sound rolls on this track will match that of the camera rolls on the workpicture track.

Kodak prints edge numbers on its camera original stocks, and "print through edge numbers" means I want these on my print as well. Release negative means I want the negative returned to me when I pay for and pick up my film; if I made no comment about this, the lab would probably assume that I want it stored in their vault for later work.

All this varies from lab to lab. It is essential that you discuss printing and handling procedures with the lab you intend to use before the shoot, especially if you are attempting something unusual when exposing your film.

Pulling Focus

There are many different variations to pulling focus, but they all involve taping and marking the focus ring on the lens to correspond to different distances needed for a given shot. Step by step, the procedure happens this way:

1) Taping the lens.

The A.C. places a thin strip of tape on the focus activator ring and a triangular shaped pointer piece of tape on an adjacent part of the lens that does not rotate, either when the lens is focused or zoomed. The strip of tape is applied *next* to the footage marks on the focus activator, not over them.

2) Finding the marks.

The director and actors start to block out the scene. This means that they will decide, among other things, where the actors will stand and move during the action. The director and D.P. will decide on camera angles (called set-ups to the crew), framing and focal length, and also any camera movement: pans, tilts, zooms, or dollies.

If an actor is going to have more than one position (subject to camera distance) in a given take, the director will usually designate the very first as position One, the next as Two, and so on. This makes it easy for him or her to communicate to the actors (as in "Let's take it from Two, Fred") as well as the cast (as in "Everybody back to one!")

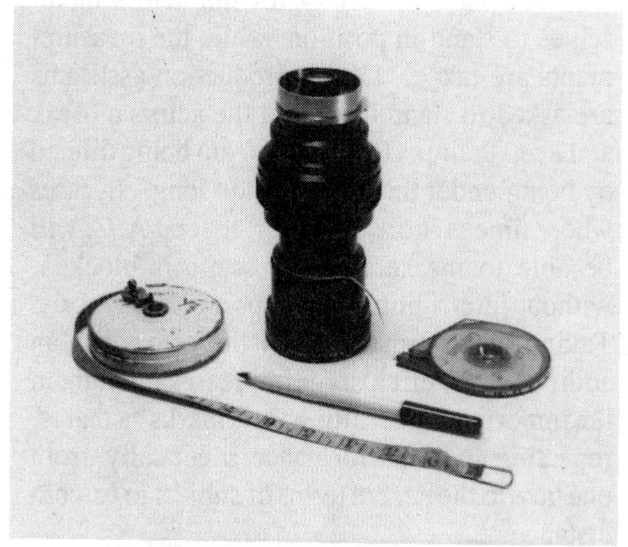

Tape Measure, Zoom, Pen, Letraset

These positions are important to almost everyone in the crew. The boom operator must know when to swing to anticipate an actor's move as well as keep the mike just beyond the camera frame for the new position. The D.P. and gaffer need to know exactly where both camera and subject will be to properly light each position. The art director needs to know precisely what is and isn't in frame with each new position (an electric light that couldn't be moved could ruin a shot that is supposed to take place in the Civil War, for example). Finally, the A.C. needs to know the precise camera to subject distance for each position within the take, and alter the focus of the lens accordingly.

He or she will measure focus with a 50' fiberglass rule stretched from the camera (specifically, the focal plane) to the eye of the actor in question. The distance is "twisted in" on the focus ring of the lens, and a mark is made on the adjacent strip of tape so that it aligns with the triangular pointer. Additional measurements are taken, and marks are added, until all the different camera/subject positions are accounted for and recorded on the lens tape. The number of marks can be only one or two or as many as ten; it is the responsibility of the A.C. to devise a system so that he or she understands the order of the marks. They can be labelled from one to ten, for example, or A to J - whatever works.

It isn't necessary for the actors themselves to stand in position while the measurements are taken. Often, production assistants are asked to stand in to give the actors a break and keep their performances from being diluted by being under the lights for too long. In cases where time is short, however, a good A.C. will be able to measure as the scene is blocked, without interrupting any important rehearsals. Taking measurements from the actors has an additional benefit also: it impresses upon them the importance of "hitting their marks" - that is, repeating their performance identically from one take to the next in terms of subject to camera distance.

This is one area where problems can arise between the cast and crew. An actor or actress may feel (and rightly so) that his or her performance is diminished by the need of the camera, lighting and sound departments for repeated, congruent action from take to take. For some talent, A.C.s, camera operators, and boom operators may be expected to compensate for surprise turns of the head, voice volume levels, and even varying positions on the set.

On one hand, virtually all actors and actresses need a certain amount of leeway in their performance; on the other, the crew knows that the talent will rarely be blamed for bad focus, poor lighting, and distorted, lost or under-modulated dialogue on the sound track.

Although one of the most important functions of the crew is to insure that the highest possible production values are obtained, the crew should never give technical instructions directly to the talent. The nature of the problem should be made clear to the director only, because

a) acting is one of the hardest things human beings can do, and it is infinitely more difficult when several different people are instructing the person who is trying to act, and

b) the director may be well aware of the problem and be unconcerned because of post-production plans (the problem may exist wholly in a section of the take that will be edited out or replaced by a reaction shot, for example). The final judgement must be left up to the director.

3) During the take.

The A.C. must use his or her peripheral vision to keep both the lens focus ring and the subject in view, while racking (twisting the focus ring) from mark to mark, keeping the subject in focus. Some people seem to have a knack for this, as well as accurately estimating any variance of the actors from their marks. For others, simple practice will increase accuracy. Be forewarned: professional Assistant Camerapeople are expected to be nothing less than perfect in all aspects of their job - especially in pulling focus.

Actually, pulling focus is quite easy, but it can be made difficult in certain situations. Lenses that are physically small may be difficult to work with - in this situation, a device called a follow focus can be of great help (see the Accessories chapter). If subject movement is wildly erratic or the lens is a telephoto and is used at a wide T stop (or both), it can often be impossible to maintain focus. Once again, the director should be made aware of the problems inherent in the take to allow him or her to make (or not make) adjustments.

Note:

What has been described above is, more or less, the standard operating procedure for focus pulling in professional, theatrical feature filmmaking. While most crews adhere to this system (with minor variations), there are many instances and situations that would cause crews to opt for other ways of focusing - for example:

- *The film is not a scripted, theatrical film.* Documentary filmmakers usually focus by eye, through the viewfinder, for the bulk of their shooting. They'll generally twist the zoom control of their lens (zooms are usually their primary lens) so that the lens is at it's most telephoto position, focus, then zoom back to the desired focal length.

- *The lens being used for the shot is so long that it is impossible to measure the distance with a tape.* In this case the operator will probably pan around from one focus point to another and have the A.C. record each mark on the lens as it is brought into focus through the viewfinder.

- *When speed is essential, and the lighting, crew and talent are already set.* If a slightly different shot is called for and everything is in place, the operator can save time by quickly eye focusing and having the A.C. record the marks.

Why is it that the above technique - focusing by eye and then recording each mark - isn't the standard operating procedure for scripted, theatrical films? The answer is simple - it requires three people instead of one.

When an A.C. uses a tape measure to find distances and record marks, he or she can work alone, either during rehearsals, or once the actors have left the set. But if focus is to be found by eye, through the viewfinder, three people are necessary: one to focus the camera, one to record the marks on the lens, and another to give the person looking through the lens something to focus on. And since no tape measure is used, nobody - especially the A.C. - has any real sense of the distances involved, so that when the talent varies from their marks (and they will), informed adjustments cannot be made. Using a tape frees up the operator and the person standing in for the talent to work on other tasks during the shoot, and gives the A.C. important footage references that can be important when actors and actresses stray from their marks.

Marking the Eyepiece.

The eyepieces of all professional motion picture cameras are adjustable, to allow persons of varying eyesight to bring the ground glass or fiber optic viewing screen into focus (see The Camera). Often, several people will be looking through the viewfinder of the camera at different times during a shoot, and this will necessitate the marking of the eyepiece for different settings.

Tape is applied to the focusing ring of the eyepiece in precisely the same way as to the lens of the camera itself. Different marks can be made for the director, camera operator, D.P., etc. This helps to eliminate confusion about focus, and speeds up the process of viewing by the different crew-people.

Focus Pulling Supplies.

Often, the A.C. will simply tear a thin strip from a wide roll of camera or even gaffer tape to go around the lens - these are cloth based and will rip in a nice, straight line. But serious professionals are now using drafting tape - a thin, smooth plastic tape that is available in many colors and widths - to record focus marks. The most common brand name is Letraset, available in just about every art supply store. It comes in a nifty plastic dispenser, and makes the taping of lenses and eyepieces very neat, and slick.

The Sharpie - an indelible felt tipped marker available in several colors - has been the pen of choice for the A.C., but many find that these are just a bit too big for marking fine focus pulls. With the availability of myriads of new markers at art supply stores, the A.C. can really go wild, and get just about any kind of color and tip combination. Watch out for markers that aren't indelible, though.

Quieting the Camera.

Despite the claims of manufacturers, all cameras make noise, enough so that *not one exists* that won't have to be subjected to some means of quieting at least some of the time.

Why is noise from cameras bad? The answer is simple, but often misunderstood by those who aren't familiar with the post-production requirements of films: a noisy camera (that goes uncorrected) can completely destroy continuity.

Motion pictures are, for the most part, shot in little bits and pieces: first a close-up, then a medium shot, a wide master, and finally a reaction shot. The film editor joins all these parts into one scene, and the initial goal is to make the viewer believe that all the pieces were somehow shot all at once - as if there were three or four cameras running simultaneously, recording the action.

Noise from the camera will always be picked up by the microphone during the take, and unfortunately, the distance from the mic to the camera will almost always vary from shot to shot. A close-up take may have fairly loud camera noise, while a medium shot has much less, because the mic and camera were quite close together for the close-up. The wide master may have very faint noise.

When the editor joins one shot to the next, the different levels of camera noise cause the sound track to "jump" - the viewer perceives not that all the different camera angles were somehow shot at once, but that each take is separate, and was recorded at a different time. In short, the illusion of continuity has been destroyed.

Many other things can destroy continuity: inconsistent lighting, changes in the set or props, varying performance, and other sources of noise on or outside of the set: air conditioning/heating vents, refrigerators, garbage trucks, airplanes, etc. - but noise from the camera presents a special problem because the camera must always be present during a take.

The solution to this problem varies from scene to scene, and even from shot to shot, because so many variables are involved. A tiny room or closet can make even the quietest camera seem like a kitchen blender, but then again if the walls and floors happen to be lined with carpet, which absorbs sound, there may be no problem. Similarly, a large room that has only hard surfaces and no drapes or rugs may seem to amplify camera noise.

The first step in solving the problem is determining the source of the noise. For example:

- *One magazine may rattle or squeak less than another* - use the quieter one for interior scenes.

- *A gear or belt may be damaged.* This is a very common cause of noise, and should be caught before the camera is taken from the rental house. The same is true for cameras that haven't received proper lubrication and maintenance.

- *Old film stock can cause many cameras to be louder.* This is usually due to shrinkage of the film over time, which reduces the distance between perforations (pitch). Instead of the claw entering each perforation cleanly, it may strike the top edge of each perf and produce a ratchety noise from the camera. This is not to say that old film should never be used - on the contrary, if it has been stored correctly (kept cool and dark and dry) older film can give results indistinguishable from fresh stock. The solution is simply to use the old stock for exterior shots, or for interior scenes where the quietness of the camera is less important (a party scene that will have music laid over it, for example).

- *A daylight spool is used.* Core loads must always be used where the quiet operation of the camera is essential. Daylight spools, no matter how straight they are (warped ones *really* make noise) will always produce a loud, un-barneyable noise that will destroy the take. Use them for the MOS shots, or outdoors.

Wrapping the Camera

Some cameras can be rented with **barneys**. These are padded fabric or leather covers that snap or velcro over the camera and reduce noise. Because they are custom fitted, and usually have special windows and flaps that aid in loading and checking footage counters, they can be quite expensive, both to rent and to own. Usually only Aaton and Arri 16SR cameras will have barneys that are readily available in rental. You'll also find that most barneys are actually too thin to really stop noise.

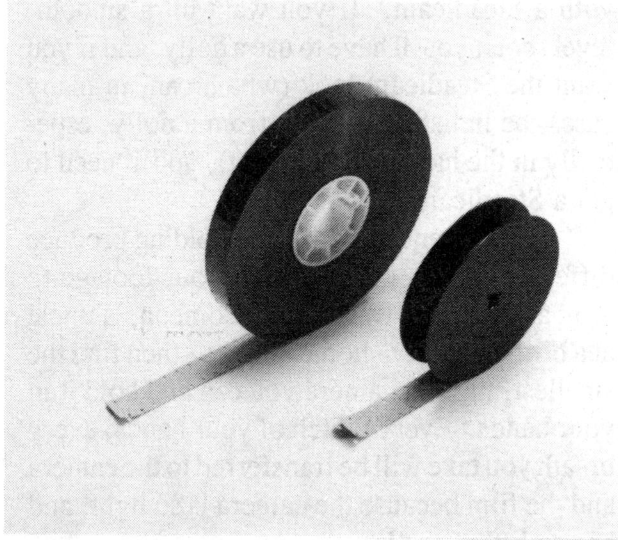

Core Load and Daylight Spool

The best thing to do is to make your own barney, especially if you plan on shooting extensively indoors. The very best barney, I've found, is an old down ski parka. For some reason, a down lining coupled with a heavy nylon shell really stops noise. The collar of the jacket is wrapped around the lens and eyepiece, and held in place with clothespins. The tripod head is covered by the front of the parka, and often the A.C. will reach through one of the armholes to start and stop the camera. In really critical situations, two parkas, or a parka and a heavy coat can be used.

Sometimes, though, this just isn't enough. The camera may be making noise in unusual ways. Since cameras vibrate, they can often send noise through the tripod and into a wooden floor. The floor acts as a sounding board, radiating noise into the scene. In this case, a sound blanket (actually a padded mover's blanket) can be thrown under the tripod, deadening any vibration.

Some cameras send noise straight out through the lens - the CP 16 and Frezzolini cameras (both mirror reflex and type A) are notorious for this. The answer is simple: Wrap and tape the neck of the parka around a series 9 or 4 1/2 retaining ring, then insert a clear filter into it. Lock it down with another retaining ring, and have the A.C. carefully hold this around - but not attach it to - the lens. The clear filter will greatly decrease noise coming from the lens, and not vibrate itself, since it does not come in contact with the camera or lens.

In the end, the noise from the camera is an ever present problem. As previously stated, the microphone will always pick up the noise from the camera in interior sync scenes. If you listen to the playback on headphones, from the Nagra itself, you'll always hear it, no matter how quiet the camera is. The goal is to have the noise be as slight as possible, so that it will ultimately be covered by the room noise, and finally by the *system noise* of the viewing environment on playback.

If you transfer your sound to 16mm fullcoat - that is, straight to magnetic film - and play it back, you'll likely hear the camera. But if you are in the same room as the dubber, or the projector on playback, you may not. If you transfer it to 16mm optical, the camera noise will probably be overwhelmed by the hum and hiss of the optical playback system. Even clean 1/4" to videotape transfers will contain a fair amount of system noise (except, perhaps, for the Hi-Fi decks - but that's another problem).

When you've finally cut, sound edited and mixed your film, then transferred it to 16mm optical and played it back to a room full of rustling people (with the air conditioning on) you'll find that any slight camera noise will probably been buried by all these other noises in the process - unless the camera noise was just too severe. Take heart - even the loudest machine designed for sync shooting can be successfully barneyed and blanketed, and give excellent results - if you take the time to do it.

HAND HOLDING

Film professionals seem to be very opinionated when it comes to hand holding. I think that the people who say they hate hand held shots are really only aware of the technique when it is done badly. They assume that whenever someone hand holds a camera, the shot will be objectionably jerky.

Sometimes, this is true. Many films have been marred by hand held shots that really should have been dolly or Steadicam shots. But hand holding is an important and unique technique; neither the Steadicam or the dolly can replace it.

Take, for example, the film ALIEN. This highly original film gets a good deal of its suspense from the camera being hand held, and not in the way you'd think. Take the scene where one of the crewmembers is revealed to be a robot: after he (it?) has been beheaded in a violent struggle, the camera is still hand held, even for stationary close ups. The technique is used here not to film wild action, or run after someone, but to give a very subtle, uncomfortable motion to the sequence that makes the viewer feel uneasy.

The television show HILL STREET BLUES always used a long, exquisitely choreographed, multi position hand held take at the start of each show to introduce characters and plots (the person holding the camera was wheeled around in a special dolly, however). This use of hand holding was chosen to imitate the techniques of documentary filmmakers, giving the footage a feel of gritty reality. You'd be hard pressed to find anyone who would feel that this hand held work is objectionably shaky.

Both these examples involve productions with professional level crews and budgets. The camera was hand held by choice, not because it was cheaper than a Steadicam, or faster than a dolly. These productions certainly could have afforded to obtain the footage with a dolly or Steadicam if they chose.

HOW TO HAND HOLD

You can hand hold the camera any way you like; there really isn't any wrong approach. However, you should know that your hand held footage won't look like it was shot on a dolly or with a Steadicam. If you want ultra smooth, level shots, you'll have to use a dolly, and if you want the Steadicam look (which can, in many cases, be indistinguishable from a dolly, especially in the hands of an expert), you'll need to get a Steadicam.

Different ways of hand holding produce different results. If you want your footage to look as though it was shot by someone's uncle at a birthday party - home movies - then find the smallest, lightest camera you can and hold it in your hands. Every twitch of your hands, every breath you take will be transferred to the camera and the film because the camera is so light, and has so little **inertia**.

The dictionary defines inertia as "the tendency of matter to retain its state of rest or velocity along a straight line so long as it isn't acted upon by an external force". The lighter an object is, the less inertia it has, and the more it will move when acted upon by an external force. Everyone who buys a one of those tiny new consumer video cameras should be issued a high tech steadying device for hand holding: a brick. Tape a brick to the bottom of one of these cameras and see how much smoother the shots become. All the so called ergonomically shaped handles and "palmrests" won't do a thing for smoothing hand held shots so long as the cameras are so light. If Sony began making all their professional Betacam cameras so that they weighed only three pounds, users everywhere would be clamping and strapping weight to their rigs until they were up to about fifteen!

To get hand held shots that are as smooth as, say, the footage on the TV show THIS OLD

HOUSE, then, you'll need a fairly heavy camera - fifteen to twenty pounds - or one that is weighed down to be this heavy. You'll also need to make the camera rest on your shoulder comfortably, and use a relatively wide angle lens.

Sixteen millimeter movie cameras that are "good" to hand hold, that deliver a smooth as opposed to home movie look when hand held - the Arri 16SR, Aaton, Eclair ACL and Cinema Products CP16 - all rest comfortably on the operator's shoulder while s/he looks through the finder. The weight of the camera is taken on the shoulder while the arms and hands are used for aiming, focussing, etc. Since the shoulder can take much more weight than the arms before fatigue and shakiness occur, cameras that are shoulderable can deliver smoother shots.

Wide focal lengths - between 8 and 12mm in the 16mm format - are also used to smooth out hand held shots. Every wiggle or bump photographed at 25mm will be twice as large as one at 12.5mm. I know of one camera operator who shot a music video hand held at 5.7mm (with a Kinoptic Tegea lens) and had several producers ask him who the Steadicam operator was!

So, for the smoothest hand held results, use a heavy, shoulderable camera or make your camera heavy and shoulderable with a piece of wood and a couple bricks, and use a wide angle lens. For shakier stuff (might be better for a fight scene or crazed killer's POV) take off the bricks or use a Filmo or a Bolex. To imitate a home movie, use at least a 25mm lens; a 50mm might be better.

DOUS, then, you'll need a fairly heavy camera—close to twenty pounds—or one that is weighted down to be that way. You'll also need to make the center rest on your shoulder comfortable and hold it relatively [illegible] angle.

Most [illegible] cameras [illegible] are good to hand hold [illegible] deliver a smooth [illegible] as opposed to the [illegible] look when hand held [illegible] the [illegible] (Detail [illegible]) [illegible] [illegible] [illegible] [illegible] the [illegible] [illegible] [illegible] and [illegible] [illegible] [illegible] [illegible] [illegible] [illegible] [illegible] [illegible] shoulder [illegible].

[illegible] used to [illegible] hand held [illegible] very [illegible] [illegible] [illegible] [illegible] 12 [illegible] [illegible] hand held at [illegible] [illegible] and [illegible] operator must.

So, for the smoothest hand-hold results, use a heavy shoulder-mount camera or make your camera heavy and shoulder-mount with a piece of wood and a couple [illegible] angle [illegible] shoulder [illegible] (might be [illegible] for a [illegible] [illegible] PDV [illegible] the [illegible] or [illegible] a Bolex [illegible] some movie [illegible] might be [illegible].

The Rental Game

Chances are, you'll rent your 16mm camera equipment rather than own it, unless you are either somewhat wealthy or only want to use a Bolex or Filmo. In fact, many camerapeople believe that they shouldn't own any photographic equipment at all (save for a few light meters) because a) they can't really afford to buy the latest, hottest camera, b) no single camera can do everything anyway, and c) there's always some new accessory out that somehow becomes indispensable, and how can you keep up with limited funds? They also argue that having a camera doesn't mean you have everything you need to make a film: what about a tripod, and maybe a dolly, and lenses, and a matte box? How about a Nagra, and microphones, and HMI lights, and fog machines, and a grip truck with stands and flags and . . . well, you get the idea. Although some people do own cameras and make a nice income renting them to themselves (when they work) and to their friends, most camerapeople decide that they'd rather have the rental house deal with ownership.

Before you call up a few establishments to find out about getting equipment, there's something you should know: rental houses are strange places. For the most part, they're populated by cynical yet dedicated managers, assistant managers, and technicians, and overseen by a president who feels that his or her business is always just on the brink of disaster. The reason the presidents feel this way is this: the camera rental business is a buyer's market (surprised?), not unlike that of warring street corner gas stations in the Fifties and Sixties.

Sitting on the shelves of these establishments, in heavy duty, metal and fiberglass road cases, is hundreds of thousands (sometimes millions) of dollars worth of camera, sound, video and support equipment. The loan payments on this equipment alone can be staggering, not to mention wear and tear, loss, insurance, employee salaries and benefits, rent and general overhead. Every day that this equipment stays on the shelves, it isn't earning money - it is costing money. The goal of all rental managers is to have it out in the field - rented - as much as possible. It would be better to have the equipment earn even a small fraction of the standard rental price, they feel, than sit on the shelf and earn nothing. Knowing this is your only real weapon: that rental managers really, *really* want to get their equipment out the door. You can call (or better yet, visit) various rental houses, getting one price after another until you find the best one; you can even tell each new company that you've been given a certain price and ask them to beat it, just like when you buy electronics equipment or new cars.

Of course, there is a difference, besides rental dollars, between a camera being in and out of the house. When it is out, it is in risk of being damaged or stolen, and it takes valuable employee time to take an order and assemble a rental package. And although rental companies invariably carry insurance against loss, it may be hard to make claims in every situation, and sometimes, serious damage may be hidden or go unnoticed at check-in. Cameras on shelves are safe and secure, and take up nobody's time. Unless you are willing to pay a certain amount, rental managers may decide that it is simply not worth the risk or time to rent the equipment to you.

But what is this certain amount? It always changes, even for the same equipment, used over the same amount of time. Different houses have different policies, and more importantly, different people. Here's a list of the things that you should know before you make that call or visit to the rental house:

There are **discounts** available. Most rental catalogs give you a one day price, and this is the most expensive way to rent. If you need to use the equipment in question for a week, you can get a weekly rate or discount, and you might save as much as 50% over the per day rate. In addition, you can simply say, "What's my discount?" This last phrase will usually only have meaning if you've dealt with the company before. In this case, the rental people know you are a (somewhat) loyal customer and that you can be trusted not to bounce a check, damage or lose the equipment, and return everything when you said you would. All these things are very important to a rental firm.

Weekends count as one day! This is the most amazing thing about motion picture camera equipment rental: you can pick up the equipment on Friday afternoon and shoot until Monday morning (you have to return everything usually before 10 a.m.) - that's two days and three nights - and only pay for a single day's rental! Many a film has been shot almost completely on weekend rentals when other businesses, used as sets, are closed also. Make sure this is the case, however; ask the rental person if the weekend definitely counts as one day (it should).

Travel days (sometimes) go uncharged. If you going to shoot in East Nowhere, a good day's journey by car and van from the rental house in downtown Bigcity, you should ask for a free travel day. If they say no, you could then ask them to ship (via Federal Express or some other expensive, time consuming way) the equipment to the location, but this may be a bluff you're not quite prepared to make - they could take you up on it! It doesn't hurt to ask for a no-charge travel day (or days if this is the case) however, and if the rental is sizable, the house may agree.

Don't forget holidays. National holidays like Labor Day, Presidents Day, etc. often go uncharged. You can schedule your shoot over a three day, holiday weekend and actually only pay for one day. You'll probably have to be making a sizable rental though. Still, it certainly doesn't hurt to ask ("Monday is Columbus Day - I don't have to pay for that, right?").

What do you get? One very tricky way that camera houses make more money on rental is to nickel and dime you to death on accessories you might assume were included in the package, or inexpensive. Get a complete list of everything you need: camera body, mags, all lenses, batteries, cables, matte box, speed controls, follow focus - everything - and make sure you are getting a price for all of it. If you are just renting a lens, ask if there's a filter adapter ring and sunshade included in the price (there should be), and see if there's an associated discount (that magic word) if you need a lens mount adapter to go with it.

What do you need? It is something of a natural state for producers and camerapeople to be at odds with each other, the cameraperson asking for, according to the producer, too damn much stuff, and getting, according to the cameraperson, nothing at all; in the end, these two people need to come together on a realistic and affordable list of equipment that meets the needs of the camera department. Is it really necessary to have an extension finder for the whole shoot? Can you get the job done without a follow focus? These extras can really add up. Much of the time, it's an unknowledgable producer or production manager calling the rental house with a list of things he or she has been given by the cameraperson to get, and which he or she has no familiarity with. If you don't know what you are asking about, you really can't bargain. If you find yourself in this situation, get the cameraperson to talk to you about each accessory (and read the rest of this book!); you may find that certain items aren't indispensable, or that substitutions (an 8-64 Canon instead of a 9-50 Cooke) are possible, and desirable.

You get what you pay for. This is always true, but sometimes, you pay much more for what you get, because you didn't ask for a discount, or didn't rent over a weekend, etc. The other thing this statement implies is that not all camera packages and rental houses are the same. Some will give you a worn, noisy 16SR, for example, with lenses that are pretty much kinda sorta collimated, for cheap. Others maintain their equipment to very high standards and expect to be paid for it. Don't automatically assume that a 16SR is always a 16SR; some are better than others.

Green is a wonderful color. Hard cash doesn't bounce. It also can be deposited into the rental house's bank immediately, unlike money that is received thirty or more days after the shoot. If you can pay even a portion of your rental charges up front, at the time you get the equipment, say so - but not at the start. Get the best price you can, and at the very end of your negotiation, say "Hey, that's a great price. Now, what about if I can pay you in cash, up front?" Often the answer will be another 10% off the one day price.

Come on down! If you call on the phone, rather than go into the house itself, you are just another faceless customer to the rental manager. You also have no idea what kind of establishment you are really dealing with - is it a big, bright, efficient rental house or the back of somebody's trailer home? If you go to the rental house, you can meet the technicians and managers, and present yourself; a real, live human (as opposed to a voice on the phone) is much harder to dismiss when rental managers negotiate rental price. You can also see just what you are getting - for example, a tripod that's shiny and new, or one that's a beat up clunker.

Niceness counts. Many producers and camerapeople treat rental employees as adversaries - and that is exactly what they end up getting. Others (perhaps to cover for their own lack of knowledge) talk down to rental people, or take on a "I am a great artist" attitude. This doesn't go over well. The people at the rental house are just that - people - and they respond better when they're treated as such. Don't expect to get good service or a good deal by bullying. There's a certain point past which rental people will just say drop dead - no additional service or negotiation is possible. It's surprising how many people, due to their tone, or attitude, will hit this wall.

I have found that the very best, most highly regarded camerapeople and Directors of Photography are also the most personable. They know they're good, and are not afraid of giving out some of their own knowledge, or asking questions about some new gadget they haven't seen before. Rental managers and technicians spend day after day preparing, repairing, and checking equipment. When someone asks them a technical question about equipment, they get a break from their work, but when the question is also aesthetic (example - "How would you go about getting a really low tracking shot that has to go under a coffee table?"), they also feel they are making a creative contribution to a production. If you have a question, ask!.

You're a student or independent. When I was in film school, everyone talked about how labs, rental houses, sound companies, etc. would give sloppy or uncaring service to people who identified themselves as students. Better to forgo any student discount and be treated like a professional, they argued. Was this true? Until I went to work at a rental house and also began finishing and starting more films, I didn't know for sure. Now I can say that the answer is no. People in the film industry almost always work at the same high level of professionalism; to do less means running the risk of more trouble and more work down the line. A bad camera or a poorly developed negative means apologies, extra rental or developing time and damage to reputation at the least - at the most, it could very well mean a lawsuit. When bad service does occur, it is almost always due to the kind of sloppiness or inattention that will affect everyone, not just a "less important" customer. To think otherwise, you have to imagine lab, rental house and mixing studio technicians saying "Aah, this guy's just a student; I'm gonna screw him over." I suppose that this does happen sometime, but in my experience I've found that the opposite is true: when these people know that you are paying for services out of your own pocket, they'll actually do more for you than somebody they've only talked to over the phone, who works for a big company and sends a messenger to get everything. When people who are working for big companies or productions attempt to whittle down their rental bills, managers know that they are just trying to save themselves a buck - the money is there, and if it isn't spent for equipment, it'll just go into the company's own profits. If you are a student or an independent with a small budget, you should say so - you just might get a better deal because rental houses know you aren't trying to gouge them. Rather, you have a legitimate request for a better deal, and you just might get it out of sympathy.

So many film service companies give student discounts that you may have to prove that you actually are enrolled in a film class because other people try to claim student status to get discounts. If you are an independent, you can try to get the this discount by stating that you are in the same financial boat as any student, and if you make a good enough case, you stand a chance of succeeding.

Insurance is extra. You probably can't rent any state of the art 35mm equipment at all without showing the rental house a copy of your insurance covering loss or damage during the shoot because it's just too risky to let a $150,000 camera package out the door without coverage. Sixteen millimeter is a different story. If a house insists that you have outside insurance to get their 16mm equipment, this is your cue that they just don't want your business. They know that insurance is very costly and that many 16mm shoots are too low budget to afford complete coverage, *and* they know that other houses often don't require it. Why wouldn't they want your business? It may be that they just don't have the equipment you're asking for, or the rental money involved just isn't enough for them to bother with. In any case, go elsewhere. No sense in pushing the point, especially if they aren't going to deal with you honestly.

Sometimes what will happen when you've finished negotiating the entire deal - all the accessories, number of days, student discount, etc. - is that the rental manager will ask you about insurance, and your answer will usually be that you have none. He or she will then say that you can buy insurance from them, the rental house. It usually ends up costing an extra 10% (or thereabouts). It's hard to say exactly what this is for, because they undoubtedly don't pay it to their own insurance company. It's just their way of assuming the risk themselves. You probably won't be able to negotiate much on this "in house" insurance, but you should budget for the possibility of paying it.

Responsibility counts. This sounds like something from a grade school lecture, but it is very important if you want to build a good relationship with a rental house.

If you don't return equipment when you say you will, you may be inconveniencing someone else who was scheduled to use it later. If you call for a specific pick-up time (especially a special, early one) be on time or you could jam up the check-out area. Pay your bill on time, or if you can't, at least pay part of it and tell the house when it can expect the rest. If you break something, point it out at check-in; the very worst customers in the eyes of the rental house are those that damage something and then turn it in, hoping that nobody notices. It's also a good idea to show up behaving responsibly. Rental house owners and managers are usually a conservative lot and, no matter how unfair it may be, generally don't take well to people who they think are weird or who look incompetent. Remember, you'll more than likely be taking a considerably expensive amount of equipment out their door, and if you look like someone who doesn't know how to correctly mount a camera (so that it falls off the tripod) or who isn't smart enough to always have someone watch the cases (so that some street thief makes off with the video tap) you won't be a welcome sight for the next rental.

From the above, it may sound as if it is an unpleasant ordeal at best to bargain with a rental house. While this is the case for many, it doesn't tell the whole story. Rental houses can also be places where you can get hands-on instruction on all kinds of camera equipment and where you can find out about an Assistant Cameraperson gig or other crew work to pay the rent. They can even be sources of employment themselves; many successful camerapeople started out sweeping floors at rental houses.

Bibliography

American Cinematographer Manual
6th edition - edited by Fred H. Detmers. Published by the ASC Press, Hollywood. For years this volume was referred to as "The Black Book". It is now red (6th edition) and so is the Professional Cameraman's handbook, leading to confusion. At any rate, this manual can be thought of as the cameraman's bible; it's a reference work with brief but informative sections on cameras, lenses, lighting, filters, exposure, underwater photography and even sound recording for motion pictures. It also contains depth of field tables, shutter angle compensator charts, English/Metric conversions, etc. Warning - the latest edition does not contain everything in the previous editions. Chances are, you won't miss anything that has been deleted, but if you really want to dig into cinematography, try to get your hands on older editions for pages on things like Depth of Focus and Frezzolini cameras. Although the latest Manual is thinner and lighter (and durably softbound), it has been typeset with rather light and less readable print than its predecessors. Nevertheless, indispensable - buy one!

American Cinematographer - magazine
ASC Holding Corp., 1782 N. Orange Dr., Hollywood, CA 90028. This glossy publication contains current industry advertising, technical features, and an excellent new series of articles on lighting that actually show fixture diagrams and footcandle levels! You'll also find in depth technical articles that are written in a longer, more understandable style than can be allowed in the American Cinematographer Manual.

Anton Wilson's Cinema Workshop
Anton Wilson. A.S.C. Holding Corporation, 1782 North Orange Drive, Hollywood, California 90078. This volume seems to be a collection of articles written for the American Cinematographer magazine. It is an excellent book that explains the technical background of a number of subjects: film, cameras, formats, lenses, and even sound, underwater shooting, and video. Contains the most clear, most extensive discussion of batteries of any work. This is not a comprehensive text - as the title suggests, it is a collection of in depth, informative and well written articles on a number of subjects. Reading it, you find yourself saying things like "aah, so that's how that works!". Highly recommended.

Feature Filmmaking at Used-Car Prices
Rick Schmidt. Published by Penguin Books. Viking Penguin Inc. 40 West 23rd, New York, NY 10010. You say you can't make your feature film because no one will give you $5,000,000? Hah! This book tells you how to make a feature in 16mm for $7,000. Okay, maybe some of what's in this book is a bit crazy, like not making a workprint to edit (huh?), but by golly, Rick Schmidt has done it himself. You may not be able to write at the top of the first page of your script INT. NUCLEAR POWER PLANT or EXT. NEW YORK 1952, but you can actually make a feature film for very little money. This book is proof that if you really want to make a feature, nothing can stop you.

Filming Practical Monitors
Kirk E. Paulsen and William C. Nusbaum - November 1984 issue of American Cinematographer. Not a book, but an article in a magazine, it contains the most readable and thorough discussion of problems encountered and results possible when filming television monitors (broadcast, VTR playback, computer screens, etc.). Although geared mainly to users of 35mm equipment, the information is easily transposed to 16mm shooting. This article is also incorporated into the 6th edition of the

American Cinematographer Manual.

Motion Picture Camera Data
David Samuelson. Published by Focal Press, London. Imagine having the owner's manuals of nearly 90 manufactures cameras, all distilled and compressed into one volume. That's the Motion Picture Camera Data book. Although the entries are necessarily brief, each is accompanied by excellent drawings showing controls, threading diagrams, etc. Included are many machines omitted in the Professional Cameraman's Handbook, such as high quality Super-8 cameras. An excellent companion to this volume.

The Mystery of Filters II
H.K. Harrison. Published by H.K. Harrison, P.O. Box 1797, Porterville, California 93258-1797. This is Harrison's guide to it's product (filters). It's a complete reference work that is not written in an abbreviated technical style.

Professional Cameraman's Handbook
Verne and Sylvia Carlson. Published by Amphoto - American Photographic Book Publishing, 1515 Broadway, New York, NY 10036. From the title, this book sounds as though it ought to contain roughly the same information as the American Cinematographer Manual - but it doesn't. This book should actually be called The Professional *Assistant* Cameraman's Handbook, for this is the person for who it was written. It has no information about exposure, filtering, or lighting - it's an extremely detailed source (complete with photographs and pointer arrows) concerning the set up and operation of professional motion picture cameras: loading, threading, cleaning, troubleshooting, etc. It also has describes the duties of the A.C: marking cans, making out camera reports, using the changing bag, etc. Although it is aimed mainly at 35mm users, is somewhat dated (the newest camera accessories and some new 35mm cameras aren't included), and has a few odd exclusions (no Aaton!), it is a text that is indispensable to the working A.C.

The 16SR Book - A Guide to the System
Jon Fauer. Edited by Stephen C. Chamberlain. Published by Arriflex Corporation, 500 Route 303, Blauvelt, NY 10913. One of the very few technical books around which is well written: no technical abbreviations and jumps of logic that assume the reader is already an expert (and therefore wouldn't need the book in the first place); clear, detailed drawings and diagrams abound. Although this work is specific to the 16SR and contains detailed information about the Arri 16SR system (it does include information about equipment not manufactured by Arri) it is so comprehensive and well done that users of other cameras would do well to read it. Also, it should be remembered that the 16SR is the primary camera used in 16mm photography today, so anyone planning on entering the field would be well served by this manual.

There's More To "Clear Pictures" Than Meets The Eye.
Kenneth Richter, October 1978 issue of American Cinematographer. In this article, Kenneth Richter lays out all the important elements of perceived on screen image sharpness, starting with the raw film and ending with the eye of the audience. Richter manufactures lens and camera testing equipment - specifically, the Richter collimator and accessories - and he is also a professional filmmaker as well. This unique combination of knowledge makes this article a must read by anyone involved in the making of films. The best way to get a copy is to write the company directly (see the Resource List); while you're at it, ask for equipment catalogues and a copy of the Richter Collimator Operating Manual as well.

Time Code In The Reel World II
Jim Tanenbaum, C.A.S. with Manfred N. Klemme, 2nd Edition
Whew! Everything you every wanted to know about time code along with the realization that there's a whole lot you wish you didn't have to know. Complete, concise, excellent; does as

good a job as is humanly possible to make time code, in all its ugly mutations, understandable. Every DP should get this work and at least try to fathom as much as possible. When Tanenbaum's new book THE PRODUCTION MIXER'S HANDBOOK comes out, snap it up. It will undoubtedly be excellent.

Student Filmmaker's Handbook
Eastman Kodak Company, Rochester, NY 14650
What's the difference between a T core and a Z core? What's specular density? A Modulation-Transfer Curve? Find out in this handbook. Although it is clearly biased toward Eastman products, it has a wide range of technical information that is difficult to find elsewhere.

Resource List

CAMERA EQUIPMENT

Aaton - 4110 W. Magnolia Blvd., Burbank, CA 91505 (818) 972-9078 fax (818) 972-2673; 2 Rue de la Paix, 38001 Grenoble, France (33) 7642-6409 fax (33) 7651-3491.

Abel Cinetech - 66 Willow Ave., Staten Island, NY 10305 (718) 273-8108. Aaton 16mm & 35mm, and accessories.

Alan Gordon Enterprises - 1430 Cahuenga Blvd., Hollywood, CA 90078 (213) 466-3561 (800) 825-MOVI fax (213) 871-2193. Motion picture equipment sales.

Angenieux - 7700 N. Kendall Drive, Miami, FL 33156 (305) 595-1144; Courrier/Mall/Postanschrift: postale 154, CH-1211 Geneva-17, Switzerland, Ph: 41(0)22 736 22 66 fax 41(0)22 786 12 49. Lens manufacturing.

Arriflex - 500 Route 303, Blauvelt, NY 10913-1123 (914) 353-1400 fax (914) 425-1250; 600 N. Victory Blvd., Burbank, CA 91502-1639 (818) 841-7070 fax (818) 848-4028.

Bolex - CH-1401 Yverdon, Switzerland (0041) 24 21 60 21 fax (0041) 24 21 68 71.

Canon - Optex, 22-26 Victoria Road, New Barnet Herts. EN4 9PF, U.K. tel. 01-441 2199 fax 01-449 3646. ZGC, Inc., 57 Plymouth St., Montclair, NJ 07042 (201) 746-4428.

Ceco International Corp. - 440 West 15th St., New York, NY 10011 (212) 206-8280. Camera, lighting & grip rental.

Century Precision Optics - 10713 Burbank Blvd., N. Hollywood, CA 91601 (818) 766-3715. Angenieux sales, service & rental.

Chambless Cine Equipment - 2488 Jewel St., Atlanta, GA 30344 (404) 767-5210 fax (404) 767-6750. Bolex sales & service.

Cinema Products Corporation - 3211 So. LaCienega Blvd., Los Angeles, CA 90016 (213) 836-7991 fax (213) 836-9512.

Cinematography Electronics - 1455 19th St., Santa Monica, CA 90404 (310) 829-1811 fax (310) 453-2601. Camera crystal sync motor manufacturing.

Clairmont Camera - 4040 Vineland, Studio City, CA 91604 (818) 761-4440; North Shore Studios, Vancouver, B.C. V7J3S5 (604) 984-4563.

CSC - (Camera Service Center) - 625 West 54th St., New York, NY 10019. Arriflex cameras and accessories.

Frezzolini, Inc. - 7 Valley St., Hawthorne, NJ 07506 (201) 427-1160.

Fries Engineering - 12032 Vose St., North Hollywood, CA 91605 (818) 765-3600 fax (818) 765-6977. Special effects 35mm & 65mm cameras.

General Camera Corp. - 540 West 36th Street, New York, NY 10018 (212) 594-8700. Camera (Arriflex & Panavision), lighting & accessory rental.

Hand Held Films - 552 Broadway, New York, NY 10012 (212) 941-0744 fax (212) 941-5472. Camera (Arriflex & Aaton) and accessory rental.

Harrison and Harrison - P.O. Box 1797, Porterville, CA 93528-1797 (209) 782-0121. Filter manufacturing.

Lee Utterbach, Inc. - 126 Russ St., San Francisco, CA 94103 (415) 553-7700 fax (415) 553-4535. Arriflex rental.

Media Logic - 17 West 20th Suite 5 East, New York, NY 10011
(212) 924-3824 fax (212) 924-3823. Support & accessory manufacturing & rental.

Norris Film Products - 1014 Green Ln., La Canada, CA 91011 (818) 790-1907 fax (818) 790-1920. Intervalometer & speed control manufacturing.

Oppenheimer Camera - Seattle (206) 467-8666 fax (206) 467-9165; Portland (503) 233-0249 fax (503) 231-4806. Camera & accessory rental.

Panavision - 6779 Hawthorn, Hollywood, CA 90028 (213) 464-3800.

Roessel CPT - 48-20 70th St., Woodside, NY 11377 (718) 424-1600 fax (718) 457-4778; 4473 Tilly Mill Rd., Atlanta, GA 30360 (404) 936-9736 fax (404) 936-9734. Arriflex cameras and accessories.

Steadicam Operators Association, Inc. - (215) 225-5226.

Swiss Professional Movie Equipment - 38 W. 32nd St., Rm. 1206, New York, NY 10001 (212) 594-6340 fax (212) 714-0719. Bolex sales & service.

TCS, Inc. - 630 9th Ave., Suite 1004, New York, NY 10036
(212) 247-6517. Aaton and Arriflex camera and accessory rental.

Tiffen Manufacturing Corporation - 90 Oser Ave., Hauppauge, New York 11788 (516) 273-2500. Filters & accessories.

Tobin Cinema Systems - 3227 49th Ave. Southwest, Seattle, WA 98116 (206) 932-7280. Camera & accessory sales & rental.

Visual Products - 46994 Peck Wadsworth Road, Wellington, OH 44090 . Used professional motion picture equipment with a guarantee.

Whitehouse Audio/Visual - 2696 Lavery Ct. Unit 8, Newbury Park, CA 91320 (805) 498 4177. Film & video equipment sales, service & rental.

ZGC (Cooke), Inc. - 57 Plymouth St., Montclair, NJ 07042 (201) 746-4428 fax (201) 746-2105. Lens manufacturing.

LIGHTING/GRIP EQUIPMENT

Birns & Sawyer - 1026 N. Highland Ave., Hollywood, CA 90038
(213) 466-8211 fax (213) 466-7049. Grip equipment.

Ceco International Corp. - 440 West 15th St., New York, NY
10011 (212) 206-8280. Camera, lighting & grip rental.

Cine-60 - 630 9th Ave., New York, NY 10036 (212) 586-8782. Lighting, accessories, & power supplies.

Cinekinetic U.S.A. - 1405 Vegas Valley Drive #177P, P.O. Box 73063, Las Vegas, NV 89170. Support & mount equipment.

Dedo Weigert - 410 Garibaldi Ave., Lodi, NJ 07644 (201) 777-2771 fax (201) 777-5585. Lighting equipment manufacturing.

General Camera Corp. - 540 West 36th Street, New York, NY 10018
(212) 594-8700. Camera (Arriflex & Panavision), lighting & accessory rental.

Kino Flo - (818) 767-6528 fax (818) 767-7517. Lighting equipment manufacturing.

Lowel-Light Manufacturing - 140 58th St., Brooklyn, NY (718) 921-0600 fax (718) 921-0303. Lighting & grip equipment manufacturing.

Matthews Studio Equipment - 2405 Empire Ave., Burbank, CA 91504 (818) 843-6715 (213) 849-6811 order hotline (800) CE-STAND fax (213) 849-1525. Lighting & grip equipment manufacturing.

Media Logic - 17 West 20th Suite 5 East, New York, NY 10011
(212) 924-3824 fax (212) 924-3823. Support & accessory manufacturing & rental.

Mole-Richardson - 937 N. Sycamore Ave., Hollywood, CA 90038-2384 (213) 851-0111 fax (213) 851-5593. Lighting & grip equipment manufacturing.

Richter Cine Equipment - 16 Ridge Road, Essex, New York, 12936
(518) 963-7080. Tripod & accessory manufacturing.

Sachtler Corp. of America - 55 N. Main St., Freeport, NY 11520 (516) 867-4900 fax (516) 623-6844 telex 140 107 sac frpt; 3316 W. Victory Blvd., Burbank, CA 91505 (818) 845-4446; Kommunikationstechnik, Germany, Gutenbergstraße 5, D-8044 Unterschleissheim bei Munchen (089) 32 158 200 fax (089) 32 158 227 telex 5 215 340 sac d. Tripod, support & lighting equipment manufacturing.

Weaver/Steadman - northeast: Dragon's Head Productions (212) 674-5681 fax (212) 674-4020; southeast: Production Services - Atlanta (404) 622-1311 fax (404) 622-1691; all other areas: Weaver/Steadman (310) 829-3296 fax (310) 828-5935. Support, crane & head manufacturing.

RAW STOCK & LABORATORIES

Du Art Laboratories - 245 West 55th Street, New York, NY 10019
(212) 767-4580. 16mm, 35mm, color & B&W processing, printing & transferring.

Eastman Kodak - 343 State St., Rochester, NY 14650 (716) 724-4000; Atlanta (404) 455-0123; Chicago (708) 218-5175; Dallas (214) 506-2372; Hollywood (213) 464-6131; Honolulu (808) 833-1661; Montreal (514) 761-3481; New York (212) 930-7500; Vancouver (604) 684-8535; Toronto (416) 766-8233; Washington (703) 908-5313. 16mm & 35mm raw stock.

Steadi-Systems - 311 W. 43rd St., Ste. 403, New York, NY 10036 (212) 974-7666 (800) 626-0946. 16mm & 35mm raw stock sales.

Technicolor Laboratories - 4050 Lankershim Blvd., N. Hollywood, CA 91608 (818) 769-8500; 321 W. 44th St., New York, NY 10036 (212) 582-7310 fax (212) 265-9089. 16mm & 35mm color processing, printing & transferring.

MISCELLANEOUS

Audio Services - 326 W. 48th St., New York, NY 10036 (212) 977-5151. Professional sound sales, service & rental.

Denecke - 5417 B Cahuenga Blvd., North Hollywood, CA 91601 (818) 766-3525 fax (818) 766-0269. Time code slate sales.

The Great American Market - 826 N. Cole Ave., Hollywood, CA 90038 (213) 461-0200 fax (213) 461-4308. Theatrical, color-correction and diffusion material manufacturing.

The International Film & Television Workshops - Rockport, ME 04856 (207) 236-8581 fax (207) 236-2558.

Rosco - (800) ROSCO NY (914) 937-1300. Theatrical, color-correction & diffusion material manufacturing.

Spectra Cine, Inc. - 820 N. Hollywood Way, Burbank, CA 91505 (818) 954-9222 fax (818) 954-0016. Metering systems manufacturing.

Lowel-Light Manufacturing — 140 [illegible], NY [illegible] fax [illegible]. Lighting & support equipment manufacturing.

Mathews Studio Equipment — 2405 [illegible] Ave., Burbank, CA [illegible] (800) [illegible] fax (213) [illegible]. Lighting & support equipment manufacturing.

Media Logic — [illegible] New York, NY [illegible] fax [illegible]. Support & accessory manufacturing.

Mole-Richardson — 937 N. Sycamore Ave., Hollywood, CA [illegible] (213) [illegible]. Lighting [illegible] manufacturing.

[illegible]

[illegible]

Wescam [illegible] Dragon [illegible] fax [illegible] (416) [illegible] fax [illegible] support [illegible] manufacturing.

RAW STOCK & LABORATORIES

[illegible] W. [illegible] St., New York, NY [illegible] (212) [illegible] fax [illegible] processing, printing & transferring.

Eastman Kodak — [illegible] Rochester, NY [illegible] Atlanta (404) 465-0121; Chicago (708) 218-5175; Dallas (214) [illegible]; Hollywood (213) 464-[illegible]; Montreal (514) [illegible] New York (212) [illegible]; Vancouver (604) 684-8535; Toronto [illegible] Washington (703) 508-5366. Film & Videotape.

[illegible] Systems — [illegible] W. [illegible] St., New York, NY [illegible] (212) [illegible] (800) [illegible] Film & videotape stock sales.

Technicolor Laboratories — [illegible] Blvd., Hollywood, CA 91608 (818) 769-8500; 321 W. 44th St., New York, NY 10036 (212) [illegible] fax (212) [illegible]. Film processing, printing & transferring.

MISCELLANEOUS

Audio Services — [illegible] W. 19th St., New York, NY 10011 (212) [illegible]. Professional sound sales, service & rental.

Cinedeck — [illegible] Blvd., North Hollywood, CA 91601 (818) 766-1525 fax (818) 766-[illegible]. Timecode slates.

The Great American Market — [illegible] N. Cole Ave., Hollywood, CA 90038 (213) 461-0200 fax (213) 461-4308. Theatrical, color correction and diffusion material manufacturing.

The International Film & Television Workshops — Rockport, ME 04856 (207) [illegible] fax (207) 236-[illegible].

Rosco — [illegible] Port Chester, NY (914) 937-1300. Theatrical, color correction & diffusion material manufacturing.

Spectra [illegible], Inc. — [illegible] Hollywood Way, Burbank, CA [illegible] (818) [illegible] fax (818) [illegible]. Metering systems manufacturing.

INDEX

Krasnogorsk 16mm
also called the K3

reflex viewing
rotating mirror shutter - 150 degrees fixed
length of exposure: 1/57.6 sec. @ 24 fps
fps: 4-48 forward only
footage counter: 0-30m
frame counter: none
power: spring wound or optional Tobin crystal motor
lens mount: 42mm screw thread
accessories: Arri standard and bayo lens adapters and video tap from MKA, Tobin crystal motor, hand grip, cable release.
standard lens: 17-69mm Meteor f-1.9 zoom

An economics teacher once told me and my fellow high school students about the origin of the expression "No free lunch". He said there used to be a drinking establishment in downtown Portland Oregon that sported the world's longest bar - something like four hundred feet long, winding around and around. Somewhere nearby was a table filled with all kinds of food with a sign over it saying FREE LUNCH. But if you tried to snag a hard boiled egg or slice of lunchmeat *before* buying a drink you were quickly escorted to the bar to make a purchase. So, there really is no free lunch.

The lesson is that no matter what any salesman tells you, nothing is free, and so it is with the Krasnogorsk. Or is it?

Something happened in recent history that was unprecedented - the Berlin wall came down. Now, there is a strange economic mix of east and west. Stories abound about how you can buy shovels made of titanium off the street in Russia for ten bucks. Leica clones can be had for twenty five. Night vision binoculars that would cost thousands here can be had for a few hundred dollars. The list goes on.

Why is everything so inexpensive? The Russian economic system was artificial - the government dictated the prices of everything rather than the consumer. Now, all this stuff - and some of it quite high tech - is available in the west at very low prices. So, there really is no free lunch except when something really once in a lifetime happens, like the collapse of the Soviet Empire.

Which brings me to the mighty Krasnogorsk, talk of film students everywhere. Why, for just five hundred bucks, you can have a brand new rotating mirror shutter 16mm movie camera with a zoom lens. It even does single frame! It has a built in light meter! And just look at all the neat accessories that come with it: a pistol grip, set of filters, single frame remote, a body brace, and a soft carry case. Wow.

Okay, now back to reality.

It just isn't made as well as a Bolex or Filmo, the two other cameras in its class that you're likely to find. The Kras supposedly self loads, like the Bolex, but I've never been able to get mine to; it always jams at a certain point in its threading path. The eyepiece is positioned so that my nose has to be scrunched against the body of the camera to get a good view. The winding apparatus isn't as easy to use as the Bolex's crank. Forget about using the lightmeter - one student told me his was almost 2 stops off. The body brace is just plain silly. I'm not sure what you're supposed to do with it. The camera will do single frame exposures for special effects and animation, but you can't backwind the camera and I'm not sure that the shutter is 100% leakproof, meaning that light may creep around the shutter between exposures during single frame work and cause a flickering effect. The zoom control on the lens is a lever, rather than a ring, and smooth zooming is difficult.

Okay. That's all the bad stuff. Now, what's good about this camera?

By golly, it really is a mirror reflex camera, which actually puts it in a class with the Arri S. This means that when the film is being exposed, there is no light-robbing beam splitter between the lens and the emulsion. The mount on the Kras is a 42mm thread, which is the same as Pentax 35mm SLR still camera mount, so you can use cheap Pentax mounted lenses. These are usually available only in longer focal lengths, like 28mm and up, but 150mm and 250mm telephoto primes can generally be had for less than $100 and screwed onto the Krasnogorsk. Also, you can make a really simple black cardboard flap that fits over the lens for single frame shooting. Just remember to lift up the flap before you squeeze off your two frames, then let it drop to cover the lens and keep light from leaking around the shutter.

The shutter angle is 150 degrees, which makes for a length of exposure of 1/57.60 of a a second at 24 fps, or very nearly 1/60 sec. which is a common exposure setting on many light meters. I've never used the built in light meter, because, as someone told me, theirs was almost 2 stops off, but others probably aren't, which brings me to the most important point about the camera: quality control - or the lack of it.

Apparently, you can get a swell running Krasnogorsk, one that has its speeds accurately marked in the fps wheel and self loads nicely and doesn't jam and focuses correctly, or you can get a lemon. Lots of stories exist about how much vodka was consumed the night before the technician assembled yours, etc. At any rate, it's possible to have a good brand new Kras or a crappy brand new Kras.

You can find, however, several individuals who claim to know how to set your Kras on track. Look in IN SYNC magazine (actually a newsprinted collection of classified film and video equipment ads, and highly recommended) to find who works on these cameras. I think the cost of putting your camera through one of these tune-ups is about $125, and although I've never heard of anyone doing so, it may be a very good idea.

More stuff about the Krasnogorsk: MKA, a company run by John Kitzen, makes a good pile of accessories for the camera. He has, among other things, a lens adapter for using Arri standard and Arri Bayonet lenses with the Kras, and also can put a Tobin crystal motor on the machine, which would make it an interesting choice for shooting playback for music videos, but not sync dialog as it is still to noisy.

So, in the end, do I reccomend the Kras? Sure. At $500 (or, let's say, $625 for a tuned-up version) the camera is a real bargain. Granted, you can't backwind it like a Bolex, and it isn't crafted as well, but it does work - and a good reflex Bolex with a zoom will set you back around $1500. Even if you owned an Arri 16SR, a Kras with an Arri adapter (so you could share lenses) would be real handy for times when you needed some rough-and-tumble hand held stuff or wanted to bolt the camera to the motorcycle fork, etc. In other words, situtations where risking an expensive machine is not prudent.

16BL Motor Update

Media Logic no longer makes their crystal replacement motor for the 16BL, but Tobin Cinema Systems has just introduced one. It's their CHT motor, and coupled with their TXM-15 controller, gives you 16 crystal speeds from 8 to 50 fps. It also will except external controls.

Also, Tobin makes crystal motors for Bolex, Arri 16S, and the Krasnogorsk. The prices are very good, considering how expensive 16mm equipment is in general. Their phone/fax number is (206) 932 7280.

BUYING USED MOTION PICTURE EQUIPMENT

The following was given to me by Mike Casey, of Visual Products, probably the largest and most well known dealer of used professional motion picture equipment in the U.S. I asked for this information so that I could write a brief chapter on buying equipment, but what he sent me is so complete that I feel compelled to print it here in its entirety:

The three most common sources for purchasing used equipment are classified ads, brokers, or dealers. All three sources have their own ways of doing things. Be sure to ask questions up front. Don't find out later as you may have no recourse.

1. CLASSIFIED ADS are usually run by individuals and offer equipment in as-is condition, many times without the opportunity for return for any reason. However, prices should be lowest.

2. BROKERS are just that - they broker the equipment and act as a middle man, advertising someone else's equipment for sale. No warranty is expressed or provided.

3. DEALERS are individuals or companies who work full time at the sale and service of montion picture equipment. Look for companies who offer a money back guarantee (not a due bill) and a warranty. Dealer's prices can be slightly higher, but often equipment is serviced prior to shipping. This can represent an actual savings when considering current service department fees. They are between $80 and $90 per hour.

A call to the manufacturer is not usually the easy road. Many of the cameras in this book are as old as the people selling them. Models and parts have been discontinued. The manufacturer's aim is to sell new cameras and accessories. They often times do not have time or knowledge to answer questions on cameras twenty years old (or older). They can, however, help in referring you to a reputable dealer.

Dealers can be an excellent resource, however, they usually work with a small staff. Try to be short and to the point with them.

Not enought can be said about being prepared. Do your homework. Read this book. Think about what you need your camera to do before purchasing.

Happy hunting.